SLAVERY,
DIPLOMACY AND
EMPIRE

To the memory of
COLIN WHITE
naval historian
1951–2008

SLAVERY, DIPLOMACY AND EMPIRE

*Britain and the Suppression
of the Slave Trade, 1807–1975*

Edited by
KEITH HAMILTON AND PATRICK SALMON

sussex
ACADEMIC
PRESS

BRIGHTON • PORTLAND

1 2 4 6 8 10 9 7 5 3

First published in 2009 by
SUSSEX ACADEMIC PRESS
PO Box 139
Eastbourne BN24 9BP

and in the United States of America by
SUSSEX ACADEMIC PRESS
920 NE 58th Ave   Suite 300
Portland, Oregon 97213-3786

British Library Cataloguing in Publication Data
A CIP catalogue record for this book is available from the British Library.

Library of Congress Cataloging-in-Publication Data
Slavery, diplomacy and empire : Britain and the suppression of the slave trade, 1807–1975 / edited by Keith Hamilton and Patrick Salmon.
p. cm.
Includes bibliographical references and index.
ISBN 978-1-84519-298-3 (h/c : alk. paper)
1. Slave trade—Great Britain—History. 2. Slavery—Great Britain—History. I. Hamilton, Keith, 1942– II. Salmon, Patrick, 1952-
HT1162.S588 2009
306.3'620941—dc22

2009017506

Typeset and designed by SAP, Brighton & Eastbourne.
Printed by TJ International, Padstow, Cornwall.
This book is printed on acid-free paper.

Contents

CONTENTS

Foreword

THE RT HON DAVID MILIBAND, MP
Secretary of State for Foreign and Commonwealth Affairs

Two years ago the bicentenary of the 1807 act abolishing the slave trade within the British empire was marked in events across the country, in academic gatherings, in exhibitions, in the opening of new museums, and in a spate of publications. They offered the opportunity for national reflection on the horrors of a commerce which George Canning, one of my many illustrious predecessors, denounced as the "scandal of the civilized world". They also reminded us of the achievements of those who campaigned for its abolition. Here in the Foreign and Commonwealth Office we commemorated the occasion with a seminar, held on 17 October 2007, on the theme of "Whitehall and the Slave Trade". Jointly hosted by our in-house team of historians and our Human Rights, Democracy and Governance Group, the seminar brought together academics, former and serving diplomats, and representatives of the media and other interested institutions. This collection of essays consists of the papers then presented along with additional contributions from seminar participants.

Britain's part in maintaining the transatlantic trade throughout the eighteenth century and the suffering thereby inflicted upon millions of Africans transported to a life of servitude in the Americas has already been rightly condemned. The economic and social consequences of the traffic remain a subject of intense academic debate. But this volume is mainly concerned with the efforts of British governments to eradicate slave trading by administrative, diplomatic and naval action, and official responses to the persistence of slavery in all its various forms. Individual chapters thus consider the international conventions aimed at suppressing slave trading; the evolution of the Foreign Office's Slave Trade Department; the mixed commission courts established to decide the fate of ships captured on suspicion of slaving; the tactics adopted by the Admiralty and naval commanders in seeking to counter trafficking in west African and Latin American waters; and the influence exercised by anti-slavery activists on Whitehall decision-making. Other contributions examine the reactions of British diplomats and statesmen to slavery and slave-trading in east Africa, south Asia and the Near and Middle East; the

vii

restrictive labour legislation of some British colonies and dependencies and that prevailing in the territories of friendly and client states; and the problems faced by Britain, first in the League of Nations and then in the United Nations, in trying to secure international agreement on measures aimed at combating and defining slavery and other types of human bondage.

The history related in these essays does not always redound to the credit of the Foreign Office. During the early nineteenth century Britain stood accused of hypocrisy by other maritime powers. The British, having established their own slave economies in the Caribbean, seemed set upon using their naval mastery to deny their rivals the opportunity to profit from the trade. Humanitarian intervention in Africa, aimed initially at suppressing the trade at source, would likewise serve eventually as a mask for imperial expansion. Then and later, Whitehall departments presided over colonial labour practices which carried with them the "taint of slavery" and, when it suited British interests, they condoned domestic slavery elsewhere. Nevertheless, there can be little doubt that throughout the nineteenth century Britain led the international fight against slave trading. The anti-slave trade declaration which at British instigation was drafted at the congress of Vienna in 1815, and which committed the sovereigns there represented to putting an end to "a scourge, which has so long desolated Africa, degraded Europe, and afflicted humanity", was more than empty rhetoric: it was a landmark in the history of humanitarian diplomacy. And the Foreign Office's Slave Trade Department, which by the early 1830s was the largest single division of the Office under a senior clerk, might well be regarded as the first human rights department of any foreign ministry.

Since then diplomacy's humanitarian agenda has expanded vastly. We have only recently been celebrating the sixtieth anniversary of the adoption of the Universal Declaration of Human Rights, a document which is far more comprehensive in its content and liberal in its intent than anything that emerged from the congress of Vienna. As, however, the authors of this volume reveal, there are limits to what diplomacy can achieve, especially when it to comes to putting universally accepted principles into universal practice in a world of sovereign states. Despite all the efforts of governments, non-governmental organizations and individual activists, slavery persists. The International Labour Organization estimates that over two million individuals have fallen victim to people traffickers, the highly organized criminal gangs which profit from subjecting human beings to degradation and misery. The fight against such exploitation continues, and the Foreign and Commonwealth Office, in collaboration with other government departments, remains committed to the cause.

Editors' Preface

KEITH HAMILTON AND PATRICK SALMON

As explained in the Foreword, this collection of essays derives from a seminar held in the Foreign and Commonwealth Office (FCO) during the autumn of 2007. Sadly, one of the principal speakers on that occasion, Colin White, director of the Royal Naval Museum at Portsmouth, died on 25 December 2008. His seminar presentation, a masterly survey of the anti-slave trade operations of the Royal Navy's "Preventive Squadron", was delivered with all the enthusiasm, vigour and panache of a devoted scholar. But illness left Colin without time to transform his paper into a chapter for publication, and we have therefore decided to dedicate this volume to the memory of his life and work.

To other contributors, seminar participants and our colleagues in FCO Historians and the Human Rights, Democracy and Governance Group, we would like to express our gratitude. We are particularly indebted to Farida Shaikh, who was responsible for much of the initial research work for the History Note, *Slavery in Diplomacy: Britain and the suppression of the transatlantic slave trade*, copies of which were distributed at the seminar and sections of which have been incorporated in the present volume; and to Grant Hibberd for his administrative assistance with regard both to the organization of the seminar and the production of the book. Thanks are also due to the Rare Books, Manuscript and Special Collections Library of Duke University, Durham, North Carolina, for permission to cite and quote extensively from the Backhouse and Bandinel papers in its custody; to Jane Hogan, the Assistant Keeper of the Archives and Special Collections of Durham University Library, for permission to cite and quote from the Wylde papers in her custody; to the National Portrait Gallery for permission to reproduce John Callcott Horsley's lithograph of James Bandinel; to the Royal Naval Museum at Portsmouth for permission to reproduce illustrations from its collection; and to Ian Ward of Nostalgia Works, Dagenham, for his help with enhancing photographic images. Finally we would like to acknowledge all the support we have consistently received from Jane Darby, head of the FCO's Information Management Group, in our efforts to complete this project.

Notes on the Contributors

Mandy Banton was formerly assistant keeper at the Public Record Office (now The National Archives (TNA)) and subsequently principal records specialist, diplomatic and colonial, in TNA. She has written and published on the regulation of labour within the British empire; is co-editor, with Karen Ordahl Kupperman and John C. Appleby, of the CD-ROM edition of the *Calendar of State Papers, Colonial: North America and the West Indies, 1574–1739* (London: Routledge, 2000); and author of *Administering the Empire, 1801–1968: A Guide to the Records of the Colonial Office in The National Archives of the UK* (London: Institute of Historical Research, 2008).

William Gervase Clarence-Smith is professor of the economic history of Asia and Africa, at the University of London's School of Oriental and African Studies. He is also chief editor of *The Journal of Global History*. He specialises in Africa and south-east Asia, with special reference to Islam, slavery, diasporas, tree crops and livestock. His most recent book is *Islam and the Abolition of Slavery* (Oxford: OUP, 2006).

Keith Hamilton is consultant historian in the Foreign and Commonwealth Office. There he co-edits the series *Documents on British Policy Overseas*, the latest volume of which, *Berlin in the Cold War, 1948–90*, was published by Routledge in January 2009. His other recent publications include an essay collection, co-edited with Edward Johnson, *Arms and Disarmament in Diplomacy* (London: Vallentine Mitchell, 2008).

Andrew Lambert is Laughton professor of naval history at King's College, London. His primary academic interests are the naval and strategic history of the British empire between the Napoleonic wars and the First World War and the early development of historical writing. He has written over a dozen books, the most recent being *Franklin; Tragic Arctic Navigator* (London: Faber & Faber, 2009). In 2004 he wrote and presented the BBC TV series *War at Sea*.

Suzanne Miers is professor emerita of history at Ohio University. She has published numerous works on slavery, the slave trade and its suppression, including *Britain and the Ending of the Slave Trade* (London: Longman, 1975), and *Slavery in the Twentieth Century: the Evolution of a Global Problem* (New York: AltaMira Press, 2003). In addition, she has co-edited, with Igor Kopytoff, *Slavery in Africa: Historical and*

Anthropological Perspectives (Madison: University of Wisconsin Press, 1977); with Richard Roberts, *The End of Slavery in Africa* (Madison: University of Wisconsin Press, 1988); with Maria Jaschok, *Women in Chinese Patriarchy: Submission Servitude and Escape* (London: Zed Books, 1994); with Martin A. Klein, *Slavery and Colonial Rule in Africa* (London: Frank Cass, 1998); and, with Gwyn Campbell and Joseph C. Miller, *Women and Slavery* (2 vols., Athens, OH: Ohio UP, 2007–8), and *Children in Slavery throughout the Ages* (2 vols., Athens, OH: Ohio UP, forthcoming 2009).

T. G. Otte is senior lecturer in diplomatic history at the University of East Anglia, specialising in the history of Great Power relations in the long nineteenth century (1815–1914) as well as modern military history. He has written or edited eight books, the latest two being *The China Question: Great Power Rivalry and British Isolation, 1894–1905* (Oxford: OUP, 2007), and, with Keith Neilson, *The Permanent Under-Secretary for Foreign Affairs, 1854–1946* (London: Routledge, 2009).

Patrick Salmon is chief historian at the Foreign and Commonwealth Office and visiting professor of international history at the University of Newcastle upon Tyne. His publications include *Scandinavia and the Great Powers 1890–1940* (Cambridge: CUP, 1997).

Farida Shaikh is a British diplomat currently based at the Foreign and Commonwealth Office in London. She has served overseas in Singapore, Zimbabwe and, most recently, in Ghana, where she was responsible for taking forward UK policy on environmental and human rights issues (including those relating to slavery in west Africa). During 2006–2007 she co-authored with Keith Hamilton FCO Historians' History Note, *Slavery in Diplomacy: The Foreign Office and the suppression of the transatlantic slave trade*.

Glyn Stone is professor of international history, University of the West of England, Bristol. His publications include: *The Oldest Ally: Britain and the Portuguese Connection, 1936–1941*(Woodbridge: Royal Historical Society, 1994); *Spain, Portugal and the Great Powers, 1931–1941* (London: Palgrave Macmillan, 2005); co-edited with Dick Richardson, *Decisions and Diplomacy: Essays in Twentieth Century International History* (London: Routledge, 1995); co-edited with Alan Sharp, *Anglo-French Relations in the Twentieth Century: Rivalry and Cooperation* (London: Routledge, 2000); co-edited with T. G. Otte, *Anglo-French Relations since the late Eighteenth Century* (London: Routledge, 2008). He is secretary of the British International History Group and a member of the Council of the Royal Historical Society.

David Turley is emeritus professor of cultural and social history and former dean of humanities at the University of Kent. His research interests are American and Atlantic social and cultural history since 1760; the history of anti-slavery movements since the eighteenth century; the African-American intelligentsia and the history of American religion. He is the author of *The Culture of English Anti-Slavery, 1780–1861* (London: Routledge, 1991), *Slavery* (Oxford: Blackwell, 2000), and editor of *American Religion: Literary Sources and Documents* (London: Helm, 1998). He has written some twenty essays and articles.

SLAVERY, DIPLOMACY AND EMPIRE

*Britain and the Suppression
of the Slave Trade, 1807–1975*

Introduction

KEITH HAMILTON AND FARIDA SHAIKH

Lyme Regis is probably better known today for its literary associations than for its radical politics. Yet, in November 1861 the town's mayor and two hundred of his fellow citizens addressed a memorial to Lord John Russell, the British foreign secretary, urging him to take steps to "teach the King of Dahomey that he is not to outrage humanity with impunity".[1] The errant monarch, King Gelele, was rumoured to be offering up human sacrifices, amongst whom were christianized Yoruba captured in raids upon their territory. Like his father, Ghezo, he was also held responsible for the sale and supply of captive Africans to those engaged in a by then dwindling transatlantic trade in slaves.[2] That the townsfolk of a Dorset seaport should have been so well informed of events in Gelele's tropical realm may be attributed to missionary zeal and the success of activists who had worked steadfastly for the slavery's abolition and the eradication of the commerce that sustained it. British governments had responded to popular concerns about the evils of slave trafficking with diplomacy, naval action and publicity. In the case of Dahomey, although the prime minister, Lord Palmerston, favoured armed intervention, he was opposed by the Admiralty and had to settle in 1862 for the despatch of a naval officer on a predictably fruitless diplomatic mission to Gelele.[3] A year earlier, the neighbouring principality of Lagos had been a more vulnerable and potentially more lucrative object of Palmerston's attention. After a decade of commercial and political involvement there, the British annexed the city-state in order to safeguard its population from the "slave traders and kidnappers who formerly oppressed them" and to foster "legitimate" trade.[4] As the essays in this volume affirm, slavery and empire were once closely related themes in international diplomacy.

That had long been so. In the fifteenth century the Portuguese had begun transporting enslaved Africans from west Africa to southern Europe. Fortified trading stations were established on the coastal littoral between the Senegal and Cameroon rivers to facilitate the commerce; São Tomé and the Cape Verde islands were acquired as transit points; and the further extension of trade routes into the Indian ocean offered

1

opportunities for the purchase of slaves in eastern and southern Africa. Other Christian nations, including the Dutch, the English, the French and the Spaniards, were soon involved in the traffic, which expanded vastly following the European discovery and colonization of America and the establishment of plantation economies on the mainland and in the islands of the Caribbean. During the seventeenth century, as they switched from tobacco to sugar cultivation, the British and French possessions in the Lesser Antilles, Antigua, Barbados, Guadeloupe, Martinique and St Kitts, emerged as the first important West Indian slave societies. The Company of Royal Adventurers, later to re-emerge as the Royal African Company, was founded in 1660 with the backing of King Charles II and a group of wealthy London merchants. It was initially granted a monopoly on the English Africa trade, and within forty years around three-fifths of the company's income was derived from the transport and sale of slaves. Encouraged by the demand of planters in their North American colonies for African slave labour, and by the expansion of their dominion there and in the Caribbean, within twenty years the British surpassed the Dutch and Portuguese as the leading shippers of slaves to the Americas. By 1807, when Parliament outlawed their participation in the trade, British slavers had probably shipped more than 2.6 million captive Africans to the Americas;[5] and until 1834 slavery, the "accumulated horrors" of which abolitionists labelled "crimes against humanity", remained legal in Britain's overseas possessions.[6]

ABOLITION'S DIPLOMACY

The business generated by this forced mass migration of labour and the concomitant commerce in commodities and finished goods contributed to the expansion of that manufacturing industry upon which Britain's international strength came to repose.[7] The trade also had a debilitating impact upon the economic development of west and central Africa, and, since it encouraged slave-raiding by local rulers, a disruptive effect upon the political and social structures of the region.[8] But public opposition to the trade in Britain initially owed less to such considerations than to the moral indignation aroused by the horrors of the traffic itself, particularly the degradation and sufferings inflicted on its human cargoes and the high mortality rates associated with the transatlantic passage. Slavery, widely assumed to have been ruled illegal in England by Lord Mansfield's judgement of 1772,[9] offended the intellectual susceptibilities of the Age of Reason.[10] It raised the ire of evangelical Anglicans, Quakers and other non-conformists, and their opinions were ably and persuasively represented in the country at large by such figures as Thomas Clarkson and

Granville Sharp, both founder members of the "Committee of the Society for the purpose of effecting the abolition of the Slave Trade", and in Parliament by William Wilberforce, the member for Yorkshire.[11] Abolitionists had, however, to overcome the resistance of a powerful commercial lobby, which contended that the British economy would suffer if the West Indian plantations were no longer able to import free African labour. Moreover, although Wilberforce was able to enlist support from influential politicians, including successive prime ministers, Pitt the Younger and Lord Grenville, and the latter's foreign secretary, Charles James Fox, he had to reckon with administrations preoccupied with war and revolution abroad and disinclined to embark on reform at home.

Parliament first took up the issue in 1788 with a debate on a bill aimed at restricting the shipping of slaves, and in 1792 the House of Commons passed a resolution calling for the abolition of the trade.[12] But practical progress towards this end had to await Nelson's triumph over the French and Spanish fleets at Trafalgar. Britain's naval mastery and ability to obstruct the supply of slaves to the colonies of rival nations, a temporary glut in the production of sugar, and the relative decline in the economic importance of the West Indies, then allowed Wilberforce, his friends and followers, to combine humanitarian with commercial and strategic arguments for abolition. Within government some still doubted the merits of their case.[13] On 16 March 1807, during the second reading of the bill to abolish the trade, William Windham, the secretary of state for war and the colonies, urged the Commons "not to go upon the abstract principles of right, but upon the consideration of the consequences of the measure, and the possible ruin of the British Empire resulting from it".[14] And even after the successful passage of the bill, the commerce persisted. The demand for slaves remained high and, in the cases of Brazil, Cuba and the cotton producing south of the United States, continued to rise until well into the 1840s. Slavers flying the flags of nations other than Britain responded to the requirements of the market. British merchants were in the meantime free to supply them with manufactured goods and to deal in products of slave economies. Abolitionists, who had yet to secure the eradication of slavery within Britain's overseas possessions, henceforth looked to diplomacy and the Royal Navy to stifle the trade upon the high seas. British governments had in any case an economic interest in ensuring that a highly profitable trade should not simply pass into the hands of foreign competitors.

Whilst the war with revolutionary France may have impeded progress towards abolition, that with Napoleonic France facilitated measures aimed at its suppression. The British were able to reduce the export of slaves from west Africa by exercising the rights they claimed as belligerents to seize enemy ships and search neutral vessels for contraband. With dubious legality the Royal Navy extended these rights to include searching ships for slaves and arresting and trying suspected slavers. The British were to some extent assisted by the fact that both Denmark and the United States had also moved to ban their citizens from engaging in the slave trade. This did not, however, give the British the right to enforce such legislation, and in 1812 a dispute over belligerent rights was to lead to war with the United States.[15] Another problem was presented by the Portuguese. Allies in the war against the French, they stood to benefit from an expanding trade in slaves between their African territories and Brazil, in whose capital, Rio de Janeiro, the Portuguese royal court resided for twelve years following its hurried departure from Lisbon in 1807. An Anglo-Portuguese alliance treaty of 1810 obliged the prince regent of Portugal to adopt the "most efficacious means for bringing about a gradual abolition of the [Slave] Trade throughout the whole of his Dominions", and disallowed his subjects from carrying on the trade on any part of the African coast not in his possession.[16] It was, however, far from easy to determine what constituted Portuguese territory. With the connivance of neighbouring African polities, Portuguese merchants established trading posts in areas which the British declined to recognize as falling under Portugal's sovereignty, and in such instances the Royal Navy, much to the obvious annoyance of the Portuguese, felt free to stop and search their ships.

Napoleon's defeat in continental Europe offered new opportunities for diplomatic initiatives directed against the slave trade. George Canning, as foreign secretary during 1807–9, had already issued instructions to British envoys urging them to enter into negotiations with their host governments to secure treaties abolishing the trade.[17] As in the case of Portugal, their efforts met with only limited success. But during 1813–14 Austria, Denmark, Prussia, Russia and Sweden all signed treaties with Britain, either promising to prohibit their subjects' participation in the trade, or pledging their cooperation in working for its abolition. Meanwhile, a royal decree was issued from The Hague forbidding Dutch nationals from slave trading on the coast of Africa and prohibiting Dutch vessels from leaving Dutch ports with the intention of engaging in the traffic. The treaty of Paris of May 1814, which brought an end to the war between France and the sixth coalition, also included an additional article by which the French expressed their intention to limit their traffic in slaves to their own colonies, and to outlaw it completely within five years. Spain too agreed in July 1814 to confine the slaving of its nationals to its own colonial empire, and the treaty of Ghent of December 1814, which formally concluded the war between Britain and the United States, stated that the two countries would "use their best endeavours" to end the

4

trade.[18] Still more important, however, was the prospect of the British being able to use the congress of Vienna to launch a new diplomatic offensive with a view to making the trade subject to comprehensive international agreement.

Lord Castlereagh, Britain's foreign secretary since 1812 and one of the principal architects of the Vienna settlement, was not known to be sympathetic to the abolitionist cause. Personally of the opinion that "morals were never well taught by the sword", he thought it would be wrong to force abolition upon nations "at the expense of their honour and of the tranquillity of the world".[19] He was nonetheless aware that he could not afford to ignore the public's strong desire for Britain to take the lead in pressing for international action against the trade. Petitions to this effect containing nearly a million signatures, had been received from around the country,[20] and in a letter to Henry Wellesley, the British envoy to Spain, he wrote on 1 August 1814 that "both Houses of Parliament [were] pledged to press it; and the Ministers must make it the basis of their policy".[21] He also sought the assistance of Wilberforce and his fellow campaigners. They supplied Castlereagh with detailed information, helped draft legal documents, and distributed propaganda abroad. His overarching aim was to effect "an immediate and general abolition" through international agreement.[22] It was in some respects an extraordinary objective. Philosophers, poets and statesmen had debated and sometimes extolled the "natural rights of man", but apart from efforts previously directed towards upholding religious liberties, there were few if any precedents for submitting an essentially human rights issue to such high-level international negotiation.[23]

Castlereagh's negotiating strategy was first to exert pressure on the French for immediate and general abolition on the assumption that if France gave way Portugal and Spain, each benefiting from the expansion of the slave-trade economies of Brazil and Cuba, would find it more difficult to resist. At the very least, he hoped to be able to persuade Portugal and Spain to commit themselves to the immediate abolition of the traffic north of the equator and to its absolute abolition within eight years. He was less optimistic about securing agreement on an earlier date. Nevertheless, he contemplated both the threat of what would amount to a Europe-wide boycott of their colonial produce, and the eventual establishment of an international mechanism for enforcing and monitoring suppression. He envisaged states formulating their own regulations to outlaw the trade and a "sort of permanent European Congress", composed of committees of the representatives of the powers, to oversee their application and "enquire into the progress made and the extent of the evil remaining". He was also eager to discover whether individual nations would be prepared to accept that each other's navies should have a reciprocal right of search of suspected slave ships. And once the trade had been abolished "by all or nearly all Christian States", it would, Castlereagh contended, be a question of how far states could be "justified in consideration of those engaged in the Traffick, of whatever nation, as engaged in an offence proscribed by Civilized Nations, and as such not to be peaceably tolerated".[24]

There was only limited sympathy for such sentiments in Vienna. Little of practical value emerged from a committee established in January 1815 to consider the question. Portugal and Spain initially resisted the participation of non-maritime powers in the committee and, along with the French, they objected to the immediate abolition of the trade and rejected the notion of reciprocal rights of search. French merchants were hoping to profit from the return to France of its colonial possessions and their government was reluctant to be seen making further concessions to a triumphant Britain, and both the Portuguese and the Spaniards viewed the idea of imposing restrictions on their colonial commerce as an infringement of their sovereignty. All they were prepared to accept was a resolution which foresaw the institution of a boycott against any country prolonging the trade beyond an agreed, yet unspecified, date for abolition. And even the permanent committee which was set up in London to keep measures against the traffic under review, proved ultimately an ineffective device.[25] These failings and shortcomings notwithstanding, Castlereagh persuaded the powers represented at Vienna to draft and sign on 8 February 1815 a declaration establishing a moral foundation for future action against the slave trade. Its signatories, the declaration pronounced, could not

> . . . do greater credit to their mission, better fulfil their duty, and manifest the principles which actuate their august Sovereigns than by . . . proclaiming, in the name of their Sovereigns, their wish of putting an end to a scourge, which has so long desolated Africa, degraded Europe, and afflicted humanity . . . [26]

This, however, was qualified by the assertion that the objective foreseen could not be attained by governments "without due regard to the interests, habits, and even the prejudices of their subjects", and that the plenipotentiaries could not therefore "prejudge the period which each particular Power [might] consider as most advisable for the definitive Abolition of the Slave Trade".[27] They were agreed that the trade was morally wrong and that it ought to be abolished, but reluctant to say how and when. As so often in humanitarian diplomacy, it was easier to proclaim principles than to settle on means for their practical application. That said, a precedent had been set. Slave trafficking had been

6

condemned and recognized as a matter of international concern, and the British henceforth had a platform from which to mount further challenges to those governments which continued to tolerate, or were complicit in, the trade. As Castlereagh explained to the prime minister, Lord Liverpool, the attention of ministers had been awakened to the subject in a degree much beyond what he had expected, "considering the Multiplicity of their Avocations and their former Ignorance of the Question".[28]

Abolitionists were disappointed by what they regarded as the small progress made at Vienna towards achieving an international accord on the suppression of the trade.[29] In the summer of 1815 it had seemed possible that the French might be ready to align themselves more closely with the British on the issue. After his return from Elba Napoleon sought to win British goodwill by declaring the French slave trade abolished and, following Waterloo, the restored Bourbon king, Louis XVIII, felt obliged to reaffirm the decision.[30] But there was only very limited support for abolition in France, and in subsequent years the French navy proved neither effective nor enthusiastic about checking a trade from which the British had so obviously profited in the recent past. Other governments were also freer with their pledges than their actions. In a treaty with Britain of July 1814 the king of Spain expressed his abhorrence at the "injustice and inhumanity" of the traffic in slaves, and promised to "prohibit his subjects from engaging in the Slave Trade, for the purpose of supplying any islands or possessions except those appertaining to Spain; and to prevent likewise, by effectual measures and regulations, the protection of the Spanish Flag being given to foreigners who [might] engage in the traffic".[31] And in January 1815 a bilateral deal was struck with Portugal whereby Britain agreed to compensate the Portuguese for ships seized since 1810, and to write off a previous loan, in return for Portugal abandoning the slave trade north of the equator and promising to determine by subsequent treaty when the Portuguese trade should cease absolutely. It was meanwhile declared unlawful for either the subjects of Portugal or vessels flying its flag to engage in the slave trade other than for the supply of Portugal's transatlantic possessions.[32] Needless to say, the re-establishment of peace was followed by a surge in slave trafficking to the Americas, and the Portuguese and Spanish flags frequently served as cover for slavers of other nations. Many of those flying Spain's colours north of the equator were in fact French or Portuguese.

It was soon apparent that if the British wished to continue their operations against the trade and enforce respect for commitments undertaken by foreign governments, the Royal Navy must have a legally defined right to detain and search suspected slavers. Particularly susceptible to British pressure, Portugal was the first amongst the principal slave trading countries to concede a mutual right of search. An Anglo-Portuguese convention of 28 July 1817 provided that warships of either nation, furnished with special warrants, might visit and search the merchant vessels of the other which they suspected of having on board slaves shipped from prohibited areas. Ships thus captured were to be taken for adjudication before one of two mixed commission courts, one sitting in Sierra Leone and another in Brazil.[33] Two months later Castlereagh's offer of £400,000 in compensation, to cover losses incurred as a result of previous British seizures and subsequent loss of trade, sufficed to persuade Spain to sign a similar treaty. Madrid agreed to the immediate abolition of the trade north of the equator, its complete abolition within Spain's dominions by 1820, the grant of reciprocal rights of search at sea, and adjudication by mixed commission courts.[34] Despite, however, the institution of these new arrangements and the presence of British naval patrols off the west African coast, Portugal and Spain remained, according to Castlereagh, "well matched in dishonesty and shabbiness" when it came to taking action.[35] James Bandinel, whose superintendence of the Foreign Office's Slave Trade Department is considered in Chapter 1, later remarked on how Spain failed to take steps to implement treaty provisions so that the sea "swarmed with slave-ships, carrying on the Slave Trade under the flag of Spain, and for account of the Spanish colonies".[36]

Bandinel likewise castigated the Portuguese authorities for endeavouring "with singular bad faith . . . by every means within their power, to frustrate the stipulations of the Convention of 1817".[37] Only the Netherlands government, which agreed in May 1818 to a treaty with Britain providing for reciprocal rights of search north and south of the equator, seemed ready to observe the spirit as well as the letter of its commitments.[38] That said, slavers of all nationalities were constantly devising ever more devious methods of evasion. These included the use of French and United States flags, which offered immunity from search by British warships, and the carrying of dual sets of flags and papers to suit circumstance and location. Moreover, Castlereagh failed in his efforts to promote a multilateral agreement between all the maritime states accepting a mutual right of visit. When the foreign ministers of the great powers met at Aix-la-Chapelle in the autumn of 1818 for the first of the post-Vienna congresses, Castlereagh's initiative was rejected, with France leading the opposition.[39] Longstanding national rivalries obstructed progress towards agreement, and in despair Castlereagh urged Wilberforce and his supporters to begin a press campaign to convert French public opinion to the suppression of the trade (an early example of the British Foreign Office delegating public diplomacy to a non-governmental organization).[40] Beyond Europe, the United States was equally troublesome. The Americans declined to concede a reciprocal right of visit, and refused to countenance participation in mixed commission courts where their citizens would be subject to a "court consisting partly of foreign judges, not liable to impeachment under the authority of the United States".[41] They, nevertheless, agreed to send a small naval squadron to patrol the west African littoral and, by the Webster-Ashburton treaty of August 1842, undertook to cooperate with Britain and maintain there an anti-slave trade force of 80 guns.[42] Meanwhile, the six Royal Naval vessels delegated to the task found it almost impossible to have a lasting impact on a trade conducted from the creeks, inlets and islands of a coast extending from Cape Verde in the north to Benguela in the south.[43]

Even when slavers failed to avoid detention, they frequently avoided prosecution. The bilateral treaties stipulated that ships could be condemned only if slaves were discovered on board. As a result, ships' masters facing imminent capture either threw their human cargo overboard or unloaded hapless Africans into small boats for transfer to the shore.[44] Indeed, George Canning, who replaced Castlereagh as foreign secretary after the latter's suicide in August 1822, reckoned that the "aggregate of human suffering and the waste of human life" in the transatlantic traffic had "increased in a ratio enormously greater than the increase of positive numbers".[45] To remedy this British diplomats persuaded the Netherlands, Portugal and Spain to append additional articles to their treaties with Britain, inflicting the same penalties and confiscation on vessels for which there was proof that slaves had once been on board as on those on which they had been found when visited. Then in January 1823, after accepting this provision, the Netherlands went a step further, agreeing that ships simply equipped for the trade might be condemned when detained by either the British or Netherlands navy. Canning's efforts to devise other means for the suppression of the slave trade, "that scandal of the civilized world", were, however, frustrated by the refusal of the French either to embrace new engagements or execute existing ones.[46] Thus the efforts of the duke of Wellington, Britain's representative at the 1822 congress of Verona, to win the adherence of the great powers to a declaration condemning the slave trade as piracy, withdrawing from slavers the protection of their respective flags, and committing them to the exclusion from their territories of the produce of slave-trading colonies, foundered on the objections of France.[47]

Only in November 1831, at a time when the newly-installed Orleans monarchy was looking for British support, did the French conclude a convention with Britain in which they accepted a very limited right of search at sea. It was to be exercised within a defined zone and a specified period by individual warships authorized for the purpose, and ships detained were to be handed over, not to mixed commissions, but to the courts of the state whose flag they flew.[48] Like the United States, France was reluctant to accept interference with its shipping by a numerically superior British navy and the subjection of its citizens to foreign judges. And although in December 1841 it joined Austria, Britain, Prussia and Russia in subscribing to a treaty extending the zone in which the right of search might be exercised and removing limits on the number of warships involved in anti-slave-trade operations, the French parliament declined ratification of the accord. Subsequent efforts to promote Anglo-French cooperation against the trade, which amounted in the 1830s and 1840s to the transport annually to the Americas of some 36–40,000 Africans, were in any case threatened by a growing perception in France that the British were resorting to measures aimed at suppression to advance their colonial and commercial interests. The Royal Navy's imposition of coastal blockades, its destruction of slave-holding barracoons, and Britain's treaties with native rulers, were all to become sources of friction. So too the British detention of ships flying American colours continued to sour relations with Washington.[49]

Action directed against slave trafficking from Africa eventually served as a catalyst to imperial rivalry. It also conflicted with established notions of state sovereignty. Even Canning, for all his opposition to great-power intervention in the domestic affairs of weaker states and his championing of Latin American liberties, was ready to contemplate "justifiable violence" against a newly-independent and slave-importing Brazil. In a despatch to Wellington, written on the eve of the congress of Verona, he contended:

> If it be true that no combination of great Powers can justify an infliction of injury upon a smaller Power: it may be affirmed on the other hand that no Power has the right (nor has it at all the more for being insignificant in strength) to interrupt by its single act, the consenting policy of all the civilized world on a matter on which the dictates of Christianity and morality are clear; and to perpetuate to a large portion of their fellow creatures misery and sufferings which all other Powers are conspiring to heal.[50]

Few British foreign secretaries have more forcibly enunciated a doctrine of humanitarian intervention.

INSTRUMENTS OF SUPPRESSION

Despite Canning's rhetoric, the transatlantic slave trade persisted until well into the 1860s and its suppression proved a costly business. According to one estimate the annual sums expended by Britain in combating the traffic between 1816 and 1862 approximately equalled its profits from the trade between 1761 and 1807.[51] The diplomatic complications arising from the exercise, particularly those leading to confrontations with Brazil, Portugal and the Spanish authorities in Cuba, are covered in subsequent chapters. But the primary concern of Chapters 1 and 2 is with the administrative and judicial instruments of suppression, the Slave Trade Department of the Foreign Office in London and the British element of the mixed commission courts in Africa and the Americas. The former, the Slave Trade Department, was, along with the Librarian's Department and the Consular Department, one of the earliest functional divisions of the Foreign Office. It was also from the 1820s into the 1830s the Office's largest department under a senior clerk. This and the fact that its clerks were amongst the worst paid in Whitehall reflected both the quantity of paper-work generated by the politics of suppression, and the initial optimism of statesmen who believed that the slave trade would soon be eliminated from the high seas. Eventually, reformed and renamed, it transmuted into the Consular and African Department, and the first head of the new department became a key player in the European partition of Africa. Britain's humanitarian diplomacy helped promote institutional change at home and the extension of empire abroad.

Amongst the department's several responsibilities was the management of the correspondence relating to the mixed commission courts. These were a legal innovation established by bilateral treaties in order to pass judgement on vessels captured on suspicion of slave trading. Those appointed by the Foreign Office to serve on the commissions were, as suggested in Chapter 2, not invariably motivated by high moral concern over the fate of the human victims of the trade. Nor were they always very effective in the fulfilment of their duties. They were nevertheless a necessary judicial complement to the anti-slave trade patrols deployed by the Royal Navy in the Atlantic and the Caribbean. Naval officers bringing captive vessels before the courts could not always count on judgement in their favour. Nor were they always equipped with ships capable of matching the speed of those employed by traffickers. However, as Colin White emphasized in his seminar presentation, the West African "Preventive Squadron" benefited from technological innovation: in 1832 it received its first steamship, the wooden paddle steamer, *HMS Pluto*, and by the 1860s the entire squadron was steam-powered. And there could be little doubting the moral fervour of officers and men, who were very often traumatized by the conditions prevailing on slave ships, and who had themselves to contend with malaria and yellow fever in their battle with the trade.

For all the enthusiasm displayed by British naval commanders in their pursuit and capture of suspect vessels, African suppliers and traders from

11

Europe and the Americas prospered as long as there were markets for slave labour in Brazil and the Caribbean. Andrew Lambert relates in his contribution how Lord Palmerston and his successor as foreign secretary, Lord Aberdeen, finally resorted to unilateral action against first the Portuguese and then the Brazilians, allowing in Brazil's case "a naval force that could be counted on the fingers of one hand to cripple a major industry". But, as Lambert stresses, broader and more pressing political and strategic constraints applied to Britain's handling of Cuba, the other major slave-importing economy of Latin America. The British were reluctant to risk either destabilising the Spanish monarchy or provoking intervention in the island by an expansionist United States. In consequence, the trade continued until the American civil war led Washington to enforce its own anti-slave trade legislation and to sign up to a treaty with Britain providing for a mutual right of search. In their dealings with Brazil, Portugal and Spain British governments had also to take domestic considerations into account. Free traders were anxious to end tariffs which discriminated against slave-produced sugar imports; Parliament questioned the cost in men and money of maintaining the West African squadron; and Quakers, though opposed to the slave trade, doubted the morality of using armed force to achieve its abolition.

Organized opposition to slavery and the slave trade, as manifested by the foundation in 1839 of Joseph Sturge's British and Foreign Anti-Slavery Society, remained a significant political force in Britain throughout the early Victorian era.[52] Indeed, as foreign secretary in the late 1830s Palmerston could hardly have afforded to ignore the abolitionists amongst the radical and non-conformist supporters of Lord Melbourne's administration. Yet, as David Turley points out in his chapter on anti-slavery activists and officials, the methods and tactics of campaigners were modified to suit what they regarded as shifting priorities. In 1814–15 activists had worked in close collaboration with ministers and diplomats in promoting suppression, combining the influence they thereby derived with public agitation. Two decades later a new breed of activists, disdainful of the political compromises of an earlier generation, placed less value on involvement in policy implementation and relied more on public lectures, pamphlets and petitions to achieve its ends. As, however, is suggested by the determined opposition of activists to British recognition of Texan independence, save on condition that Texas first conclude an anti-slave trade treaty, they seem to have had little appreciation of the other factors, such as Britain's relations with France and the United States, which Palmerston and Aberdeen had to take into account. British governments remained committed to an abolitionist agenda, but the international situation was rarely such that they could subordinate other external interests to one overriding moral imperative.

Empires of Evasion

Nowhere did the British find it more difficult to reconcile their humanitarian aspirations with their perceived strategic needs than in the Near and Middle East. There they sought to preserve the Ottoman and Persian empires as bulwarks against the further extension of Russian influence, and to maintain the authority of Muslim potentates of the African and Arabian littorals as a guarantee against their lands falling prey to other European rivals. Yet British efforts to end the slave trade and to mitigate some of the worst excesses of slavery in the Muslim world challenged local customs and values, and had the potential to destabilize the politics of the region. These are issues which T. G. Otte addresses in his chapter. He points out that, unlike the slavery practised in Brazil, the Caribbean and the southern states of the United States, that of the Muslim world was in general, though not invariably, domestic rather than economic. Moreover, since any challenge to domestic slavery could be represented as challenging the family structure of Muslim households, Muslim rulers were reluctant to be seen as bending to foreign remonstrations. Where the trade itself was concerned, Britain was well able to use its extensive consular network to monitor its size and assist in relieving the sufferings of some of its victims, and the Royal Navy intervened actively to curb the traffic in the Indian ocean, the Red sea and the Persian gulf. Successful naval action, nevertheless, required a legal framework and, as Otte argues, that in turn depended on British diplomats being able to utilize prevailing international circumstances, most obviously Ottoman vulnerability to Russian military advances, in order to squeeze treaties from sultans, shahs and khedives.

Unfortunately, as British consuls learned to their cost, the authority of Muslim rulers was rarely respected throughout the entirety of their realms. Ottoman provincial governors and their subordinates frequently neglected, or otherwise evaded, the implementation of the Porte's *firmans* proscribing and restricting the slave trade. British officials could, however, also be distinctly cautious when faced by the persistence of slavery in Muslim Africa and Asia. Indeed, William Gervase Clarence-Smith maintains that so fearful were some of the political consequences of tampering with servitude that they manipulated Islamic beliefs and institutions to delay slavery's abolition. Others, he relates, attempted to discover abolitionist potential in Islam's holy texts. Sir Sidney Smith, the hero of the siege of Acre, tried to demonstrate to the Ottoman sultan that slavery was not at one with the humanitarian principles of the Qur'an; Sir Justin Sheil, the British minister in Tehran, endeavoured to persuade Muhammad Shah that the importation of slaves was contrary to Islam;

and Sir Bartle Frere put similar arguments to Egypt's khedive and the sultan of Zanzibar. But there is little evidence to suggest that the subsequent actions of any of these princes was seriously influenced by lectures from unbelievers on the ethics of Islam. Although in 1848 Persia's shah prohibited the import of slaves by sea, he seems as likely to have been swayed in this direction by the counsels of an eminent sufi as by the diplomacy of Sheil.

There was in any case an element of hypocrisy in the British berating non-Christians on the evils of slavery. The British were themselves ready to tolerate domestic slavery, though not the slave trade, in African and Asian territories which fell under their protection. Moreover, the act of 1833 abolishing slavery in Britain's colonial possessions did not offer complete or immediate freedom to those thereby manumitted. It established an apprenticeship system, with skilled slaves serving their masters for a further four years, and field slaves for six; and emancipated slaves remained subject to the very restrictive "master and servant" legislation prevailing within the empire. Mandy Banton, in an essay in which she examines the significance of this and subsequent colonial legislation, contrasts the enlightened approach of Lord Glenelg, the colonial secretary during 1835–39, and Sir James Stephen, his permanent under-secretary, towards labour issues, with the "distrust of humanitarianism and emphasis on economic concerns" exhibited by their late nineteenth- and twentieth-century successors. Laws enacted by colonial assemblies in Africa and the West Indies were underpinned by racist notions, including the assumption that "primitive" peoples required more stringent regulation than their counterparts in advanced economies, and by the desire of employers for cheap and unskilled labour. In the Cape Colony and elsewhere in Africa penal sanctions were introduced to enforce contracts of employment and harsh and summary punishment could be meted out to employees for comparatively trivial offences. James Maxton, the Independent Labour Party MP, complained in 1929 that such legislation perpetuated the "economic slavery of the people". But, as Banton indicates, British governments were unenthusiastic about international conventions aimed at reforming colonial labour law, much of which would remain in force until the eve of decolonization.

British official attitudes towards the use of forced labour in the neighbouring Portuguese empire seem likewise to suggest that by the 1890s humanitarian concerns mattered less in Whitehall than they had done in the 1830s. The recruitment of "contract labour" in Angola by methods which very often amounted to enslavement, and the subsequent shipment of the unfortunate captives to the equatorial islands of São Tomé and Príncipe for employment in the cocoa plantations there, was an embarrassment for chocolate-manufacturing Quaker families in England.

It was also a matter of increasing concern to anti-slavery campaigners in general. However, as Glyn Stone reveals in a chapter in which he reviews in detail consular reporting and parliamentary and press criticism of the traffic, the late nineteenth-century Foreign Office was very cautious in its handling of the question. Portugal was an ancient ally; it was strategically important to Britain in Africa and the Atlantic; and its Mozambican subjects were a valuable source of labour for the mines of southern Africa. As foreign secretary from 1905, Sir Edward Grey was more inclined than his immediate predecessors to remonstrate with the Portuguese and, following the overthrow of the monarchy in 1910, the new republican administration in Lisbon signalled its readiness to modify colonial labour practices. Senior British officials seemed, nonetheless, reluctant to pursue the issue with the vigour that Portugal's critics felt it deserved.

Labour conditions in Portugal's overseas possessions remained an inconvenience and an irritant to the British government, but in the aftermath of the First World War it was generally believed that the traffic in enslaved Africans had been virtually eliminated. The partition of Africa by the European powers and their negotiation and signing of the Brussels act of 1890 for the repression of the trade were assumed to have achieved this end. In the concluding chapter of this volume Suzanne Miers demonstrates how false was this impression. During the inter-war years slave raiding continued in east Africa and the Sudan, with traffickers serving markets in the Hejaz and elsewhere in the Arabian peninsula. Moreover, although the League of Nations, influenced by British anti-slavery activists, pressed ahead with international measures aimed at combating slavery in all its various forms, government departments in London were lukewarm in their support. The suppression of the slave trade had once offered a pretext and a reason for imperial expansion. Yet it had long since become apparent that the maintenance of empire required respect for, and sometimes the exploitation of, native customs, and that could all too often mean Britain's acquiescence in slavery's persistence. Not that the end of empire and decolonization made Britain's task any the easier in this respect. British governments were henceforth reluctant to appear to be interfering in the internal affairs of former colonies and dependencies, and until the 1970s they were exposed to international criticism because slavery had yet to be outlawed in what were perceived as Britain's client states in Oman and the Persian gulf. Meanwhile, attempts within the United Nations to devise new mechanisms for monitoring and rooting out slavery in all its various forms were hampered by the ideological divisions of the Cold War, and by the determination of some of the newly-independent states of Africa and Asia to so broaden the definition of slavery as to include within its scope *Apartheid* and colonialism.

Slavery and the slave trade were nevertheless still capable of arousing public passions in Britain. In 1962, just over a century after the citizens of Lyme Regis drafted their memorial, evidence of children being traded in west Africa generated letters of protest to the Foreign Office, petitions, deputations and parliamentary questions.[53] The modern phenomenon of people trafficking, more usually equated with the control, rather than the possession and trading, of individuals, has also become a matter of increasing domestic and global concern. And the international human rights agenda, into which slavery and related matters have been subsumed, continues to confront governments and diplomats with issues which would not have been foreign to Castlereagh and Canning. Foremost amongst these is that of when, whether and on what legal and moral basis, humanitarian intervention in the affairs of other sovereign states might be undertaken. In 1822 Canning contemplated "justifiable violence" against Brazil's maritime slave trade on the grounds that it contradicted "the consenting policy of all the civilized world on a matter on which the dictates of Christianity and morality [were] clear". Since then the "civilized world" has become more diverse, the "consenting policies" therefore more difficult to achieve, and the requirements of religion and morality far less easy to discern. Even when it was otherwise Dahomey's slave-trading sovereigns survived the wrath of Christian England.[54]

Notes

1   The National Archives (TNA), FO 84/1160, memorial from the inhabitants of Lyme Regis, 27 Nov. 1861.

2   On Dahomey's role in the slave trade, see Karl Polanyi, *Dahomey and the Slave Trade: an analysis of an archaic economy* (Washington: University of Washington Press, 1966).

3   FO 84/1160, memo. by Palmerston, 9 Aug. 1861. David Murray, *Odious Commerce: Britain, Spain and the abolition of the Cuban Slave Trade* (Cambridge: CUP, 1980), pp. 302–4.

4   John D. Hargreaves, *Prelude to the Partition of West Africa* (London: Macmillan, 1966), pp. 53–6. Suzanne Miers, *Britain and the Ending of the Slave Trade* (London: Longman, 1975), pp. 49–50.

5   David Richardson, "The British Empire and the Atlantic Slave Trade, 1660–1807", *The Oxford History of the British Empire*, vol. ii, *The Eighteenth Century* (Oxford: OUP, 1998), ed. P. J. Marshall, pp. 441–64. Between 1791 and 1800 British vessels conveyed an annual average of 32,550 Africans into slavery. Ronald Hyam, *Britain's Imperial Century: A Study of Empire and Expansion* (London: B.T. Batsford, 1976), p. 40.

6   Letter from Thomas Clarkson *et al.*, *The Times*, 20 July 1846, p. 6, col. e. The emancipation bill, which passed into law on 29 August 1833, provided that as from 1 August 1834, slavery, as a legal status, would cease to exist

throughout the British colonies. On the background to this legislation, see Howard Temperley, *British antislavery, 1833–1870* (London: Longman, 1972), pp. 1–18.

7 This is not, however, to endorse the thesis advanced by Eric Williams in his seminal study *Capitalism and Slavery* (Chapel Hill, NC: University of North Carolina Press, 1944) that the capital inflow resulting from the slave trade and the slave economies of the West Indies was a vital stimulus to Britain's industrial revolution. For a summary analysis of recent academic research on the significance of the slave trade for Britain's economic development, see Kenneth Morgan, *Slavery, Atlantic Trade and the British Economy, 1600–1800* (Cambridge: CUP, 2000), especially pp. 94–8.

8 Herbert S. Klein, *The Atlantic Slave Trade* (Cambridge: CUP, 1999), pp. 71–2.

9 Peter Fryer, *Staying Power: The History of Black People in Britain* (London: Pluto Press, 1987), pp. 120–6.

10 Hugh Thomas, *The Slave Trade: The History of the Atlantic Slave Trade, 1440–1870* (London: Papermac, 1997), p. 463. Adam Hochschild, *Bury the Chains: Prophets and Rebels in the Fight to Free an Empire's Slaves* (London: Pan Books, 2006), p. 87.

11 William Hague, *William Wilberforce: the life of the great anti-slave trade campaigner* (London: Harper Perennial, 2008), pp. 142–68.

12 Thomas, *Slave Trade*, pp. 507–9.

13 Andrew Porter, "Trusteeship, Anti-Slavery and Humanitarianism", *The Oxford History of the British Empire*, vol. iii, *The Nineteenth Century* (Oxford: OUP, 1999), ed. Andrew Porter, pp. 198–221.

14 W. E. F. Ward, *The Royal Navy and the Slavers: The Suppression of the Atlantic Slave Trade* (London: George Allen and Unwin, 1969), p. 15. Thomas, *Slave Trade*, p. 554.

15 Tara Helfman, "The Court of Vice Admiralty at Sierra Leone and the Abolition of the West African Slave Trade", *The Yale Law Journal*, vol. 115 (2006), pp. 1122–56.

16 James Bandinel, *Some Account of the Trade in Slaves from Africa as connected with Europe and America* (London: Longman, Brown & Co., 1842), pp. 127–8.

17 Ibid., p. 125.

18 Ibid., pp. 129–41. See also Lewis Hertslet, *A Complete Collection of the Treaties and Conventions at present subsisting between Great Britain & Foreign Powers; so far as they relate to Commerce and Navigation; to the Repression and Abolition of the Slave Trade; and to the Privileges and Interests of the Subjects of the High Contracting Parties* (2 vols., London: Egerton, 1820), vol. i, pp. 261–3.

19 Cited in Leslie Bethell, *The Abolition of the Brazilian Slave Trade: Britain and the Brazilian Slave Trade Question, 1897–1869* (Cambridge: CUP, 1979), p. 12.

20 Suzanne Miers, *Britain and the Ending of the Slave Trade* (London: Longman, 1975), p. 11.

21 Cited in Jerome Reich, "The Slave Trade at the Congress of Vienna: a study in English public opinion", *Journal of Negro History*, vol. 53 (1968), pp. 129–43.

22 Paul Michael Kielstra, *The Politics of Slave Trade Suppression in Britain and France, 1814–48: Diplomacy, Morality and Economics* (London: Macmillan, 2000), pp. 34–36, 44, 51.

23 Bertrand Badie, *La diplomatie des droits de l'homme: entre éthique et volonté de puissance* (Paris: Fayard, 2002), pp. 19–46.

24 C. K. Webster (ed.), *British Diplomacy, 1813–1815: select documents dealing with the reconstruction of Europe* (London: Bell, 1921), pp. 233–5.

25 Miers, Britain and the Ending of the Slave Trade, pp. 10–13. C. K. Webster, *The Foreign Policy of Castlereagh, 1815–1822*, vol. ii, *Britain and the European Alliance* (London: Bell, 1958), pp. 454–8. Reich, "The Slave Trade", p. 142.

26 Hertslet, *Treaties*, vol. i, pp. 9–13.

27 Ibid.

28 TNA, FO 92/11, Castlereagh to Liverpool, letter, 26 Jan. 1815.

29 David Turley, *The Culture of English Antislavery, 1780–1860* (London: Routledge, 1991), pp. 76–7. C. K. Webster, *The Foreign Policy of Castlereagh, 1812–1814*, vol. i, *Britain and the reconstruction of Europe* (London: Bell, 1931), pp. 423–24.

30 Kielstra, *Slave Trade Suppression*, pp. 56–8.

31 Bandinel, *Some Account of the Trade in Slaves*, pp. 131–2.

32 Ibid., pp. 151–2.

33 Ibid., pp. 152–6. Bethell, *Brazilian Slave Trade*, pp. 18–19.

34 Bandinel, *Some Account of the Trade in Slaves*, pp. 159–64.

35 Cited in Thomas, *Slave Trade*, p. 592.

36 Ibid., p. 601.

37 Bandinel, *Some Account of the Trade in Slaves*, pp. 154–5.

38 Ibid., pp. 163–4.

39 *Papers Relating to the Slave Trade, presented to Parliament, Feb. 1819*: No. II, *Protocol of the Conference between the Plenipotentiaries of the Five Powers, 4 Feb. 1818*, enclosure 1, annex A, p. 13; No. VI, Castlereagh to Richard Rush, letter, 20 June 1818, p. 45; No. XI, Conference at Aix-la-Chapelle, Nov. 1818, enclosure 11, p. 83.

40 Webster, *Castlereagh*, vol. ii, pp. 464–5.

41 *Papers Relating to the Slave Trade, presented to Parliament, Feb. 1819*: No. VIII, Rush to Castlereagh, letter, 21 Dec. 1818, p. 50.

42 Miers, *Britain and the Ending of the Slave Trade*, p. 18.

43 Thomas, *Slave Trade*, p. 593.

44 Ward, *Royal Navy*, p. 82.

45 Duke of Wellington (ed.), *Despatches, Correspondence and Memoranda of Field Marshal Arthur Duke of Wellington, K.G.*, vol. i (London: John Murray, 1867), p. 323.

46 Harold Temperley, *The Foreign Policy of Canning, 1822–1827* (2nd edition, London: Frank Cass, 1966), pp. 313–14.

47 Wendy Hinde, *George Canning* (London: Collins, 1973), pp. 341–2.

48 Bandinel, *Some Account of the Trade in Slaves*, pp. 242–5. Kielstra, *Slave Trade Suppression*, p. 157. Ward, *Royal Navy*, p. 121.

49 Miers, *Britain and the Ending of the Slave Trade*, pp. 15–18. Muriel E. Chamberlain, *Lord Aberdeen: A political biography* (London: Longman, 1983), pp. 312–21.

50 Wellington, *Despatches,* p. 329.
51 David Eltis, *Economic Growth and the Ending of the Transatlantic Slave Trade* (Oxford: OUP, 1987), p. 97.
52 Howard Temperley, *British antislavery*, pp. 62–92.
53 Suzanne Miers, *Slavery in the Twentieth Century: The Evolution of a Global Problem* (Walnut Creek, CA: AltaMira Press, 2003), pp. 360–1.
54 Gelele, despite further quarrels with Britain, remained king of Dahomey until his death in 1889. His successor, Behanzin, was deposed in 1894 following the French conquest and dismemberment of his kingdom. Hargreaves, *Prelude*, pp. 201–7, 344. In 1999 the BBC was still reporting on the sale of children into domestic slavery in the Republic of Benin, the name adopted in 1975 by the Republic of Dahomey.

CHAPTER ONE

Zealots and Helots
The Slave Trade Department of the Ninetenth-Century Foreign Office

KEITH HAMILTON

During the first half of the nineteenth century British governments translated a moral crusade against the slave trade from the domestic to the
international sphere. This involved the negotiation of declarations and
conventions aimed at facilitating the Royal Navy's role in policing the
coasts of Africa and Latin America, and the establishment of mixed
commission courts, first in Sierra Leone then elsewhere, for the adjudication and condemnation of ships detained on suspicion of slaving. It led
to disputes with France, Portugal, Spain and the United States; coercion
in Africa; and what amounted to the chastisement of Brazil, one of the
principal slave-importing countries. And only in the 1860s was the
Atlantic slave trade finally eradicated with the halting of that with Cuba
during the American civil war. All this, British reactions to the supply of
slaves from within and without the Muslim world, and the relationship
between humanitarian intervention and the expansion of empire, has
been examined in detail in numerous scholarly works. By the 1840s, anti-
slave trade diplomacy was, in the words of one British foreign secretary,
Lord Aberdeen, a "new and vast branch of international relations".[1] Its
study has since become a well-established branch of imperial and international history. Yet the Slave Trade Department of the Foreign Office,
the body which oversaw correspondence relating to the traffic and
managed the mixed commissions, and which was largely responsible for
mounting a major campaign of public diplomacy against the trade, has
seemed only to attract the interest of administrative historians.

This is hardly surprising. Until 1854 the clerks of the department were
in, but not truly of, the Foreign Office. Their work was very often dull
and routine, requiring little intellectual effort. They registered, reproduced and recycled the enormous documentation generated by the
diplomacy of abolition, but their contribution to policy remains difficult
to discern. And while some were described as zealous in the execution

20

of their duties, their pay and grading were lower than those of their colleagues of the regular establishment. The department, according to one permanent under-secretary, Henry Unwin Addington, bore "the mark . . . of *helotry*".[2] However, in its early years it was the largest defined division of the Foreign Office headed by a senior clerk, and its formation predated that of the geopolitical departments which later characterized the Office. Moreover, if, as has recently been suggested, the mixed commission courts should be regarded as the first international human rights courts,[3] then the Foreign Office's Slave Trade Department could be considered the first human rights department of any modern foreign ministry. The bureaucratic lynch-pin of the mechanisms devised by the British in their diplomatic endeavour to eliminate slave trafficking, it was instrumental in the elaboration of Britain's policy towards sub-Saharan Africa.

BANDINEL'S DEPARTMENT

James Bandinel, the first head of the department, was also the author of one of the earliest published histories of Britain's anti-slave trade diplomacy. His 1842 book on the *Trade in Slaves from Africa* remains an authoritative account of the accords which, by bribery, cajolery and moral suasion, Britain extracted from other powers with a view to limiting and ultimately abolishing the trade upon the high seas.[4] A man of conviction when it came to dealing with the slave trade, his frequent appeals to Christian morality may have been reinforced by his several filial links with the Almighty. Born in 1783, the son of the Reverend Dr James Bandinel, the rector of Netherbury, he was younger brother to the Reverend Bulkeley Bandinel, the Librarian of the Bodleian in Oxford, and son-in-law to the Reverend Robert Hunter, the rector of Burton Bradstock in Dorset. His son, another James, followed in the family's clerical tradition becoming eventually rector of Emley in Yorkshire and a minor, though noted, theologian.[5] Yet Bandinel's career was probably more influenced by Mammon than any Anglican deity. Having secured appointment as a Foreign Office clerk in April 1799, he had been deeply troubled by his failure to gain early advancement and he was desperate to enlarge his income.[6] His hopes of preferment may well have been encouraged when in 1819, during Lord Castlereagh's tenure as foreign secretary, he was asked by him to take on "extra employment" in superintending the details of the execution of the various slave trade treaties and the management of the mixed commission courts. Three years later he was promoted to be one of the Office's four senior clerks. Then in the autumn of 1824 George Canning, Castlereagh's immediate successor,

decided to compensate him for his additional duties with a payment of
£1,000 and an annual allowance of £200. The £1,000 was paid from
monies arising from the sale of condemned slave vessels, and the annual
allowance was to be included in the expenses voted yearly by Parliament
to cover the costs of the mixed commissions.[7] The award gave Bandinel
more than a moral stake in the suppression of the slave trade.

Those who served under Bandinel in London received less generous
treatment. The Foreign Office was of course itself only forty years old
when Bandinel secured his senior clerkship. Its administrative structure
remained rudimentary, there being under two under-secretaries just
eighteen clerks of the regular establishment, to which another four were
added in 1826.[8] As for the Slave Trade Department, it was as Addington
later remarked, at its inception a "mere nullity . . . a Dept. of secondary
consideration and welded on, as it were, to the Office as an excrescence
aggregated to a body of higher quality and nature".[9] This was in part due
to the way in which slave trade clerks were recruited and remunerated.
Charles Pettingal, George Frere, and Bandinel's nephew, John James Le
Mesurier, who were engaged to assist Bandinel in the years 1825–27,
were all drawn from outside the Office with this specific task in view.
Their salaries were defrayed from the parliamentary vote for suppression
of the slave trade, their employment was regarded as temporary, and their
work essentially that of copyists rather than that of "persons requiring
education and capacity".[10] Bandinel continued to execute most of the
important duties himself, and the salaries of his juniors were inferior to
other clerks in the Office, as also were their prospects of promotion. In
1843 clerks of the regular establishment received on their first appointment £100 per annum, and by annual increments, ranging from £10 to
£50, they could eventually hope to attain the office of chief clerk with
a maximum salary of £1,250 a year. By contrast, slave trade clerks entered
the Office on £80 a year, and could never attain a salary higher than
£300, or a position more elevated than that of first clerk within their
department.[11]

Some were tempted to improve their income through appointment
overseas as judges, arbitrators and registrars of the mixed commission
courts. But in so doing they risked falling victim to disease and sometimes violence in the tropics. Insurance companies were reluctant to
maintain life cover for appointees to such places as Freetown in Sierra
Leone and Surinam in Dutch Guiana;[12] and in August 1855 George
Canning Backhouse, the son of the Office's very first permanent under-
secretary, was murdered only eighteen months after arriving at his post
as commissary judge in Havana.[13] Those who remained in the Foreign
Office had to cope with a steadily increasing workload. The British
government was far too optimistic in its estimate of the impact of diplo-

macy and naval action upon the slave trade. Treaties relating to its suppression multiplied as did the paper-work associated with them. In consequence, the business of Bandinel's department, which included the direction of all the relevant correspondence with foreign powers and the mixed commissions and, in response to public demand, the preparation of a large body of parliamentary papers, seemed relentlessly to expand. Despatches and letters received and sent by the department rose from 844 in 1830 to 2,205 in 1840, and to 4,198 in 1845, and between 1830 and 1845 the printed slave trade papers published and laid before Parliament rose from 338 to 1,335 printed pages. (There was no Freedom of Information Act in 1845. There was no need for one.) Bandinel was, in addition, responsible for the distribution of parliamentary grants averaging £20–30,000 a year in the form of contingency expenses, salaries and pensions, to commission personnel.[14] In effect, he himself acted as paymaster to the commissioners, collecting a 1 per cent fee on their salaries, an arrangement of which the Treasury was unaware until in 1843 it assumed direct responsibility for such disbursements.[15]

Bandinel's grasp of the slave trade and the economic and political issues associated with it made him an authority on African matters in general. He was the only person in the Foreign Office with any specialized knowledge of Africa and he was frequently consulted by both the Treasury and the Colonial Office. Lord Palmerston, who was foreign secretary for all but nine months of the period between November 1830 and August 1841, sought his advice on British policy towards French expansion in west Africa and, more particularly, with regard to French incursions into the area bordering the River Gambia.[16] On another occasion Bandinel was charged with the preparation of a memorandum on the political and legal status of Fernando Po and Annabon, islands which the British government considered purchasing with a view to relocating there the mixed commission courts of Sierra Leone and thereby easing the sufferings of Africans liberated on captured slave ships. Although the islands had been ceded by Portugal to Spain in 1778, they had not been under continuous European occupation and, in Palmerston's opinion, Spain appeared to have "the same kind of claim" to them as Britain then had to the Falkland Islands.[17] British explorers also met with Bandinel and, at the invitation of Thomas Fowell Buxton, in 1839 he attended the first meeting of the British and Foreign Anti-Slavery Society, the organization founded to campaign for world-wide emancipation.[18]

Buxton was personally of the opinion that the suppression of the Atlantic slave trade might be better facilitated by attacking it at its source, and by persuading local African rulers to turn their attention to agriculture and other forms of commerce.[19] The idea appealed to Lord Glenelg, the colonial secretary, and at his request Bandinel began work on drafting comprehensive instructions for the negotiation of treaties with African chiefs and kings within the bights of Benin and Biafra.[20] The papers with which Bandinel supplied the Colonial Office included, in addition to a model treaty (based on one concluded in 1840 with the sultan of Muscat) prohibiting the slave trade and providing for the "opening of friendly communications for innocent and useful Commerce", proposals for Britain's acquisition of Fernando Po and for the erection of a small fort above the delta of the River Niger (or Quorra as it was then known).[21] These reflected Cabinet thinking on the matter. Nevertheless, Bandinel evidently perceived his work on what became the Niger expedition as extending somewhat beyond his customary administrative duties. He was left free to draft on his own initiative and, in his dealings with Glenelg and his successors, Lord Normanby and Lord John Russell, he assumed more of an advisory role than might at that time have been expected of a senior clerk in the Foreign Office. He also made a number of suggestions as to what might be offered to local African rulers with a view to securing their adhesion. Native tribes could, he thought, be offered protection against their neighbours if this would induce them to give up the slave trade, but only when Britain could conveniently fulfil such a condition "on account of immediate contiguity" or "other special circumstances". Likewise, he counselled against more than "anxious and affectionate advice" when pressing for the abolition of "human sacrifices" where such practices existed. The "prejudices of the Natives" might, he speculated, "be so strong in favour of the Custom that the Abolition of it may in some cases create a Risking of breaking off the negotiations".[22]

Conscious that he might be close to overstepping the boundary which separated clerical from ministerial responsibilities, Bandinel was apologetic, almost obsequious, in proffering this advice. "I do not know", he wrote, "whether I ought to beg pardon for these Observations, but I must add that I shall readily obey any Directions which Lord John Russell may give me for altering the draft of the Agreement in the way that he shall desire".[23] Yet Buxton and his fellow anti-slave trade campaigner, Stephen Lushington, considered Bandinel's draft instructions too modest. They believed that any settlements intended to demonstrate the benefits of agriculture and commerce "must be kept apart from the contamination of prevailing native practices"; and, to that end, they urged the government to purchase the "sovereignty of a territory not exceeding one hundred miles square". Even this represented a retreat from their belief that the establishment of British sovereignty over whole kingdoms was the "greatest boon" which could be conferred on Africa and "the surest as well as the speediest mode of effecting the eradication of the Slave Trade". The alternative might in any case mean leaving Africa to the French, the Portuguese and, in the case of Liberia, the Americans. There were, in addition, the newly independent "Texians", who might "ere long covet portions of the African soil, for the very purpose of giving facility to the Slave Trade". Already the intellectual, if not yet the political, seeds, were being sown which would one day help transform the Slave Trade Department from a repository of information into an agent of empire in Africa.[24]

Two years later, in 1842, Lord Aberdeen, Palmerston's successor as foreign secretary, appointed Bandinel to the commission, which was to meet in 10 Downing Street, to revise the instructions of the British fleets engaged in suppression of the trade. "We must", Aberdeen observed, "by the perfect justice and openness of our proceedings induce foreign powers to join Great Britain in the Christian and humane tasks which, at immense cost and labour, she has imposed upon herself."[25] There was never any doubt in Bandinel's mind about the righteousness of this endeavour. The suppression of the slave trade became for him an act of reparation for sins previously committed by British traders in Africa. When, in retirement, he testified before the House of Commons Select Committee on the Slave Trade, a body which was highly critical of the costs and efficacy of the naval squadrons maintained off the coasts of west Africa and South America, he was passionate in opposing any relaxation of British efforts to eradicate the commerce. On 13 April 1848 he responded to questioning on the subject that there was a "retribution" which Britain owed to Africans. "[W]e owe it", he added, "to every principle of humanity; we owe it to what we have done and have been able to do; we owe it also to the general feeling of this country; we owe it to the character which we hold among the nations of the world, to be still foremost in endeavouring to extinguish the trade, and we should do what is practicable".[26] He was no less anxious to ensure respect for treaties already concluded. In the case of Brazil, whose governments had done little to fulfil their international obligations with regard to halting the traffic, he thought that Britain would be justified "in making redress by force of arms".[27] Unlike Quaker abolitionists, Bandinel had no qualms about resorting to naval action in defence of what would now be defined as human rights.

Bandinel was in other respects far from being a paragon of bureaucratic virtue. Despite his literary venture, his drafting skills were evidently not always up to the standards expected within the Office. Palmerston could be quite tyrannical in such matters, and in a minute in which he complained of having to correct the English of his staff, one parliamentary under-secretary noted that Bandinel "expresse[d] himself very awkwardly", and that it was disagreeable to have to correct all his sentences "as if he was a schoolboy". Yet if this were not done, Palmerston would send it back, "slashed about with very cutting observations". So upset was Bandinel by Palmerston's comments on one of his drafts that he ordered it "to be kept *for the hereafter*".[28] It may be that the moralizing, and in later years abstemious, Bandinel was peculiarly sensitive to criticism. His relations with his estranged wife hardly suggest that he was the most accommodating of individuals. Jealousy on his part reputedly led to their separation, and both were subsequently to engage in the bitterest of recriminations. According to his niece and future daughter-in-law, Julia Le Mesurier, James Bandinel's affairs with Lady Arabella Harvey and Lady Mary Shephard also ended in squabbles and tears. "Just like all women", he complained of a Lady Mary, distraught at his refusal to run off with her, "so unreasonable! If a man will not give up every thing, character & station, & all his hopes of succeeding in life, they are infuriated and will hate you more bitterly than they loved you warmly!"[29] Bandinel's personal ambitions, especially where money was concerned, do indeed appear to have overshadowed his relations with colleagues, family, friends and lovers. In middle age he was determined that nothing should be allowed to threaten either his position or acquired perquisites. This, in part, explains his resistance to the efforts of John Backhouse, the permanent under-secretary, to achieve a "proper system and Establishment for the Office".[30]

CLERICAL ERRORS

Backhouse, who characterized the opposition of Bandinel and John Bidwell, the first senior clerk, to the promotion of a new chief clerk as "mean and tricky", had hoped that with the backing of Palmerston he could achieve a general improvement in working conditions throughout the Office. This included the abolition of special allowances and the ending of the anomalous status of a separately-funded Slave Trade Department.[31] For the moment, however, Bandinel's department was neither a happy nor a healthy fiefdom. Pettingal survived the longest in post. Subject to attacks of "Rheumatic Inflammation attended with great Debility", he remained in the department until October 1843 when he left, possibly with a view to escaping to a better climate and securing a higher salary, to become arbitrator of the recently-established mixed commission court at Boa Vista in the Cape Verde islands.[32] Frere, who suffered "disappointment and discouragement" at being shut out from the prospect of advancement in the Office, also left in 1842 to join the mixed commission at the Cape of Good Hope.[33] Meanwhile, Le Mesurier had passed away. Taken seriously ill, in 1833 he gained temporary appointment as an attaché in Buenos Aires, but died next year aboard a ship bound for Madeira.[34] Two other appointees to the department,

John Browne and Daniel Dowling, both had serious financial troubles. The former, a negligent and dilatory character who was the subject of several reprimands, was a chronic debtor, and in June 1835, at the beginning of a two and a half year absence from the Office, found himself in such distress in France that Palmerston was moved to seek employment for him in Dunkirk.[35] By November 1839, ten months before he finally left the Office, he was having £20 annually deducted from his salary for payment to the commissioners of the insolvency court.[36] Hardly less embarrassing was Dowling's situation. On 20 May 1845 he had to send Bandinel a note explaining that his creditors had made it impossible for him to come into the Office. They, he wrote, "have been watching in the Street for me and all my hopes of settling everything satisfactorily depend in great measure in my not being in actual restraint from them".[37] Five months later, still unable to resolve his "pecuniary difficulties" in a manner that would allow him to fulfil his Office duties, he resigned.[38]

These were relatively minor domestic problems of little or no significance when set aside those resulting from the actions of two other slave trade clerks, Charles Henry Parnther and Henry Charles Scott. A barrister's son, Parnther was educated at Eton and Trinity College, Cambridge, and, a keen cricketer, he played for his university and the MCC. He first gained employment in Bandinel's department in April 1835, but was dismissed in 1836 after having been accused of mishandling agency fees. His father, an old friend of Palmerston, intervened, and in 1837 he was reinstated on appeal.[39] Within six years, following the departure in quick succession of Pettingal, Frere and Browne, he found himself first clerk in the department, managing an impecunious Dowling and, from November 1842, an inexperienced Scott. He also acted as principal assistant to Bandinel, substituting for him as superintendent whenever he was absent. Intent on making the most of his new position, he soon began lobbying for a salary increase or, at any rate, an additional allowance, to compensate for his new responsibilities.[40] His senior colleagues were sympathetic to his plea. Charles Canning, the son of the former foreign secretary and the then parliamentary under-secretary, complimented Parnther on the "zealous and most efficient manner" in which he had invariably discharged his duties. But another twelve months were to pass before, on 17 November 1844, he wrote to tell Parnther that, having spoken to Aberdeen, he was confident that before the end of the year the question "would be determined and acted upon in a manner which will make your position in the Office more satisfactory to you".[41] A month later Parnther was awarded an additional annual allowance of £100, backdated to January and to be drawn on the Office's contingent fund.[42]

Parnther's additional allowance was intended to be "quite independent of any general change in the Slave Trade Department".[43] Reform was again in consideration. Already in March 1842 the expenses of the department had been transferred from the mixed commissions' grant to the Foreign Office, and in 1843 the Treasury assumed direct responsibility for funding the British element of the courts.[44] The slave trade clerks nevertheless remained inferior in income and status to those in other divisions of the Office. With a view to remedying what he saw as an obvious injustice Addington, Backhouse's successor as permanent under-secretary, recommended the department's integration with the regular establishment.[45] But while Canning favoured promoting Parnther and Dowling, he doubted if others in the department could be considered anything more than copyists. "I am", he noted, "confident that all the head work of the Dept. can be efficiently done by the Superintendent, one Assistant & the 2nd Clerk, if this last is a Person of intelligence and industry."[46] It was in any case apparent that the Treasury would be reluctant to fund even Parnther's upgrading and the proposal was not pursued.[47] Indeed, it was not until March 1847 that Parnther, along with Dowling's successor, Scott, returned to the offensive. Together they addressed a minute to Palmerston, who had returned to the Foreign Office in the previous summer, drawing attention to the "great and discouraging difference" between their terms of employment and those of the established clerks.[48] Addington and Thomas Staveley, who had replaced Bandinel in December 1845, favoured the two clerks being placed as supernumeraries on a level, or at least nearly so, with their coevals in the Office until they reached the top of the scale of second class clerks.[49]

Palmerston was no less supportive. He personally subscribed to the notion that an "Office ought to be like a Regiment, one Body, the members of which should in their respective Grades be liable to perform any of the Duties for which the Body is constituted, and to be shifted from one Duty to another as occasion may require".[50] Unfortunately for Parnther, whose salary in 1847 was still no more than that of a third class clerk in any other department, Addington withheld from making any formal application to the Treasury until October 1848.[51] Discussions regarding the establishment and differences over the reporting of a Treasury commission of enquiry into the workings of the Foreign Office made for further delay, and it was not until March 1853 that it was finally settled that Parnther and Scott should be assimilated to the scales of second and third class establishment clerks and benefit from their promotion from January 1850.[52] By then Parnther was thoroughly disgruntled. He was particularly disappointed to learn that as part of the exercise he was to be deprived of the £100 annual allowance he had been awarded eight years earlier, leaving him, he wrongly reckoned, £5 a year worse off. He was equally put out by the news that his colleague Scott was, after only eleven years in the department, also to be retrospectively promoted to the grade of second class clerk.[53]

After an interview with the chief clerk, the one-legged and short-tempered Ulsterman, George Lenox-Conyngham, Parnther was reassured that his prospects were in fact improved.[54] Nonetheless, his long struggle for a pay rise may have affected his attitude towards his work. It may also have contributed to a decline in his physical, and possibly his mental, well-being. In July 1852 he took sick leave, but this was followed by his absence from the Office without satisfactory explanation for a full 151 days. Reprimanded by Addington, in February 1853 he was threatened with dismissal if the offence were repeated.[55] But whether Parnther's absence from, or his general dissatisfaction with, his position had any bearing on subsequent revelations that he and Scott were involved in embezzling slave trade funds remains open to speculation. The fraud first came to light when in August 1853 Lord Clarendon, foreign secretary since the previous February, received a letter from the Reverend Charles Jackson of Bentley near Farnham in Hampshire. This revealed that his uncle, Sir George Jackson, since 1845 the British commissary judge at Luanda, had been alarmed to find that £450 was missing from the account which Parnther and Scott managed for him in London.[56] As was customary at this time, the two clerks had acted as agents for Jackson and his colleagues, ensuring payment of salaries and settlement of outstanding bills. However, on investigation by Lenox-Conyngham it was discovered that Parnther and Scott were in debt to Jackson for the sum of £498 19s. 1d., and that in addition they owed Edmund Gabriel, the court arbitrator at Luanda, and William Smith, the registrar there, £622 18s. 11d. and £414 19s. 1d. respectively. All the evidence suggested that the monies had been misappropriated by Parnther and Scott for their own uses over a period of eighteen to twenty months. "The lamentable extent of the irregularity", noted the chief clerk, " . . . is quite inexplicable".[57] Parnther and Scott were in no position to make good the missing funds and on 16 September 1853 both received notice of their dismissal on the grounds that they were "guilty of fraudulent and disgraceful behaviour".[58] Needless to say, neither was in the Office to receive the news. Parnther was again absent without leave, and Scott simply absconded.

There was some irony in the fact that George Jackson should have been a casualty of the fraud. Formerly, as commissary judge in Rio de Janeiro, Jackson had enjoyed an income four times larger than that of the highest paid slave trade clerk, yet he had persistently protested his poverty and pressed for improved remuneration. Other British functionaries had been irritated by his petulant behaviour and delays and inconsistencies in his adjudications, and when in 1841 he was accused of accepting bribes from Brazilian slavers Palmerston promptly instigated his transfer.[59] An underpaid and overworked Parnther may possibly have considered an overpaid and under-performing Jackson fair game for peculation. But it did him little good. Parnther was just a fortnight short of his fortieth birthday when he learned of his dismissal. Within fourteen months he was dead. He suffered a ruptured aorta, and his body was found on 10 November 1854 in a public house, the Red Lion at Walham Green, not far from where he had once resided in Brompton.[60] It seems unlikely that Bandinel would have approved of the establishment. However, by 1854 he was long since deceased. He died on 29 July 1849 after having had the misfortune to contract Asian cholera at Salisbury while attending a meeting of the Archaeological Institute.[61] And in April 1851 his immediate successor, Staveley, was replaced by Thomas Ward, the third son of Viscount Bangor and a veteran of several diplomatic missions.[62] These changes, and particularly those associated with the agency accounts scandal, offered Clarendon both an opportunity and a pretext for seeking once and for all to transform the department. He began by appointing in Parnther's stead Francis Alston, a very able second class clerk of the regular establishment, who would eventually succeed Lenox-Conyngham. Then, in the following year, 1854, the Slave Trade Department was, with Treasury concurrence, reconstituted as a regular department of the Office.[63]

POST-MORTEM PERMUTATIONS

Only one slave trade clerk, George Skelton, who had been appointed to the department in 1845 and who, as longest serving clerk, now succeeded to Scott's position, seemed unlikely to benefit from the change. He was not offered the opportunity to join the establishment, but it was agreed in 1854 that he should receive the salary of a second class clerk.[64] Two years later he left the Office to follow the same path as many of his under-appreciated predecessors, becoming arbitrator of the mixed commission courts in Sierra Leone, where he died of fever in 1865.[65] A more fortunate slave trade clerk was Henry Percy Anderson. Like Bandinel, a clergyman's son, he had joined the department in October 1852 and in April 1854 was, as a result of Clarendon's reform, appointed to the regular establishment as a fourth class clerk. Within thirty years he was to rise to become head of the Office's Consular and African Department, into which the Slave Trade Department had by then been absorbed and transformed, and, as such, he was a key figure in the European partition of Africa.[66] Parnther's disgrace proved to be Anderson's salvation. Yet, even in a reformed Slave Trade Department, grievances over pay and grading persisted. William Henry Wylde, who in 1855 was appointed assistant senior clerk in the department, nourished what became a long-standing grudge against the Office over its refusal to confirm his earlier probabtionary promotion to the rank of senior clerk. Instead, he found himself acting and paid as second in command, first to Ward, and then to Ward's sickly successor, Adolphus "Dolphie" Oom. During the latter's prolonged illness, Wylde had effectively to take over the direction of the department, and although in April 1859 he replaced Oom as senior clerk, he had by then been passed over for promotion by at least three junior colleagues. The Treasury opposed his being offered any financial recompense for fear of creating a precedent, and a resentful Wylde had, like previous members of his department, to content himself with a salary inferior to his peers.[67]

Wylde had been introduced early to clerical work. Born in April 1819, the son of Colonel (later Major-General) William Wylde of the Royal Artillery, he had, aged sixteen, accompanied his father to northern Spain when in 1835 Colonel Wylde was despatched there as part of the British Auxiliary Legion serving under Queen Isabella during her struggle with the Carlists. The young Wylde was present at many military operations.[68] He also acted as his father's private secretary before returning to England in 1838 to take up appointment in the Foreign Office, first as a supernumerary clerk in the Slave Trade Department, and then, from April 1839, as junior clerk of the establishment. In 1846 he returned to the Iberian peninsula, again as assistant to his father, whom Palmerston sent on a special mission to a Portugal teetering on the edge of civil war.[69] All this and Wylde's fluency in Spanish might seem particularly pertinent to one who would spend a good part of his subsequent career gathering and collating information on developments in Portugal's African colonies and on the slave trade with Spain's remaining imperial possessions.[70] Certainly in 1859 that with Cuba was his department's main concern. During the two previous years it had increased considerably, and Wylde was vigorous in pressing for arrangements which would ensure a regular supply of intelligence from Havana and, at a time when the Cuban trade was conducted largely in vessels flying American colours, New York.[71] He likewise advocated punitive action against west African rulers complicit in the trade.[72] Indeed, Wylde's minutes and memoranda suggest that he was far less circumspect than Bandinel had been in counselling ministers and senior colleagues on the subject. Palmerston, who was prime minister during 1859–65, continued to busy himself with the slave trade. But Wylde and his departmental associates had a detailed understanding of the traffic which four successive and less formidable secretaries of state, Malmesbury, Russell, Stanley and Clarendon, could ill-afford to ignore.

Wylde was also, despite his earlier setback in securing substantive promotion, well-regarded in the Office. When in 1873 Edmund Hammond retired as permanent under-secretary both Staveley and Alston, the chief clerk since 1866, were of the opinion that Wylde ought to apply for the vacant post of assistant under-secretary.[73] By then the Slave Trade Department's geographical focus of attention had shifted eastwards. As the transatlantic traffic in slaves declined, particularly during the American civil war, so did official interest in curbing that of the Muslim world increase. Palmerston had long since launched an attack on the largely Arab-controlled trade in Africans, and to that end agreements had been concluded with the Ottoman and Persian empires and their neighbours and feudatories in Arabia.[74] But it was the revelations of David Livingstone and the grim tales he had to tell about the east African slave trade which in the mid-1860s re-ignited public concern for the sufferings of the native peoples of the region. Zanzibar, whose sultan was a quasi-independent tributary of the ruler of Muscat, was at the hub of the trade and, when the results of naval patrolling off the east African coast proved disappointing, Wylde was drawn into the Whitehall-wide debate on how best to deal with the sultan and the Arab slavers. His advice was blunt and forthright. In a memorandum of 6 April 1869 he argued that Britain must behave liberally towards the sultan in order to win his assistance in taking further measures against the trade, and at the same time deliver warnings to the chiefs of the Arabian coast and Persian gulf that the Royal Navy intended to enforce existing treaties. He was convinced that such measures, along with a well-organized distribution of a small squadron, would suffice to suppress the east African trade. "There were", he declared, "never wanting Prophets who prophesised that it would be impossible to put an end to the Slave Trade on the West Coast, but the result has proved the contrary, and I have no doubt the same success will attend our efforts on the East Coast should it be decided by H.M.'s Govt. to make the attempt."[75]

Wylde's memorandum was far more robust in style and content than anything drafted by Bandinel during his stewardship of the Slave Trade Department. It was a policy document whose emphasis was as much on strategy as tactics. Others soon followed, and Wylde, who represented the Foreign Office on an interdepartmental committee established by Clarendon specifically to look at means of combating the east African trade, was still being consulted on the issue two years after leaving the Slave Trade Department. In a paper of 28 September 1871 he urged the government not to allow the sultan of Zanzibar "perpetually to violate his Treaty engagements . . . to spread misery and ruin over a large portion of the African Continent".[76] The advice, supported by the Admiralty and colleagues in the Office, was not ignored, and in 1873 the sultan was persuaded under threat of a naval blockade to accept a treaty prohibiting the export of slaves from his possessions on the mainland of Africa.[77] Yet Wylde's department was peripheral to the main political work of the Office. Indeed, with the elimination of the transatlantic trade it, like the navy's west African squadron, had lost its original *raison d'être*. Measured on the basis of despatches received and sent, the Slave Trade Department's share of Foreign Office correspondence had shrunk from 17.63 per cent in 1845 to 4.68 per cent in 1865.[78] Wylde's staff consisted of no more than an assistant, and two junior, clerks, and after he left the department in July 1869 to take over the superintendence of the Commercial and Consular Department, his replacement, Hussey Crespigny Vivian, who had been every bit as vocal as himself in pressing for more vigorous action in east Africa,[79] stayed no more than three years in post before moving to the more prestigious German Department.[80] A single Consular and Slave Trade Department was subsequently established under Wylde, and in 1876 its work was divided between a Slave Trade Department, under Wylde's personal supervision, and a Consular Subdivision.[81]

Within this combined super-department other administrative permutations were to follow, including the creation in 1879 of a Slave Trade and Sanitary Department. It, in addition to dealing with the slave trade, had responsibility for correspondence relating to cattle plague, quarantine and pilgrims, thus bringing under common administration a bizarre amalgam of agricultural, humanitarian, religious and social issues.[82] Wylde, for his part, was fully alive both to the extent to which religious beliefs and practices impinged upon the trafficking in people particularly in the Near and Middle East, and of the importance of consular persuasion and reporting in combating the trade. Reports from the Hejaz indicated that captive Africans were being shipped across the Red sea in vessels flying the Ottoman flag and that they were being traded on to lands elsewhere in the region by pilgrims returning from Mecca. It was in part with a view to reinforcing the navy in its efforts to contain the trade that Wylde initiated negotiations which led to the conclusion in March 1880 of a new Anglo-Ottoman convention.[83] It provided *inter alia* for a mutual right of search of vessels in waters other than the Mediterranean.[84] To the evident disappointment of Victorian reformers, the agreement did nothing to tackle the white slave traffic, the sale and supply of women, mostly of Circassian and Georgian origin, for marriage and concubinage in Turkey. But Sir Henry Layard, the British ambassador in Constantinople, was reluctant to offend Muslim opinion. He feared that by raising the matter he would have "the whole Turkish people up in arms against us". There were in any case, as Layard pointed out to Wylde, parallels in the West. "In England", he wrote, "mothers take their daughters to balls & garden parties to get them off their hands. Here fathers (Circassians) sell their daughters to get them good establishments."[85]

When Wylde finally retired in March 1880 a further reorganization was effected in the Foreign Office, and by 1882 two quite separate departments, a Commercial and Sanitary Department and a Consular and Slave Trade Department, had come into existence.[86] This reflected the growing importance of commercial work, and the assumption, confidently expressed by Lord Granville, the foreign secretary in Gladstone's second administration, that the management of a diminishing slave trade correspondence would soon be distributed elsewhere within the Office.[87] Granville had evidently neither foreseen the extent to which developments in tropical Africa would impinge upon British diplomacy during the 1880s, nor reckoned with the ambitions and calibre of Percy Anderson, who though nominated in 1882 senior clerk in charge of the Consular and Slave Trade Department, was in fact appointed in 1883 first head of a renamed Consular and African Department.[88] The change in departmental nomenclature was a matter of some significance. Henceforth, the slave trade and its suppression would increasingly be treated in the Foreign Office as but one, albeit important, element of a broadening African agenda. Ever since the 1840s the promotion of other forms of trade and the establishment of British settlements had been seen as means of combating the traffic in Africa. Palmerston and Russell had encouraged with subsidies and, on occasions, warships, the penetration of the Niger basin by British explorers, merchants and missionaries. And when in June 1854 Livingstone arrived at Luanda, after having traversed the African interior, he was quick to impress on Edmund Gabriel, the principal victim of the agency accounts fraud, that "if Legitimate Commerce were once established in the Congo, there [was] a high degree of probability that the Slave Trade would be effectually checked throughout the whole extent of that Country".[89] It was likewise characteristic of Wylde that, soon after taking over the Consular Department in 1869, he argued strongly in favour of maintaining a naval presence on the Niger because with a little more energy the river could be rendered a "most valuable mart for British manufacturers".[90] Thirteen years later another slave trade clerk, Clement Hill, contended that the battle against the east African trade might be best continued by the appointment of "travelling Vice-Consuls" attached to the British agency at Zanzibar and with residencies on the mainland. Were Sir John Kirk, the agent there, also provided with a steam vessel, Hill thought this would be of advantage "in preventing native outbreaks and missionary quarrels, in encouraging British subjects, in developing trade, in keeping the Sultan's authorities up to the mark and in supporting British influence on the mainland". Commerce, Christianity and empire were the handmaidens of humanitarian intervention.[91]

One further concern of both Hill and Kirk was the need to check the "intrigues of the French" in east Africa and the Indian ocean.[92] It had for some time been apparent that the naval campaign against the slave trade had encouraged native dhows to seek French protection.[93] By the 1880s the paramountcy that the British had formerly exercised over much of the African littoral was being increasingly challenged by other European powers with commercial and ultimately political designs upon the continent. Indeed, barely had Anderson settled into his new department before he was confronted by what looked like a French bid for hegemony over the mouth of the Congo, and in the ensuing scramble for land and influence he gave priority to safeguarding Britain's power and prestige. He may only have had a third class degree in classics, but in the words of William Roger Louis, he had a "first class chess-board mentality" when it came to dealing with imperial rivals.[94] He and his department gained much credit for their part in the Berlin West Africa conference of 1884–85. Sometimes perceived as a watershed in the European partition of Africa, the conference followed on from the objections of other great powers to Britain's efforts to block the territorial aspirations of France by advancing the historic claims of Portugal. Agreement was eventually reached on a mix of measures, including internationalization and neutralization, which were intended to ensure free trade in the Congo and Niger basins. In practice they may well have hastened the transition from informal to formal empire across the continent.[95] The British, nevertheless, still managed to introduce humanitarian content into the conference proceedings, and the Berlin act pronounced that the maritime slave trade was forbidden by international law, and that operations which furnished slaves for it on land and water "ought likewise to be regarded as forbidden".[96] After over half-a-century of fighting the slave trade, the Foreign Office still clung to the moral high ground whilst defending tenaciously Britain's interests in the market-place of empire.

In these respects the British derived considerable advantage from having had in the Slave Trade Department a knowledge-based division with unrivalled experience in marshalling public opinion behind the causes it pursued. No other European foreign ministry had the equivalent resident expertise for engaging in the complex diplomatic wrangles which arose over Africa, east and west, during the next two decades. Bandinel's department, associated with patronage and prone to financial malpractice, may sometimes have seemed to belong more to the eighteenth than to the nineteenth century. But the department, recast in the 1850s and renamed in the 1880s, emerged as the very model of a twentieth-century Foreign Office department, in which its senior staff would have the opportunity to influence policy in a manner virtually unknown elsewhere in the Office. Anderson and Clement Hill, his immediate successor as head of the Consular and African Department, were in practice diplomats as well as bureaucrats, participants in bilateral and multilateral negotiations and intermediaries between the official and public arenas.[97] There was also a significant broadening of their departmental agenda. The Brussels conference of 1889–90, the first such intergovernmental gathering devoted specifically to curbing the slave trade, prefigured later League of Nations' debates by addressing the related issue of arms trafficking in Africa.[98] In the long process of reform and transition, humanitarian intervention was refined both as an instrument of diplomacy and a means of imperial control. A century before the late Robin Cook proclaimed that a Labour government would put "human rights at the heart of [its] foreign policy", his Victorian predecessors had learnt to count the costs and reap the benefits of giving their diplomacy an "ethical dimension".[99]

Notes

1 Cited in Andrew Porter, "Trusteeship, Anti-Slavery and Humanitarianism", *The Oxford History of the British Empire*, vol. iii, *The Nineteenth Century* (Oxford: OUP, 1999), ed. Andrew Porter, pp. 198–221.

2 The National Archives (TNA), FO 83/313, Addington to Aberdeen, draft letter, autumn 1843, attached to minute by Addington, 16 March 1846.

3 Jenny S. Martinez, "Antislavery Courts and the Dawn of International Human Rights Law", *The Yale Law Journal*, vol. 117 (2007), pp. 550–641.

4 The full and typically wordy title of Bandinel's study is: *Some Account of the Trade in Slaves as connected with Europe and America; from the introduction of the trade into modern Europe down to the present time; especially with reference to the efforts of the British Government for its extinction* (London: Longmans, Brown & Co. for HMSO, 1842).

5 *Oxford Dictionary of National Biography*, vol. iii, pp. 664–5. The name Bandinel is derived from Bandinelli, that of an Italian protestant family, whose descendants arrived in England in the seventeenth century, having previously resided in Languedoc and the Channel Islands.

6 Duke University Library (Durham, NC), Rare Book, Manuscript, and Special Collections Library, Bandinel MSS, Bandinel to Marian Hunter (later Mrs J. Bandinel), letters, 2 June and n.d. 1812.

7 FO 83/40, Joseph Planta to Bandinel, minute, 4 Dec. 1824. Measured in terms of retail purchasing power, £1,000 in 1824 is roughly equivalent to £70,165.49 in 2007.

8 Charles R. Middleton, "The Foundation of the Foreign Office", *The Foreign Office, 1782–1982* (Frederick, Maryland: University Publications of America, 1984), ed. Roger Bullen, pp. 1–18.

9 See note 2 above.

10 Ibid. TNA, FO 366/386, Palmerston to Treasury, draft letter, 9 Aug. 1841.

11 Ibid.

12 TNA, FO 84/447, Sir George Jackson to Lord Aberdeen, letter, 2 March 1842.

13 Duke University, Backhouse MSS., Box 17, Thomas Callaghan (Havana) to Thomas Staveley, letter, 8 Sept. 1855.

14 FO 366/313, Charles Parnther and Henry C. Scott to Palmerston, minute, 17 March 1847.

15 Charles R. Middleton, *The Administration of British Foreign Policy, 1782–1846* (Durham, NC: Duke UP, 1977), pp. 198–99. FO 84/489, Sir C. Trevelyan (Treasury) to Charles Canning, letter, 23 Nov. 1843.

16 Middleton, *Administration of British Foreign Policy*, pp. 199–200 and 264.

17 FO 84/299, FO to Colonial Office, 30 Jan. 1839, letter covering memo. by Bandinel, 24 Jan. 1839.

18 FO 84/305, Buxton to Bandinel, letter, 20 June 1839, and minutes by W.T.H. Fox-Strangways and Palmerston, 21 June 1839.

19 Howard Temperley, *White Dreams, Black Africa. The Antislavery Expedition to the Niger 1841–1842* (New Haven and London: Yale UP), pp. 9–19.

20 Bandinel MSS., minute by Glenelg, 18 Feb. 1839, enclosed in Bandinel to Aberdeen, letter, 28 Nov. 1843.

21 TNA, FO 881/521, memo., "Africa. Expedition and Mission Proposed: Some Points for Consideration", 1 Feb. 1839, and Annexes A and B, draft instructions for negotiators and draft Treaty. FO 84/336, Bandinel to James Stephen (Colonial Office), letter, 10 April 1840. Palmerston was subsequently to request that the term "agreement" be substituted for "treaty" since the latter implied a negotiation under the Foreign Office. FO 84/337, Lord John Russell to Bandinel, extract from minute, 13 Dec. 1840.

22 FO 84/336, Bandinel to Stephen, letter, 10 April 1840.

23 Ibid.

24 FO 84/337, Lushington and Buxton to Russell, letter, 7 Aug. 1840, enclosed in Russell to commissioners of the Niger expedition, letter, nd. Dec. 1840.

25 Bandinel MSS., Aberdeen to Bandinel, minute, 6 Dec. 1842. FO 84/446, Aberdeen to Lushington, letter, 14 Dec. 1842; C. Canning to the commissioners, letter, 29 Dec. 1842. The full story of the ill-fated Niger expedition is related in detail in Temperley, *White Dreams, Black Africa*.

26 *Parliamentary Papers, 1847–48*, xxii (272), *House of Commons Select Committee on the Slave Trade*, 1st Report, para. 3281.

27 Ibid., para. 3387.

28 Kenneth Bourne, *Palmerston. The Early Years, 1784–1841* (London: Allen Lane, 1982), p. 425.

29 Bandinel MSS., Julia Le Mesurier to Mrs J. Bandinel, letter, 30 Dec. 1839.

30 Backhouse MSS., Box 12, J. Backhouse to G. C. Backhouse, letter, 17 July 1841.

31 Ibid., FO 366/386, Palmerston to Treasury, draft letter, 9 Aug. 1841.

32 Middleton, *Administration of British Foreign Policy*, p. 301. FO 84/389, Pettingal to Bandinel, letter, 7 Feb. 1841; Pettingal to Palmerston, letter, 5 May 1841. As early as 1826 Pettingal had been offered the job of clerk with

the mixed commission court in Havana, but he declined the appointment because of worries relating to the climate, expenses and the well-being of his family and other dependants. He was also "engaged in a Chancery Suit respecting some property" which he assumed would eventually be his. FO 84/61, Pettingal to Planta, minute, 14 June 1826.

33 FO 366/674, Frere to Palmerston, letter, 28 Aug. 1841. Middleton, *Administration of British Foreign Policy*, p. 280.
34 Ibid., pp. 291–2.
35 TNA, FO 27/510, Bidwell to V.-Consul Pettingal (Dunkirk), letter, 4 June 1835.
36 FO 84/305, Palmerston to commissioners of the Court for the Relief of Insolvent Debtors, draft letter, 16 Nov. 1839.
37 Middleton, *Administration of British Foreign Policy*, p. 301.
38 FO 366/674, Charles Canning to Dowling, letter, 1 Nov. 1845.
39 Middleton, *Administration of British Foreign Policy*, p. 301. Bourne, *Palmerston*, p. 447.
40 FO 366/313, Canning to Parnther, letter, 8 Nov. 1843.
41 Ibid., Canning to Parnther, letter, 13 Nov. 1844.
42 Ibid., minute by Addington, 19 Dec. 1844.
43 Ibid., Canning to Parnther, letter, 13 Nov. 1844.
44 FO 84/489, Sir C. Trevelyan to Addington, letter, 2 Aug. 1843; Trevelyan to Canning, letter, 23 Nov. 1843.
45 FO 366/313, Addington to Aberdeen, draft letter, nd., autumn, 1843.
46 Ibid., memo. by Canning, nd., April 1844.
47 Ibid., memo. by Addington, 18 March 1847.
48 Ibid., Parnther and Scott to Palmerston, minute, 17 March 1847.
49 Ibid., memos. by Addington and Staveley, 18 March and 3 May 1847.
50 Ibid., memo. by Palmerston, 6 May 1847.
51 Ibid., Addington to Staveley, minute, 12 Feb. 1848.
52 Ibid., Palmerston to Treasury, draft letter, 22 March 1851; Addington to Palmerston, minute, 8 Nov. 1851; G. Cornewall-Lewis to Palmerston, letter, 17 Dec. 1851; Lord Stanley to Treasury, letter, 24 Dec. 1851; memo. by Trevelyan, 7 Feb. 1852; memo. by G. Lenox-Conyngham, 23 Feb. 1852; minute by Lord Clarendon, 15 March 1853.
53 Ibid., Parnther to Addington, minute, 15 April 1853.
54 Ibid., Parnther to Addington, letter, 21 April 1853.
55 FO 366/449, Addington to Parnther, minute, 9 Aug. 1852; Addington to Parnther, letter, 21 Feb. 1853.
56 Ibid., C. Jackson to Lord Clarendon, letter, 10 Aug. 1853.
57 Ibid., memo. by Lenox-Conyngham, 31 Aug. 1853.
58 Ibid., minute by Clarendon, 16 Sept. 1853; Addington to Parnther and Scott, letter, 16 Sept. 1853; Addington to G. Jackson, 27 Sept. 1853.
59 FO 84/445, memos. on Sir G. Jackson, 13 March 1842. Leslie Bethell, *The Abolition of the Brazilian Slave Trade. Britain, Brazil and the Slave Trade Question, 1807–1869* (Cambridge: CUP, 1979), pp. 201–2.
60 General Register Office, Death Certificate for Parnther, 11 Nov. 1854. The public house has since been refurbished and appropriately renamed the

Fiesta Havana. Situated in the Fulham Road it was in 2007 offering its clientele Cuban cocktails and salsa dancing.

61 *Gentleman's Magazine*, 1849, pt. 2, p. 327. Middleton, *Administration of British Foreign Policy*, p. 264.
62 Ibid., p. 316.
63 FO 366/449, Addington to Lenox-Conyngham, minute, 31 Oct. 1853; Clarendon to Treasury, letter, 9 March 1854; W.E. Gladstone to Clarendon, minute, 5 April 1854.
64 Ibid., Skelton to Clarendon, minute, 28 June 1854; note by E. Hammond, 30 June 1854.
65 Ibid., Lord Shelburne to Skelton, minute, 1 Dec. 1856. Middleton, *Administration of British Foreign Policy*, p. 308.
66 Wm. Roger Louis, "Sir Percy Anderson's Grand Africa Strategy, 1883–1896", *English Historical Review*, vol. lxxxi (1966), pp. 292–314.
67 FO 366/675, Hammond to Lord Malmesbury, minute, 26 July 1858. FO 366/676, memo. by Wylde, 8 Dec. 1868, attached to Hammond to Clarendon, minute, 22 Dec. 1868; Hammond to Treasury, letter, 28 Dec. 1868; Geo. A. Hamilton (Treasury) to Hammond, letter, 20 Jan. 1869.
68 *The Times*, 4 March 1909, p. 13, col. e.
69 Colonel Wylde was also an equerry to Albert, the prince consort. On the diplomatic background to his mission to Portugal, see: Roger Bullen, *Palmerston, Guizot and the Collapse of the Entente Cordiale* (London: Athlone Press, 1974), pp. 213–92.
70 University of Durham Library, Archives and Special Collections, Wylde MSS., Lord Granville to Treasury, letter, 23 May 1873.
71 FO 84/1082, memos. by Wylde, 26 May, 23 June and 29 Aug. 1859.
72 FO 84/1160, memo. by Wylde, 7 Aug. 1861.
73 Wylde MSS., Staveley to Wylde, letter, 24 Oct. 1873. In the event Thomas Villiers Lister, who had previously served under Wylde, was appointed to the post.
74 Ehud R. Toledano, *The Ottoman Slave Trade and its Suppression, 1840–1890* (Princeton: Princeton UP, 1982), pp. 91–123.
75 FO 84/1310, memo. by Wylde, 31 March 1869.
76 Wylde MSS., memo. by Wylde on the *Report of E. Africa Slave Trade Cttee.*, 28 Sept. 1871.
77 Suzanne Miers, *Britain and the Ending of the Slave Trade* (London: Longman, 1975), pp. 89–91.
78 Wylde MSS., *Return of the Number of Despatches &c Received and Sent from the Foreign Office, in each Year from 1826 to 1873*.
79 See for example, Wylde MSS., memo. by Vivian on the east African slave trade question, 18 Oct. 1871.
80 FO 366/676, minute by Clarendon, 27 July 1869. FO 366/677, minute by Lord Granville, 9 Feb. 1872.
81 Ray Jones, *The Nineteenth-Century Foreign Office. An Administrative History* (London: Weidenfeld and Nicolson, 1971), pp. 88–9.
82 Ibid., p. 90. FO 366/677, minute by Lord Derby, 15 Dec. 1876. FO 366/678, minute by Lord Tenterden, 13 Dec. 1879.

83 FO 84/1510, Layard to Wylde, tel., 18 May 1878, with minutes by Wylde, Lord Salisbury and Julian Pauncefote. Wylde was every bit as resolute in pressing for the suppression of the Red Sea slave trade as he had been in urging action against that of the Indian Ocean. Despite the pessimism some-times expressed by Colonel Charles Gordon, the Egyptian governor-general of the Sudan, regarding his own efforts to counter the traffic, Wylde believed that its eradication could be achieved "if we make up our mind to spending a little more money on the necessary measures for its repression". However, his proposal for branding negroes liberated in Arabia so that they would "carry always with them a badge of freedom" and not be subject to re-enslavement was not endorsed by either Julian Pauncefote, the permanent under-secretary, or Lord Salisbury, the foreign secretary. FO 84/1544, memo. by Wylde, 11 June 1879; and minutes by Wylde, Pauncefote and Salisbury on Zorab (Jeddah) to Salisbury, despt. No. 12, 30 May 1879.

84 Miers, *Britain and the Ending of the Slave Trade*, pp. 82–6. Toledano, *Ottoman Slave Trade*, pp. 233–7.

85 Wylde MSS., Layard to Wylde, letter, 18 Feb. 1880. On Layard's views on the white slave traffic, Wylde noted: "It must be left to time to effect a change in this demoralizing social institution, and I would propose to say so to Sir H. Layard." FO 84/1570, minute by Wylde, 1 March 1880.

86 R. W. Lingen (Treasury) to Tenterden, letter, 20 April 1880.

87 FO 366/678, Granville to J. Bergne, letter, 10 March 1881.

88 Ibid., minutes by Alston, 30 Nov. 1882, and Granville, 20 and 21 Dec. 1882.

89 FO 84/931, Gabriel to Clarendon, despt., 22 June 1854.

90 FO 84/1311, memo. by Wylde, 2 Oct. 1869. See also on the Foreign Office and the Niger, John D. Hargreaves, *Prelude to the Partition of West Africa* (London: Macmillan, 1966), pp. 34–8.

91 FO 84/1694, memo. by Hill, 23 Aug. 1882.

92 Ibid.

93 Miers, *Britain and the Ending of the Slave Trade*, p. 105.

94 Louis, "Percy Anderson", pp. 292–4.

95 Wm. Roger Louis, "The Berlin Congo Conference", *Britain and France in Africa. Imperial Rivalry and Colonial Rule* (New Haven: Yale UP, 1971), eds. Prosser Gifford and Wm. Roger Louis, pp. 167–220.

96 Miers, *Britain and the Ending of the Slave Trade*, pp. 172–3.

97 In addition to representing Britain at the Berlin West Africa conference, Anderson also participated in the Berlin negotiations of 1890 which resulted in the Anglo-German agreement on Africa and Heligoland. Hill, who in 1872–73 was a member of Sir Bartle Frere's special mission to the sultans of Muscat and Zanzibar, served as special commissioner to Haiti in 1886 and represented Britain at the 1900 London conference for the protection of wild animals in Africa. From 1900 to 1905 he was superintendent of the African protectorates under the Foreign Office, and in retirement he was president of the African Society.

98 Suzanne Miers, "The Brussels Conference of 1889–1890: The Place of the Slave Trade in the Policies of Great Britain and Germany", *Britain and Germany in Africa. Imperial Rivalry and Colonial Rule* (New Haven and

London: Yale University Press, 1967), eds. Prosser Gifford and Wm. Roger Louis, pp. 82–118.

99 Robin Cook, "Putting Principle into Practice: The Role of Human Rights in Foreign Policy", *Cambridge Review of International Affairs*, vol. xv, no. 1 (2002), pp. 45–51. Mark Wickham-Jones, "Labour's trajectory in foreign affairs: the moral crusade of a pivotal power", *New Labour's Foreign Policy: A New Moral Crusade?* (Manchester: Manchester UP, 2000), eds. Richard Little and Mark Wickham-Jones, pp. 3–32.

CHAPTER TWO

Judicial Diplomacy
British Officials and the Mixed Commission Courts

FARIDA SHAIKH

Britain's fight against the slave trade helped shape the structure of the nineteenth-century Foreign Office. It also led to a unique experiment in judicial diplomacy through the establishment of mixed commission courts. These resulted from bilateral treaties which Britain concluded successively with Portugal (1817 and 1842), Spain (1817), the Netherlands (1818), Brazil (1826) and the United States (1862), permitting the search and seizure by their respective navies of vessels of their nationals suspected of trading illegally in slaves. In each instance the treaties provided for the creation of at least two jointly-staffed courts, one within the territory of each of the contracting parties, which were charged with determining the fate of ships thus detained. British officials appointed to the mixed commission courts were, like those initially serving in the Slave Trade Department, a breed apart from other servants of diplomacy. Their names eventually appeared in the *Foreign Office List* alongside those of ambassadors, ministers and consuls, but, save in those instances when consuls doubled as judges or court arbitrators, commissioners were not considered members of either the diplomatic or consular services. Nor were they invariably men with legal experience or training. They adjudicated, arbitrated and assessed; they gathered intelligence on the slave trade; and they reported to the Foreign Office. Some developed a strong personal commitment to the suppression of the trade: this, however, was not a prerequisite of their selection. Better remunerated than most clerks in Whitehall, and with fewer opportunities for long-term career advancement than their colleagues in legations, they were wary participants in what has since been perceived as one of the earliest attempts to enforce international human rights law.[1]

STAFFING COURTS

Anglo-Portuguese, Anglo-Spanish, Anglo-Netherlands, Anglo-Brazilian and, from 1862, Anglo-American, mixed commissions were set up in Freetown, the capital of the British crown colony of Sierra Leone. The port was selected for a number of reasons. First, Sierra Leone had been established in 1772 by the philanthropic Sierra Leone Company as a settlement for liberated slaves, and as a crown colony it had acquired a relatively developed administrative infrastructure which made it an ideal reception centre for both naval crews and the freed captives of slave ships. Secondly, there was already a precedent since a vice-admiralty court had been established there after the 1807 abolition act in order to adjudicate cases of British, and sometimes foreign, slavers.[2] Finally, most captures of slave vessels took place along a 2,000 mile stretch of west African coast, so a "local" depot where warships could bring in slavers and their cargoes was necessary. An Anglo-Netherlands commission also sat in Surinam, an Anglo-Spanish commission in Havana, an Anglo-Portuguese (later Anglo-Brazilian) commission in Rio de Janeiro, and, from 1842, Anglo-Portuguese commissions sat in Boa Vista (Cape Verde islands), the Cape of Good Hope, Luanda and Spanish Town (Jamaica). In time, there were also Anglo-American commissions in Sierra Leone, the Cape of Good Hope and New York. Each court comprised a commissary judge and a commissioner of arbitration (arbitrator) from each signatory country, and a registrar, responsible for recording court decisions, was appointed by the sovereign government of the territory in which the commission resided. The contingent expenses of the courts were shared equally between the two countries concerned, except in Freetown where Britain paid one third, and Portugal, Spain, Brazil and the Netherlands one sixth each. Responsibility for the payment of the salaries of British commissioners, borne initially by the funds voted by parliament for the suppression of the slave trade, rested with the Foreign Office.

The early years of operation saw a number of teething problems. Whilst Castlereagh keenly pursued implementation of the new treaties, including the prompt appointment of court officials, other countries party to the treaties were less conscientious. In February 1819 Thomas Gregory was appointed first British commissary judge in Freetown, along with Edward Fitzgerald, the commissioner of arbitration, and Daniel Molloy Hamilton, the registrar.[3] But when, by November that same year, Portugal had still not appointed its court personnel, British officials at post were left confused about how best to proceed. The foreign secretary, Lord Castlereagh, after consulting the Portuguese minister in London, the Marquis de Palmella, instructed the British commissioners to hear

cases involving Portuguese ships even in the absence of Portuguese officials, and to fill their positions until they arrived.[4] This proved to be a
lasting arrangement that would apply at various times to all of the mixed
commissions in Sierra Leone.[5] Although Netherlands and Spanish
commissioners were appointed in 1819, and the Portuguese commissioners the following year, frequent absences through illness and a failure
by governments to replace deceased staff meant that British commissioners often sat alone.[6] And the Brazilians, who in 1826, after securing
their independence from Portugal, agreed to subscribe to Portuguese
commitments regarding the slave trade, delayed appointing a commissary
judge in Freetown for another two years.[7] Then on arrival at post the
Brazilian judge, José de Paiva, challenged the legality of all previous adjudications concerning Brazilian slavers, arguing that they could not have
received a satisfactory hearing in his absence. This claim the British
rejected. If Brazilian ship owners felt they had sustained an injury by the
absence of one of their nationals as a commissioner, the responsibility,
they contended, rested with their government.[8] Meanwhile, de Paiva did
little to improve his standing with the local community when in
September 1829, within weeks of his wife's death, he married his
adopted, and by then several months pregnant, daughter.[9]

Other governments rarely seem to have matched the crusading zeal of
the British when it came to suppressing the trade. And where the courts
in Sierra Leone were concerned they had difficulty in finding people
ready to brave far from attractive postings in what was popularly
perceived as the white man's grave. The British were fortunate in being
able to recruit personnel from the pool of officials already *in situ* in the
colonial administration.[10] They also offered them extremely attractive
remuneration. While in 1819 Sierra Leone's colonial governor had an
annual salary of £2,000, the commissary judge at Freetown was paid
£3,000 a year, plus an outfit allowance of £500. His colleagues, the arbitrator and the registrar, received respectively £1,000 and £500, and, like
the judge, they could draw pensions after six years' service at post.[11]
British commissioners in Rio de Janeiro and Havana, whilst spared, at
least to some extent, a severe and debilitating climate, were often more
at risk of personal violence than their counterparts in Freetown. During
the 1830s, for example, Sir George Jackson, the commissary judge, and
Frederick Grigg, the arbitrator, in Rio de Janeiro, frequently called on
the national guard to escort them through angry crowds which were apt
to hurl stones at the courthouse when the mixed commission was in
session.[12] Around this time the commissary judge's salary in Rio de
Janeiro was £1,200, and that of the commissioner of arbitration £800.
In Havana the equivalent salaries were £1,600 and £1,200.[13]

Despite these relatively high earnings, personnel were not shy of asking for more. George Jackson, who held appointments as commissary judge over the best part of thirty years, was a regular Oliver Twist. A career diplomat who had served in Paris, Berlin and Madrid, he had first become acquainted professionally with matters relating to slavery when for four years, 1823–27, he was Britain's principal representative on a commission established in Washington to settle claims for compensation arising out of the war of 1812. It was work which involved, among other things, assessing what payments should be made to American plantation owners whose slaves had been freed as a result of British military action. Never an unduly modest man, Jackson equated his position with that of minister, the rank then held by most heads of British diplomatic missions, and after his return from Washington in 1827 he was to assert that he had achieved far more favourable terms than his government had originally contemplated.[14] This, Jackson evidently believed, entitled him to further preferment and a larger emolument. Lord Dudley, the foreign secretary, disagreed, but he was prepared to recommend him for the then vacant position of commissary judge in Sierra Leone.[15] Jackson prevaricated. He wanted an outfit allowance equal to half a year's salary, and the prospect of a substantially enhanced diplomatic pension if he were unable to remain at post for the requisite number of years.[16] Indeed, he turned down the job when, in March 1828, it was made plain to him that neither his appointment as commissary judge, nor any services he might perform in Sierra Leone, could be considered "Diplomatick".[17]

Jackson soon changed his mind. Unemployment, even on a diplomatic pension of £700 per annum, must have seemed less attractive than the salary of a non-diplomatic commissary judge.[18] But Jackson still managed to delay his departure for Sierra Leone until June 1828 and, after arriving in Freetown on 26 August,[19] he came rapidly to the conclusion that a fever-ridden west Africa did not suit his constitution.[20] He requested leave of absence on 31 January 1829 and, though this was turned down, he departed for England in June on grounds of ill-health.[21] For the next twelve months, he drew the half-pay due to an absentee commissioner, and would doubtless have continued to do so had the Foreign Office not forced him to choose between returning to Sierra Leone and reverting to his pension.[22] Thereafter, having relinquished his position, he began again to badger the government either for another appointment or what he regarded as just financial recompense.[23] Almost two years were to pass before in 1832 the foreign secretary, Lord Palmerston, responded positively to his application for the then vacant post of commissary judge in Rio de Janeiro.[24] Jackson, who would almost certainly have preferred a fully-fledged diplomatic appointment, once more complained about the outfit allowance on offer (this time a meagre £300).[25] Residence in Rio also proved costly and it was with a view to remedying his "very distressing" personal situation there that, while on leave in London in 1837, he sought, albeit unsuccessfully, to persuade Palmerston to permit him to receive simultaneously both his salary and half his pension, pending possible promotion to a full diplomatic posting.[26]

Jackson was noted for his "peculiar and morbid sense of official or personal dignity and [his] excessively captious and querulous irritability of temperament".[27] He was nonetheless far from alone amongst mixed commission staff in feeling that his services were insufficiently appreciated. William Smith, his immediate successor at Freetown, had served in Sierra Leone since 1825 when he was appointed registrar to the mixed commission. Later, as arbitrator, he survived the fever epidemic of 1829, which killed the colony's chief justice, drove its lieutenant-governor mad, and sent Jackson fleeing back to England,[28] and by 1834, when sickness finally forced Smith to retire, he could claim to have overseen the adjudication of 145 slave ships and emancipation of 26,000 captive Africans.[29] Yet, as he had not served as a judge for the qualifying period, his request for a full pension appears to have been rejected.[30] An arguably more deserving case was presented by the family of George Canning Backhouse. The son of the Foreign Office's first permanent under-secretary, Backhouse had grown tired of the Office clerkship which in 1838 his father had pressed him to accept. Anxious for a position abroad, he was overjoyed when in December 1852 he was offered the post of commissary judge with the Anglo-Spanish court in Havana.[31] The appointment allowed him to more than treble his current income, and meant that after twelve years he would be able to retire on a pension of £600 per annum. But he was unduly optimistic. Neither he nor his wife had reckoned with the expense of setting up home in Cuba or the rich variety of fauna which would plague their early days on the island.[32] When on 31 August 1855 he died of a knife wound inflicted by intruders into his house, he left his young widow with mounting debts and three children to raise.[33] She, however, was unable to wring from the government more than a lump sum of £1,200, the most, she was informed, that had "ever been granted on similar grounds to the family of an Officer of the Slave Trade Department".[34]

JUDGING CAPTIVES

At the time of his murder Backhouse had no court arbitrator and he was the last British official appointed to Havana solely with the function of commissary judge. The mixed commission courts were by then being progressively run down. But in the 1820s, as their needs had become clearer, additional staff had been recruited, including clerks, court marshals, messengers, translators and, at Freetown, a mixed commission surgeon to take care of slaves during the period of adjudication.[35] The functions of the courts and matters concerning procedure were outlined in the several bilateral treaties, and further clarified by guidelines which issued from the law officers of the crown.[36] On arrival in port, the captured slave ship, together with any slaves it carried, became the responsibility of the marshal of the court. The officer in command of the prize crew had to make an affidavit before the registrar, and hand over any papers found on board the captured vessel together with a certificate, drawn up at the time of capture, stating where and when the ship was searched, its condition, and the number of slaves found on board. Ships' papers were crucial pieces of evidence: dual sets would imply attempts to switch nationality and evade search, valid passports might sanction the legal trade in slaves. The Anglo-Portuguese convention of July 1817 did not apply to Portuguese vessels either trading in slaves south of the equator, or transporting slaves between Portugal's colonies in the southern and northern hemispheres. Log books could therefore provide evidence of a ship's deviation from its permitted route and into illicit slave-trading waters. The captain and two or three individuals from the captured vessel also had to make depositions on oath. A standard set of "Interrogatories for the Use of the British Commissioners, to be administered to the Witnesses belonging to the Vessel taken" was drawn up in order to help ascertain the facts in court. All items of evidence were presented to the court which had to decide, without appeal, and within twenty days of the ship being brought into port, on the legality of capture, and whether the vessel in question was guilty of illegal slave-trading. Except in special circumstances, a final sentence had to be delivered within two months. If judges found themselves unable to agree on the sentence, or on any matter relating to the enforcement of the treaties, they had to draw by lot the name of one of the two commissioners of arbitration to settle the matter.

Vessels found guilty of illegal trading, and which had been lawfully seized, were condemned as legal prize, their cargo (except slaves) was sold by public auction, and the profits divided equally between the two governments concerned. Britain's moiety was paid to the captors as reward for their work, whilst the foreign governments disposed of their shares as they saw fit. Additional separate funds from the Treasury were provided as bounty or head-money for each slave found on board and, after the introduction of equipment clauses into treaties (whereby slavers could be condemned in virtue of their being equipped for slaving, even if no slaves were found on board), a sum calculated according to the ship's tonnage, was payable.[37] Slaves found on board condemned vessels were listed, along with their details, in a slave register. They were then liberated, issued with certificates of emancipation, and handed over to the government in whose territory the commission sat, to be employed as servants or free labourers. In Freetown they were registered as British and offered the possible options of apprenticeship in the West Indies, a placement with a regiment of black soldiers, or a plot of land for cultivation in Sierra Leone.[38] But "free labourers" were often nothing more than slaves by a different name, as Richard Robert Madden, an ardent abolitionist, would testify before a parliamentary select committee in 1836. Moreover, those who chose to stay in Sierra Leone were not particularly successful with their farming endeavours, and also ran the risk of being recaptured by slave-traders. Sometimes they were tempted by the prospect of substantial profits to take up slave-trading themselves. In total, nearly 65,000 slaves were liberated in Freetown, and more than 10,000 and 3,000 were freed in Havana and Rio de Janeiro respectively.[39]

Mixed commission courts did not have jurisdiction over the owners, masters, or crews of condemned vessels; it was, instead, for the national courts to try and punish such individuals. But British commissioners made it their business to remind foreign governments of their own domestic legal obligations. So, for example, when in 1834 two Portuguese vessels were found guilty of slave-trading off São Tomé and Príncipe, British commissioners at Sierra Leone wrote to the Portuguese governor of the islands reminding him to "see the necessity of causing the penalties of Portuguese law to be carried into effect", namely the banishment of the master and pilot of the slavers to Mozambique and the imposition upon them of a hefty fine.[40] Ships that were not proven to be engaged in the illegal trade, or which were judged to have been seized illegally, were restored to their proprietors along with their cargo (including slaves). Such owners had a right to claim compensation for legal costs, losses incurred, such as those arising from the interim death of slaves and the daily costs of feeding the slaves and crew during the trial. And the commission courts were responsible for determining the levels of compensation warranted. The "captor himself" (i.e. the captain of the naval ship which made the seizure) was responsible for paying these costs, although in practice the British government often footed the bill, or at least made a contribution. Thus, between December 1838 and December 1844, a total of 12 out of 274 ships brought before the courts were restored, and the compensation in three of these cases was paid in full by the British government.[41] The Royal Navy's concentration upon the west coast of Africa meant that most adjudications took place in Freetown. Some 528 cases were handled there during the years 1819–45: 241 by the Anglo-Spanish commission, 155 by the Anglo-Portuguese commission, 111 by the Anglo-Brazilian commission, and 21 by the

Anglo–Netherlands commission. In the same period the commissions at Havana and Rio de Janeiro were responsible respectively for 50 and 44 adjudications, and that at Surinam for one.[42]

In many instances the effective running of the mixed commissions involved close collaboration between British court officials, colonial administrators, and members of the consular and diplomatic services. Consuls were an especially valuable source of information on local slave trafficking, and consular clerical staff sometimes made up for staffing deficiencies in the mixed commissions. But the conditions and terms of their employment were very different from those of commissary judges and arbitrators.[43] On occasions, these differences were a source of friction. During his travels through Cuba in the late 1830s, the prominent abolitionist, David Turnbull, praised Charles David Tolmé, the then British consul at Havana, as "most efficient, intelligent, and courteous", yet despaired that "his salary [was] so limited, being not more than 300L a year, that he ha[d] been compelled to engage in business as a merchant and a planter, in order to enable him to occupy that station in society which the nature of his office imperatively require[d]". Like all planters and merchants in Cuba, Tolmé employed slaves, and he imported goods that would most likely be used in the purchase of slaves from Africa in complete contradiction of Britain's abolition policy. It was therefore, Turnbull observed, "impossible that there [could] be much cordiality between him and the other British functionaries, whose duty, of course, it [was] to set their faces against slavery in all its accursed forms".[44] Colonial administrators were, by contrast, sometimes required actively to assist the mixed commissions in taking care of the victims of the trade. The governor of Sierra Leone had, for example, to provide accommodation to alleviate the sufferings of Africans otherwise confined aboard slave vessels under adjudication, an obligation which in 1828 was almost impossible to fulfil since the governor had only space available for 150 and there were 803 captives aboard ships awaiting court decisions.[45] The administration in Freetown was likewise responsible for feeding and clothing liberated Africans, and for paying them to tend plots of land until more permanent apprenticeships could be secured.

The colonial authorities could, however, find themselves at odds with the mixed commissions over the treatment of vessels detained for adjudication, especially when it came to interpreting domestic and international law. This is well illustrated by the case of the *Activo*, a Brazilian brig which in 1826 Captain James Arthur Murray, the commander of *HMS Atholl*, seized more than four degrees south of the equator. The ship, which was equipped for slaving and had a cargo of captive Africans, was brought before the Anglo-Portuguese commission at Freetown. But before a verdict could be reached, the Africans aboard rebelled and all 163 of them escaped to shore where the customs officer within the colonial administration took custody of them. The governor and his staff clearly had their own opinions and methods regarding suppression of the illicit traffic, and a request from Murray's agent for the return of the cargo was rejected on the grounds that once landed on British soil slaves were automatically free men.[46] In the absence of legal precedents or established norms for settling such issues and with no procedures for appeal beyond the mixed commission courts, the British government sought the opinion of the Doctors' Commons, the society of civil lawyers in London who were accustomed to advising on the rulings of vice-admiralty courts. Its view was that the colonial authorities were acting contrary to the law establishing the tribunal at Freetown, and that they were bound by treaty and the directions of Parliament to restore the freed Africans to the "Claimant as Slaves, or as having been illegally captured or detained by a British Vessel".[47] As this would have been neither politically nor practically expedient the escapees retained their freedom. This was nevertheless embarrassing to Murray since the mixed commission court subsequently ruled that while the *Activo* had been guilty of trading illegally in slaves, its seizure had been illegal because it had been made south of the equator.[48]

The court also ordered the restitution of the *Activo* to its master, José Pinto de Araujo, and that Murray should pay unconditionally a sum of £256 2s. 8d to cover de Araujo's legal expenses. But further compensation for the 163 escaped slaves, demurrage of the brig, and interest "on the estimated Capital employed in the purchase and maintenance of the Cargo", amounted to £10,787 15s. This sum, the court ruled, should be paid by Murray, provided the governments of Britain and Brazil agreed and declared that "the said sums ought to be so paid according to the intent and meaning of the said convention, but not otherwise".[49] The mixed commission was in effect seeking legal advice from the governments concerned as to whether, though wrongfully seized, illicit slave-traders were to be compensated for financial losses thereby incurred. Attempts by the British minister at Rio de Janeiro to discuss the matter with the Brazilian authorities were spurned, and in consequence Lord Aberdeen, who was appointed foreign secretary in June 1828, dismissed as "perfectly unwarrantable" Brazil's persistent demands for the total indemnification.[50] A similar case had, in fact, arisen with the Portuguese in 1823, when Britain had refused to pay compensation, and Aberdeen had no intention of making concessions to Brazil.[51] British commissioners, not always mindful of previous precedents, had to be advised accordingly to ensure their correct interpretation of the convention in future cases. While, however, the master of *Activo* was not compensated for the loss of his slaves, the British government (not

Captain Murray) finally paid him an indemnity of £413 11s. (£157 8s. 4d. more than the court had ordered be paid unconditionally for legal expenses).[52]

CURBING ABUSES

British commissioners tended to be more hostile towards suspected slave traders than their foreign counterparts, and in disputed cases the nationality of the commissioner of arbitration (literally decided by the drawing of lots) could be the most decisive factor in determining the fate of a ship. As Turnbull noted during his travels through Cuba in 1840, "it may be fairly said that the condemnation of a slaver depends not nearly so much on fact, or law, or the merits of the case, as on the less fallible doctrine of chances".[53] A ship was far less likely to be restored to its master in Sierra Leone where British commissioners often sat alone, than in Havana or Rio de Janeiro (see the table below). Moreover, while it was common knowledge that Spanish, Portuguese and Brazilian vessels were adept at evading the law, information gathered by Britain's commissioners and consuls suggested that foreign governments were very often complicit in such illegalities. The treaty with Spain of 1817 permitted those holding royal licenses to continue slave-trading south of the equator until 1820. But it was discovered that the Spanish authorities continued to issue them well after this date. In 1822 George Canning, Castlereagh's successor as foreign secretary, protested against this "very considerable Abuse practised by the colonial Authorities of Spain".[54] British protests were however of little avail.

Ships Adjudicated, Condemned, and Restored at Various Mixed Courts, 1831–1841[55]

Court	Ships adjudicated	Ships condemned	Ships restored	% of ships restored
Sierra Leone	272	267	5	1.8
Havana	30	27	3	10
Rio de Janeiro	25	17	88	32

Similar problems persisted elsewhere. In 1826 Henry Chamberlain, the British consul-general in Rio de Janeiro, alerted the Foreign Office to a highly irregular passport service being offered by the president of the Brazilian province of Bahia. According to Chamberlain, on the advice of local merchants likely to be "most interested in the continuance of the very abuse we are endeavouring to put down",[56] he had been issuing passports permitting slave-traders, in direct contravention of the treaty, to trade at ports north of the equator. British commissioners were informed, and instructions issued to naval officers "so that upon the meeting with any vessels irregularly licensed, such vessels may be dealt with according to Treaty upon that particular point".[57] Brazil's refusal to end this activity resulted in some heated diplomatic exchanges, with Aberdeen eventually promising strong enforcement measures to counter the Brazilian government's blatant breaches of its treaty obligations.[58] Portuguese officials were equally complicit in such irregularities. The Cape Verde islands had for many years been a major transit depot for the slave trade, and the Portuguese authorities had long been, often openly, abetting the slavers.[59] In one instance in 1839, cooperation between the Britain's commissioners in Sierra Leone and its consul at Cape Verde led to the discovery that the Portuguese governor of the islands had been issuing fraudulent passports to visiting slavers. Confronted with the evidence (passports with his signature found on board condemned vessels), the governor denied all involvement, blaming instead the chief magistrate of the islands who had, he claimed, performed the "work of an artist" in forging his signature.[60] The following year the British consul reported that not only were fraudulent passports still being issued, but ships belonging to the Portuguese government were being used to traffic slaves.[61]

Such reports heightened the sense of frustration felt by the British over their apparent inability to halt the slave trade with Brazil, which continued to flourish under the Portuguese flag. Despite the fact that in January 1815 the Portuguese had engaged to "determine by a subsequent Treaty the period at which Portuguese Slave Trade should cease universally", governments in Lisbon were in no hurry to agree on an extension of the limits on the trade set in the convention of 1817.[62] When in 1839 negotiations for a new Anglo-Portuguese treaty collapsed, Palmerston resorted to unilateral action. Legislation was enacted permitting the Royal Navy to detain all Portuguese and stateless vessels engaged in, or equipped for, slave trafficking, and providing for their condemnation by vice-admiralty courts. These measures sufficed to persuade Portugal to re-open negotiations, and a new Anglo-Portuguese treaty of 1842 extended the mutual right of search to the southern hemisphere and established the mixed commission courts in Luanda, Boa Vista, Spanish Town and Cape Town. Meanwhile, the British chose to reinterpret the Anglo-Brazilian treaty of 1826. By that treaty the newly-independent Brazil had agreed to the terms of the Anglo-Portuguese convention of 1817, and, following Brazil's formal abolition of its slave trade in 1830, the British had assumed the right to search and seize Brazilian slavers south of the equator. Nonetheless, prior to 1842 vessels bound for Brazil, even when detained laden with captive Africans, were still able to escape condemnation by asserting Portuguese nationality. A slaver might thus depart for Africa flying Brazilian colours, and return under those of Portugal. It was in part to counter such practices that in 1839 the British insisted that, on the basis of existing treaties, they were free to seize and bring before the courts ships leaving Brazil's ports equipped for slaving.[63]

Brazilians were already sore at the British naval presence in their country's territorial waters, and within the mixed commissions they resisted what they regarded as illegal interference with legitimate commerce. In consequence, Royal Naval officers delivering suspected slavers could never be certain of their condemnation. Nor could they always rely upon the British element in the courts. Jackson, as Britain's commissary judge in Rio de Janeiro, had taken the initiative in claiming for the Royal Navy the right to detain Brazilian vessels simply on the basis of their being equipped for slaving.[64] But he was subsequently much criticized by locally-based British diplomats and naval commanders for the inconsistency of his decisions. William Ouseley, the British chargé d'affaires in Rio de Janeiro, declared in April 1841 that "it would be difficult to find a Commissioner so totally unfitted, whether influenced by his own peculiar ideas or those of others as the present Commissary Judge". Jackson's acquiescence in the release of vessels captured by the Royal Navy and brought before the mixed commission court in 1838 and 1839, and a long delay in handling the case against another in 1840, led Palmerston to threaten to remove him from his post. Allegations that Jackson had accepted bribes from Brazilian slave ship owners were never substantiated, but, according to Brazil's foreign minister, Jackson's cohabiting lady friend was in their pay.[65]

Turnbull and other abolitionists also accused Jackson and his associates of having slaves in their employ. This latter charge, Jackson strenuously denied. Like other British officials in slave-owning countries, he had found it far from easy to hire domestic servants. He believed that he had been deliberately discriminated against in this respect, and claimed that it was "next to impossible to meet with white servants in Brazil".[66] "Free people", protested the wife of the British minister in Rio, "are very difficult to be met with, & uncommonly expensive."[67] Jackson, for his part, had resorted to purchasing the services of liberated Africans, providing the latter with a daily allowance as well as their board and clothing. He was nevertheless ready to comply with Palmerston's instructions that he henceforth abandon their services.[68] But this seems to have landed him in even more trouble. In a letter to the British minister in Rio de Janeiro, he wrote describing how, on 3 September 1841,

> . . . a Lady in [his] family, worn out by the fatigue and worry consequent on the loss of [his] blacks and the impossibility of getting free servants,

was suddenly attacked with a fit of momentary insanity under the impulse of which she seized upon a sword, threatening mischief to herself and others.

The ensuing fracas, during which a pistol was substituted for the sword, led to mob intervention, the summoning of the local militia, and its manhandling and attempted arrest of Jackson.[69]

Palmerston had by then already decided to dispense with his delinquent judge. In August 1841 Jackson was ordered to Surinam,[70] and John Salmo, the commissary judge there, replaced him in Rio de Janeiro. Salmo, a former king's advocate in Sierra Leone, was not noted for his professional competence.[71] Nor could Surinam have afforded him much experience in adjudicating on suspected slavers. But the Brazilians were in any case in no mood to yield to pressure, and in March 1844 gave notice to Britain of the expiration of the Anglo-Portuguese convention of 1817, which remained the basis of their participation in the mixed commission courts system. It was in response to this that Aberdeen, who was again foreign secretary, resolved that Brazilian slavers should, as stipulated in 1826, be treated as pirates, and in August 1845 Parliament passed an act providing for their trial by vice-admiralty courts.[72] Five years later, after Palmerston's return to the Foreign Office, the British government stretched even further the meaning of the 1826 treaty so as to permit the Royal Navy to resort to coercion. In June 1850 British warships entered Brazilian ports to flush out vessels being fitted for the slave trade, and the subsequent burning and scuttling of ships achieved its end. Despite calls in Brazil for war with Britain, that summer the government in Rio de Janeiro proceeded to introduce a comprehensive ban on the importation of slaves, and within two years the commerce was virtually at an end.[73]

EXPOSING CORRUPTION

Insofar as the transatlantic slave trade was concerned, British attention was henceforth focused primarily upon that with Spain's remaining Caribbean possessions. Of particular interest to abolitionists was the fate of those freed by the mixed commission courts. Slaves liberated in Havana could, as also in Rio de Janeiro, all too easily be re-enslaved or engaged as what amounted to forced labour. It was with a view to remedying this abuse that the British insisted on including in an Anglo-Spanish treaty of June 1835 the stipulation that *emancipados* (Africans emancipated by the mixed commissions) should be delivered to the government whose cruiser made the seizure. The treaty, which also extended rights of mutual search of suspected slavers to south of the equator and permitted the condemnation of vessels simply when they were equipped for slave trading, led to the creation in 1836 of the new office of super-intendent of liberated Africans in Havana. Madden, a Colonial Office appointee, was the first to take up the position.[74] But his zeal soon led to disputes with both the Cubans and his colleagues on the island.[75] Almost immediately there developed a remarkably acrid relationship between Madden, a fiery Irishman, and Edward Schenley, the British court arbi-trator. Whilst Madden was only too ready to challenge the Spanish authorities, Schenley, who had been severely wounded at Waterloo, favoured cautious diplomacy and declined to support him in his quarrel with Miguel Tacón, the island's captain-general, over the grant of a parcel of land for the temporary accommodation of *emancipados* awaiting transfer to British colonies.[76] Undeterred, Madden finally succeeded in persuading the British government to send a warship, *HMS Romney*, to Havana, where, manned by black soldiers, it served as a floating transit centre for liberated slaves.[77]

Relations between Madden and Schenley deteriorated further when in July 1836 the commissary judge went on sick leave, leaving Schenley in charge, with Madden temporarily appointed as arbitrator.[78] Schenley was particularly irked when he discovered that Madden had recruited contacts from amongst the various mercantile houses, and was reporting separately to London on arrivals and departures of suspected slavers in a manner which implied incompetence on his part.[79] Their mutual antag-onism was probably fuelled by jealousy, and in the end, Palmerston had to intervene personally in the dispute which otherwise could not but "fail to impair the authority of the Commission".[80] In fact, the commission faced many obstacles to its effective operation without this in-fighting adding to its burden. The Anglo-Spanish treaty had not been promul-gated in Cuba and, in spite of receiving evidence from Madrid to the contrary, Tacón repeatedly insisted that he had not yet received instruc-tions from the Spanish government on the matter.[81] Slave dealers attempted to conceal their illicit trade by claiming that the Africans found on seized slave ships or sold at market were *ladinos* (either long-settled legally enslaved or *emancipados* in extended servitude), who were merely being transported within the island, not *bozals* (newly-imported Africans). And, in order to avoid being detained, Spanish slave ships increasingly sailed under Portuguese and American colours. Until 1842 Portugal's treaty obligations regarding the suppression of the slave trade were more limited in scope than the latest Anglo-Spanish agreement, and although the United States government had long since outlawed the slave trade, it had as yet no treaty with Britain providing for the mutual right of search.

Madden and Schenley both protested to Nicholas Trist, the United

States consul in Havana over the abuse of the American flag by slavers.[82] So also did James Kennedy, who was appointed British commissary judge in 1837, and Campbell Dalrymple, Schenley's successor as registrar. But Trist was impervious to their complaints.[83] Indeed, Trist, who added to his considerable income by assuming the duties of Portuguese consul, was actively engaged in facilitating the slave trade.[84] He endorsed Spanish slavers as American, testified to the legitimacy of voyages undertaken by their Portuguese counterparts, and he was suspected by the British of issuing false documents of emancipation to assist a slave-smuggling operation between Cuba, Texas and the southern United States.[85] Madden did, however, find the opportunity to expose Trist's fraud in an American court when, in 1839, recently-imported *bozals* on board the Baltimore schooner *Amistad* rebelled and, after killing the captain and the cook, took charge of the vessel. The ship was subsequently intercepted by the US Navy and the Africans jailed pending the resolution of the case. The Spanish government held that the slaves were *ladinos* and pressed for their despatch to Cuba to face charges of mutiny and murder. Against the advice of Kennedy, Madden acted as an expert witness when their case came to court in New York, and his testimony, in which he drew attention to the involvement of Trist and the Cuban authorities in the issue of false documents, doubtless helped the enslaved Africans to win their freedom.[86] His allegations also led to Trist's removal from Cuba and a congressional enquiry into his conduct. But this was not allowed to obstruct his later appointment as chief clerk of the State Department.[87]

Trist was not the only consul to be pilloried by Madden. He also launched a personal offensive against Tolmé, who, in addition to possessing slaves, was noted for his socializing with local slave traders and suspected of abetting their activities.[88] Soon after Madden's arrival in Cuba, Tolmé had made it clear to the British commissioners that he had no wish to be associated with them. His object, he wrote in a letter of November 1836, was "the protection and promotion of general interests, for which a certain degree of popularity [was] requisite".[89] Yet, it was not until August 1840 that Palmerston was persuaded to withdraw him from Cuba.[90] The Colonial Office in the meantime selected Madden to head a commission of enquiry in west Africa, and both his and Tolmé's positions in Havana were taken jointly by Turnbull, whose recently-published book, *Travels in the West*, had done much to expose the iniquities of the Cuban slave trade. His selection was every bit as controversial as Madden's had been. The Spanish colonial administration rightly feared that Turnbull would prove excessively troublesome, and at their behest Madrid rejected a British proposal, inspired by Turnbull, that the Havana mixed commission be accorded powers to investigate the status of negroes suspected of being illegally enslaved.[91] Palmerston, despite being set on his appointment, was likewise perturbed lest Turnbull "get himself into Difficulties by an overweening fondness for display".[92] In the event, Turnbull's championing of the cause of re-enslaved *emancipados*, one of whom he accused Kennedy of having in his service, irritated his colleagues in the commission, thoroughly alienated two successive captains-general of the island, and contributed to mounting political and social unrest.[93] He was also blamed for helping to foment slave rebellions whose savage repression in 1844 was dubbed "la Escalara". Those caught in revolt were often strapped to a ladder (*escalara*) and lashed to death. Turnbull, though stripped of his consular post, threatened with death by angry plantation-owners, and hounded from the island, was luckier: Aberdeen made him commissary judge in Spanish Town, Jamaica.[94]

DECLINING ADJUDICATION

The task awaiting Turnbull in Jamaica was hardly an arduous one. He himself had previously been very critical of the mixed commission system, dismissing the Anglo-Spanish courts as mere sinecures,[95] and Britain's resort to vice-admiralty courts in its campaign against the Brazilian slave trade was a measure of the decline in their importance. The introduction into Portugal (1839) and Spain (1845) of legislation providing for the punishment of masters and crews of slave ships led their nationals to trade increasingly without flags or under that of the United States. Henceforth, few of the vessels detained by the Royal Navy fell within the jurisdiction of the mixed commission courts. During the whole decade following 1840 the tribunal at Havana dealt with no more than seven cases: three vessels were condemned, three were freed, and the court was unable to adjudicate in the case of another.[96] Indeed, following Dalrymple's death in 1847 nobody was appointed to succeed him as arbitrator. As for Kennedy, he devoted much of his time in Cuba to the study of ornithology and the preparation of a book on the archaeology of the Yucatán. These, however, were less inappropriate pursuits than those of the Spanish commissary judges, José María Herrera y Herrera and José Buenaventura Esteva, who were two of the largest slave-owners on the island.[97] Moreover, although Backhouse, Kennedy's immediate successor, would have few opportunities to exercise his judicial functions, he readily embraced the cause of aggrieved *emancipados*, and his intervention may well have secured the liberation of several of their number.[98]

In addition to the Anglo-Brazilian mixed commissions, which were dissolved in 1845, the Anglo-Portuguese court at Freetown was wound up in 1844, and those at Boa Vista and Spanish Town, neither of which was ever of any practical value, were closed in 1851. Nevertheless, following the conclusion in April 1862 of a treaty between Britain and the United States for the suppression of the slave trade, Anglo–American mixed commission courts were established at New York and Cape Town, and the British consul-general in Havana retained the office and title of commissary judge until 1892. The survival of the courts was in large part due to the persistence of the trade. During the 1850s the Cuban slave economy continued to prosper and, according to one estimate, in 1858–59 Cuba imported between twelve and fifteen thousand enslaved Africans. Corruption, particularly the bribing of officials to overlook the landing of slave cargoes, was rife, and remained so until in 1866 the government in Madrid introduced legislation outlawing the trade in terms which substantially reduced scope for evasion. British efforts to halt the trade were meanwhile constrained by the fact that much of it was carried on by vessels armed with American papers. Only with the outbreak of the American civil war and the signing of the treaty of 1862 did the United States concede a mutual right of search of vessels under suspicion.[99] The new tribunals may have done little or no business, but they were a key component of a strategy designed as much to deter as to seize and prosecute slavers. They in any case came at little extra cost to the Treasury since the British already had commissioners at Cape Town, and Edward Archibald, their consul in New York, simply added the duties of commissary judge to his existing functions.

Archibald possessed a detailed knowledge of that city's role in the transatlantic slave trade.[100] Well-primed by a paid informant of Cuban descent, from March 1859 onwards he kept the Foreign Office amply supplied with intelligence on American-registered vessels fitted for slaving.[101] Elsewhere, when there was little adjudicating to be done, Britain's representatives in the mixed commissions seemed readily to turn to collecting, and disseminating information on slavery and the slave trade. George Jackson, whose conduct at Rio de Janeiro and subsequent refusal to proceed to Surinam did not stand in the way of his re-employment by the Foreign Office, was in 1846 appointed commissary judge in Luanda.[102] There, during the next thirteen years, he spent a good deal of his working life reporting on slave trafficking on the coast of Angola and in the Congo basin. If by 1856 the trade at Luanda was "in a state of nearly abeyance", it still gave 'indications of life and of a readiness to spring up afresh as vigorously as before', and in the interior and at other points on the coast there was every sign of its being actively pursued.[103] Angola remained, in Jackson's words, in "a state of Society . . . where the majority of the inhabitants are looked upon by the scanty white population as little better than beasts of burden existing only for their good pleasure and profit".[104] Vigilance came to matter more than prosecution, and Jackson did not shy from remonstrating with the colony's governors over infringements of treaty obligations and domestic legislation.[105] He was also keen to demonstrate his humanitarian credentials. In a characteristically effusive letter of 14 May 1851, he wrote to the local American naval commander of how a quarter of a century earlier he had in Washington been "engaged in appraising human beings like myself as mere Goods and Chattels", adding:

> I have since that time been chiefly employed in restoring the same unhappy class to freedom, and their natural rights, and in giving effect under the auspices of the Eminent Statesman to whose untiring energy our present promising prospects may be mainly attributed, to that unceasing and disinterested perseverance, in this righteous cause on the part of my Government and Country which will ever form one of the brightest pages in its history.[106]

The letter, which was later copied to London, was possibly, at least in part, intended to flatter Palmerston, a statesman whom Jackson had otherwise rarely managed to impress. Jackson's idealism, like that of many others who served with the mixed commissions and in the Slave Trade Department, was underpinned by self-interest. But idealism there was.

Notes

1 See, for example, Jenny S. Martinez, "Antislavery Courts and the Dawn of International Human Rights Law", *The Yale Law Journal*, vol. 117 (2007), pp. 550–641.

2 Tara Helfman, "The Court of Vice Admiralty at Sierra Leone and the Abolition of the West African Slave Trade", *The Yale Law Journal*, vol. 115 (2006), pp. 1122–56.

3 The National Archives (TNA), FO 315/1, passim.

4 Ibid., Castlereagh to Thomas Gregory and Edward Fitzgerald, despt. No. 1 (Portugal), 18 Nov. 1819.

5 Ibid., George Canning to commissioners, Sierra Leone, despt. No. 1 (General), 26 Nov. 1822.

6 Leslie Bethell, "The Mixed Commissions for the Suppression of the Transatlantic Slave Trade in the Nineteenth Century", *The Journal of African History*, vol. vii (1966), pp. 79–93.

7 FO 315/2, Lord Aberdeen to commissioners, Sierra Leone, despt. No. 8, 25 Sept. 1828.

8 Ibid., Aberdeen to commissioners, despt. No. 14, 2 Dec. 1829.

9 TNA, FO 353/95, pt. 1, William Smith to George Jackson, letters, 24 Aug. and 5 Nov. 1829.

10 C. W. Newbury (ed.), *British Policy Towards West Africa: Select Documents 1786–1874* (Oxford: Clarendon Press, 1965), p. 494. Edward Fitzgerald,

appointed first Commissioner of Arbitration in 1819, was named as chief justice in the "Constitution of the Colony and Sierra Leone and its Dependencies" on 17 October 1821, and Daniel Molloy Hamilton, the first registrar at the mixed commission in 1819, was also the advocate of the colony.

11 *Slave Trade Papers presented to the House of Commons, 10 June 1842: Return on the Amount paid for Salaries and Incidental Expenses for the Commissions established on the part of Her Majesty under the Treaties with Foreign Powers for suppressing the Traffic in Slaves ¼ up to January 1842*, HP 426, p. 2. See also Bethell, *Mixed Commissions*, p. 81, footnote 5, although these figures are at odds with the above.

12 Bethell, "Mixed Commissions", p. 84, citing TNA, FO 84/275, Jackson and Grigg to Palmerston, despt. No. 21, 24 April 1839.

13 See note 11.

14 FO 353/96, Jackson to Palmerston, letter, 9 June 1832.

15 FO 353/95, pt. 1, John Backhouse to Jackson, letters, 5, 16 and 29 Jan. 1828.

16 Ibid., Backhouse to Jackson, letter, 14 March 1828.

17 Ibid., Backhouse to Jackson, letter, 8 March 1828.

18 Ibid., Backhouse to Jackson, letter, 3 May 1828; Jackson to Backhouse, letter, 6 May 1828.

19 Ibid., Jackson to Aberdeen, despt. No. 36, 2 Sept. 1828.

20 Ibid., Jackson to Aberdeen, letter, nd. 1828.

21 FO 353/95, pt. 2, Jackson to Aberdeen, letter, 24 Aug. 1829. FO 84/445, memo. on Sir George Jackson's services and pension, 13 March 1842.

22 FO 353/96, Backhouse to Jackson, letter, 5 July 1830; Lord Dunglas to Jackson, letter, 13 Oct. 1830.

23 Ibid., Jackson to Palmerston, letter, 9 June 1832.

24 Ibid., Jackson to Palmerston, letter, 21 June 1832; G. Shee to Jackson, letter, 30 June 1832.

25 Ibid., Jackson to Shee, letter, 5 July 1832.

26 Jackson also asked Palmerston to waive the rule by which he received only half pay while on leave. But the most that the Foreign Office was prepared to concede was that, during his absence from post, Jackson might receive as much of his pension as together with his half salary would equal his full pension (i.e. £700 p.a.). Ibid., Jackson to Palmerston, letters, 7 and 14 April 1837; Jackson to Backhouse, letter, 9 May 1837; Palmerston to Jackson, letter, 13 April and 28 May 1837; Backhouse to Jackson, letter, 4 May 1837; W. Fox-Strangways to Jackson, letter, 16 May 1837.

27 FO 84/445, memo. on the circumstances which led to Sir George Jackson's removal from Rio de Janeiro, 13 March 1842.

28 FO 353/95, pt. 1, Smith to Jackson, letters, 5 Nov. 1829 and 11 June 1830.

29 TNA, T1/4221, Sierra Leone Mixed Commission Bundles, Smith to duke of Wellington, letter, 22 Dec. 1834.

30 Smith's pension in 1835 was £850 p.a., £150 less than a full pension for a commissary judge. *Slave Trade Papers presented to the House of Commons, 10*

June 1842: Return on the Number of Persons now receiving Pensions for Service in the said Commissions, HP 426, p. 7.

31 Duke University (Durham, NC), Rare Book, Manuscript and Special Collections Library, Backhouse MSS, Box 17, George Backhouse to Mrs J. Backhouse, letters, 18 and 21 Dec. 1852.

32 Backhouse MSS, Box 17, G. Backhouse to Mary Backhouse, letter, 1 May 1853. John V. Crawford, who was acting consul-general in Havana during long periods in the 1860s, reckoned Havana "without exception . . . the most expensive city in the world", and that an income of £1,500 per annum, less income tax, would "just keep a man free from debt". University of Durham Library, Archives and Special Collections, Wylde MSS., J.V. Crawford to W.H. Wylde, letter, 25 Aug. 1864.

33 Ibid., J. J. Crawford to Lord Clarendon, letter, 1 Sept. 1855. Luis Martínez-Fernández, *Fighting Slavery in the Caribbean. The Life and Times of a British Family in Nineteenth-Century Havana* (Armonk, NY: M.E. Sharpe, 1998), pp. 143–50.

34 Backhouse MSS, Box 18, Lord Wodehouse to Mrs Grace Backhouse, letter, 10 Jan. 1856.

35 Senior clerks received their salaries from the Foreign Office, but less senior staff were paid from the contingent expenses of the court. In 1824 the salary of a senior clerk in Sierra Leone was £400 p.a., that of a junior clerk £150 pa, and that of a surgeon £100 p.a. Information about salaries in FO 315/1.

36 Bethell, "Mixed Commissions", p. 84.

37 *Slave Trade papers presented to the House of Commons, 24 August 1846: A Return of all sums of money paid in each year since 1807 to Captors of Vessels condemned for Violation of the Laws and Treaties prohibiting the Slave Trade..*, HP 653, p. 4. Act 1st & 2d of Geo. 4, c. 61, and the 5th of Geo. 4, c. 113 of 1824 entitled the captor to the British moiety of the proceeds from a condemned vessel. Tonnage bounty became payable after the passing of Act of the 1st & 2nd Vict. C.47, on 27 July 1838. In January 1823 the Netherlands became the first country to agree with Britain that ships equipped for the slave trade, though not found actually engaged in it, should be condemned when detained by cruisers. Similar provisions were made in the treaty concluded with Spain in June 1835 and in additional, but unratified, articles to the Anglo-Brazilian treaty of 1826 agreed in July 1835. James Bandinel, *Some Account of the Trade in Slaves from Africa as connected with Europe and America* (London: Longman, Brown & Co., 1842), pp. 164, 230–1 and 238–9.

38 Hugh Thomas, *The Slave Trade. The History of the Atlantic Slave Trade, 1440–1870* (London: Papermac, 1997), p. 688.

39 Bethell, "Mixed Commissions", p. 89.

40 FO 315/12, Sierra Leone commissioners to governors of São Tomé and Príncipe, letter, 19 July 1834.

41 *Slave Trade Papers presented to the House of Commons, 13 March 1845: A Return of the Number of Vessels Captured in each of the said Years, stating whether they were ultimately Released or Condemned, and with an Account of the Net Proceeds . . .*, HP 471, pp. 6–8; and *A Return of the Amounts, as nearly as they can be*

given, paid for Illegal Captures; distinguishing the Compensations paid by the Captors from those paid by the British Government, p. 12.

42 Bethell, "Mixed Commissions", p. 84.

43 R. Fynn, *British Consuls Abroad; their Origin, Rank and Privileges, Duties, Jurisdiction and Emoluments* (London: J. Wertheimer & Co, 1846). Consuls generally received fairly good salaries but subordinate consular staff, including vice-consuls, were either not paid at all, or paid very little. In the 1840s a consul in Paris earned £100 per annum, in Madrid £350, in Cape Verde £400, in Rio de Janeiro £800; the consul-general in Havana earned £1,200. Governors were very well paid.

44 David Turnbull, *Travels in the West: Cuba, with Notices of Porto Rico and the Slave Trade* (London: Longman, 1840, reproduced as Elibron Classics series by Adamant Media Corporation, 2005), pp. 43–4.

45 FO 353/95, pt. 1, Jackson to Aberdeen, letter, 20 Sept. 1828.

46 FO 315/2, Joseph Planta to R. W. Hay (Colonial Office), letter, 26 Feb. 1827.

47 Ibid., Doctors' Commons to Canning, letter, 20 Jan. 1827.

48 Ibid., record of Anglo-Portuguese commission at Sierra Leone, 7 July 1826.

49 Ibid.

50 FO 315/2, Aberdeen to Viscount d'Itabayana, letter, 1 Dec. 1828.

51 FO 315/2, Aberdeen to Lord Ponsonby (British minister, Rio de Janeiro), despt., No. 3 (Slave Trade), 6 Dec. 1828.

52 *Slave Trade Papers presented to the House of Commons, 24 Aug 1846: A Return of all Sums of Money paid by the Crown to or on behalf of Captors, in Satisfaction or Indemnification of Expenses or Damages arising from the Prosecution or Seizure of Vessels alleged to be engaged in the Slave Trade*, HP 653, pp. 5–7.

53 Turnbull, *Travels*, pp. 40–41.

54 FO 315/1, Canning to commissioners, Sierra Leone, despt. No. 1 (Spain) 25 Sept. 1822, and enclosures; Francisco Martinez de la Rosa to L. Hervey, letter, 3 June 1822.

55 Figures calculated from *Slave Trade Papers presented to the House of Commons on 3 May and 6 August 1842: A Return of the Number of Slave Vessels Captured by Her Majesty's Cruisers since the Year 1831 inclusive . . .*, HP 561, pp. 6–11.

56 FO 315/2, Canning to commissioners, Sierra Leone, despt. No. 1, 12 Jan. 1826, and enclosures.

57 Ibid., Planta to secretary, Admiralty, letter, 12 Jan. 1826.

58 Ibid., record of Anglo-Brazilian Mixed Commission, Sierra Leone, 24 Jan. 1827, case involving Brazilian brig *Heroina*.

59 See for example *Slave Trade Papers laid before the House of Commons, Nov. 1825–July 1827: (A) Communications received by the Admiralty from Naval Officers, since November 1825. Enc. No. 29 – copy of a Letter from J.P. Clarke, Esquire; dated at British Consulate, St Jago, Cape de Verds, 13 May 1827, addressed to Commodore Bullen, C.B.*, HP 366, p. 17.

60 FO 315/13, commissioners, Sierra Leone, to Rendall (British consul, Cape Verde), letter, 31 Dec. 1839.

61 FO 84/310, British commissioners, Sierra Leone, to Palmerston, despt. No.

113 (Portugal), 1 Dec. 1840; FO 84/340, British commissioners, Sierra Leone, to FO, letter, 22 June 1840.

62 Bandinel, *Trade in Slaves*, pp. 150–1.

63 Leslie Bethell, *The Abolition of the Brazilian Slave Trade. Britain, Brazil and the Slave Trade Question, 1807–1869* (Cambridge: CUP, 1970), pp. 154–220.

64 Ibid., p. 167.

65 FO 84/445, memo. on the circumstances which led to Sir George Jackson's removal from Rio de Janeiro, 13 March 1842.

66 FO 353/96, Jackson to Palmerston, letter, 28 Oct. 1840.

67 Backhouse MSS., Box 12, Mrs W. Hamilton-Hamilton to Mrs J. Backhouse, letter, 6 Sept. 1841.

68 Jackson had in his employ five emancipated Africans, three male and two female. After their dismissal, they were sent by ship to Demerara. FO 353/96, Jackson to Canning, letter, 13 Dec. 1842.

69 Ibid., Jackson to Hamilton-Hamilton, letter, 11 Oct. 1841.

70 Ibid., Palmerston to Jackson, letters, 4 Aug. 1841.

71 J. W. St.G. Walker, *The Black Loyalists. The Search for a Promised Land in Nova Scotia and in Sierra Leone, 1783–1870* (Toronto: University of Toronto Press, 1992), p. 339.

72 Muriel E. Chamberlain, *Lord Aberdeen. A political biography* (London: Longman, 1983), pp. 368–69. Bethell, *Brazilian Slave Trade*, pp. 218–59.

73 Ibid., pp. 327–63.

74 Luis Martínez-Fernández, "The Havana Anglo-Spanish Mixed Commission for the Suppression of the Slave Trade and Cuba's *Emancipados*", *Slavery and Abolition*, vol. xvi, no. 2 (1995), pp. 205–25.

75 D. R. Murray, "Richard Robert Madden: His Career as a Slavery Abolitionist", *Studies*, vol. lxi (1972), pp. 41–53.

76 FO 84/195, Schenley to Palmerston, letter, 8 Oct. 1836; Schenley to Fox-Strangways, letter, 31 Oct. 1836.

77 Murray, "Madden", p. 50.

78 FO 84/195, Madden to Palmerston, letter, 5 Nov. 1836.

79 Ibid., Madden to Palmerston, letter, 22 Oct. 1836; Schenley to Macleay, letter, 28 Oct. 1836.

80 Ibid., Palmerston to Schenley & Madden, letter, 15 Dec. 1836.

81 TNA, CO 318/146, Madden (as superintendent for liberated Africans) to FO, letter, 27 Feb. 1839; FO 84/195, Palmerston to British commissioners, Havana, despt. No. 6, 9 May 1836.

82 FO 84/195, Schenley and Madden to Palmerston, letter, 30 Nov. 1836; Trist to Schenley and Madden, letter, 29 Nov. 1836.

83 FO 84/274, Trist to British commissioners, Havana, letter, 8 Jan. 1839; Kennedy to Palmerston, despt. No. 7, 19 Jan. 1839; Trist to Kennedy and Dalrymple, letter, 2 July 1839.

84 Ibid., Kennedy and Dalrymple to Palmerston, despt. No. 35, 27 Oct. 1839.

85 Ibid. FO 84/196, Macleay & Schenley to Palmerston, despt. No. 1, 1 Jan. 1836. FO 315/13, W. Lewis (Sierra Leone) to G. Elliot, letter, 26 May 1840.

86 CO 318/146, Madden to Kennedy, note, 25 Sept. 1839; Madden to

Blackwood (Colonial Office), letter, 3 Oct. 1839; Madden to Lord John Russell, letter, 20 Dec. 1839.

87 Robert L. Paquette, *Sugar is Made with Blood: The Conspiracy of La Escalera and the Confict between Empires over Slavery in Cuba* (Middletown, Conn.: Wesleyan UP, 1988), pp. 188–9.

88 FO 84/274, Kennedy to Palmerston, despts., 16 March & 29 May 1839. CO 318/149, Madden to Vernon Smyth (Colonial Office), letter, 20 March 1840, with notes by Vernon Smyth.

89 FO 84/197, Tolmé to British commissioners, Havana, letter, 2 Nov. 1836.

90 TNA, FO 72/559, Palmerston to Tolmé, despt. No. 1, 22 Aug. 1840.

91 Paquette, *Sugar*, p. 139. *Slave Trade Papers, Correspondence with Foreign Powers – Spain –Class B, 1 Jan.–31 Dec. 1841, presented to both Houses of Paliament, 1842*, pp. 17–19 and 383–8.

92 FO 72/559, minute by Palmerston, 19 Aug. 1840.

93 CO 318/149, de Giron to Turnbull, letter, 22 Dec. 1840. FO 84/356, Turnbull to Palmerston, letter, 12 March 1841. David Murray, *Odious Commerce. Britain, Spain and the Abolition of the Cuban Slave Trade* (Cambridge: CUP, 1980), pp. 154–55.

94 Ibid., pp. 154–5 and 160. Paquette, *Sugar*, pp. 159–67, 174 and 209–32.

95 Turnbull, *Travels*, p. 342.

96 Martínez-Fernández, "Havana Anglo-Spanish Mixed Commission", p. 207.

97 Martínez-Fernández, *Fighting Slavery in the Caribbean*, pp. 46–8.

98 Martínez-Fernández, "Havana Anglo-Spanish Mixed Commission", pp. 214–20.

99 Regis A. Courtemanche, *No Need of Glory. The British Navy in American Waters, 1860–1864* (Annapolis, Maryland: Naval Institute Press, 1977), pp. 89–92.

100 Prior to his appointment to New York, Archibald had served for ten years as Newfoundland's advocate general. Eugene H. Berwanger, *The British Foreign Service and the American Civil War* (Lexington, Ken.: University of Kentucky Press, 1994), p. 9.

101 FO 84/1086, Archibald to Russell, Slave Trade despt. No. 19, 11 July 1859; Archibald to Lyons, letter, 4 Oct. 1859.

102 On his return from Rio de Janeiro to London Jackson had engaged in a long wrangle with the Office over his pay and pension. He also sought another diplomatic appointment, but initially turned down Aberdeen's offer to him of the commissary judgeship at Luanda on the grounds that it would further impair his health. FO 353/96, Jackson to Aberdeen, letters, 2 March 1842 and 26 Oct. 1844; Aberdeen to Jackson, 21 Jan. 1843; Addington to Jackson, letter, 18 Nov. 1843.

103 FO 353/97, pt. 2, British commissioners, Luanda, to Lord Clarendon, despt. No. 14, 16 Feb. 1856.

104 FO 353/97, pt. 1, Jackson to Clarendon, despt. No. 12, 21 July 1854.

105 FO 353/97, pt. 2, British commissioners, Luanda, to Clarendon, despt., 31 March 1854; despt. No. 39, 29 Oct. 1855; despt. No. 41, 13 Nov. 1855; Jackson to J. Rodrigues Coelho do Amarl, letter, 26 July 1856.

106 Ibid., Jackson to Arthur H. Toole, letter, 14 May 1851; Jackson to Russell, letter, 28 Jan. 1853.

CHAPTER THREE

Slavery, Free Trade and Naval Strategy, 1840–1860

ANDREW LAMBERT

By the late 1830s British attempts to end the transatlantic slave trade by a combination of international agreement and standing naval patrols had reached an impasse. There were several fundamental problems. Firstly there were still open markets for enslaved Africans in the New World, the sugar plantations of Cuba and Brazil, while African kingdoms relied on the trade for their prosperity. With a ready market and an open source of supply shipping could always be found, at the right price to connect the two. While these conditions persisted the slave trade would endure; hard as it tried the Royal Navy could only reduce the flow, a situation analogous to the contemporary traffic in narcotics. Ultimately success would only be achieved when the demand had ceased, and the supply largely stopped. Efforts to achieve those ends were seriously hampered by diplomatic problems and operational weaknesses. This paper will address the development of naval action against the trade against the background of international agreements, the legal framework provided by the Crown's law officers, and the type and scale of force available.

THE LIMITS OF NAVAL POWER

While the legal regime in place by 1840 appeared to provide for effective action fundamental structural problems limited the impact of British action. Several nations either refused to allow British cruisers to search suspected slavers under their flag, or connived in the violation of international agreements signed with Britain. British cruisers could not stop American flagged vessels, while those of Portugal and Brazil were safe below the equator. To make matters worse the standing patrol off the west African coast was small, and many of the warships used were too slow to catch the latest generation of slavers, usually swift American built schooners. This situation infuriated three times foreign secretary (1830–34, 1835–41 and 1846–51), Lord Palmerston. A committed abolitionist, Palmerston worked hard to improve the diplomatic context of the campaign, but he recognised the limits of national power and the wider interests that were involved in any sustained effort. The states that resisted British demands did so for powerful reasons. All nations believed that behind the smokescreen of moral fervour and righteous indignation the British were serving their own commercial ends. After the bitter experience of being the only significant neutral carrier for most of the French Revolutionary and Napoleonic wars (1793–1815) the United States refused to allow the British to exercise a right of search on American flagged vessels.[1] Freedom of the seas had become an American mantra, one that would only be ended by the civil war of 1861–65. Furthermore, while the United States had outlawed the importation of slaves many years before the country remained deeply divided on the issue of slavery. The delicate balance between free and slave states before 1861 ensured no effective action was ever taken against American slave ships, or foreign vessels that fraudulently hoisted American colours. As President Tyler declared in his 1841 annual message to Congress the Stars and Stripes was being "grossly abused by the abandoned and profligate of other nations".[2] By blaming the vice on Iberian rogues he could turn a blind eye to the builders and operators of the ships in question, most of whom were American citizens, and avoid taking any action. Suitably embarrassed by British seizures of such fraudulent "American" ships an American anti-slavery patrol was set up in 1842, but it was never intended to be effective, to avoid upsetting sectional interests, and only became active after slavers openly landed slaves in Georgia in 1858.[3] The American position proved to be the final obstacle to the closure of the Atlantic trade because the United States was simply too powerful to be coerced, and too divided to be persuaded. American shipping sustained the Cuban slave market into the 1860s. The intransigence of Washington marked the limits of British power, short of all-out war.

By contrast Brazil and Portugal, despite signing treaties with Britain outlawing the trade, connived in its continuance for economic and political reasons. Both powers feared Britain planned to seize Portugal's African settlements under the pretext of abolition, and establish alternative sources for colonial produce, sugar, coffee and cotton, cutting Brazil's markets. At the same time both countries were anxious for British political support and closely tied to the British economy. Both were vulnerable to British coercion.

Further pressure for action came from the British West Indies, where the economic woes of the newly emancipated colonies were ameliorated by preferential import duties on their primary export, sugar. This sop to the waning political power of the West Indian planters was under attack from free traders, and the Anti-Corn Law League, which pressed for cheap food, as a way of lowering the wages of the working classes, and increasing the profits of industry. In the event, neither the compensation provided for abolishing slavery, nor the preferential duties did much good to the heavily indebted West Indian planters or the local economy. Economic power passed into the hands of merchants and bankers.[4]

Above all British foreign secretaries recognized the links between the abolition of the slave trade and wider national interests. Political and economic concerns in Africa, the West Indies and America were deeply enmeshed with European and even Asian concerns. Ending the slave trade was not an absolute priority: it was subordinate to the maintenance of peace and stability in Europe, and the economic interests of the state. In consequence it frequently took a back seat. The abolition of the slave trade must be seen in the wider context of British domestic and external policy.

The diplomatic and legal complexities of conducting what were, in essence, warlike operations on the high seas against the merchant ships of many nations ensured that the abolition of the slave trade would cost the Royal Navy a great deal of blood, sweat and treasure over the fifty years that followed the British legislation. Turning a noble gesture into a concrete fact was hard work. For fifty years the anti-slave trade patrol on the coast of west Africa was exposed to virulent tropical diseases, especially yellow fever and malaria, entirely unaware that the vector was the humble mosquito. Various miasma theories were developed to explain why ships and men that spent the night inshore or up river were stricken by these lethal complaints. Men died in droves, the human cost ultimately ran into thousands, prompting some liberal, humanitarian politicians to question the value of the effort. At the same time Quaker abolitionists questioned the morality of using force to achieve the object. Cost and lives were a big issue for "Little Englanders" then as now.

THE TRADE

The trade in enslaved Africans was demand driven: Cuban, Brazilian and American plantation economies were propelled by sweated slave labour, and used the resource to destruction. Not only were these economies expanding, but the slave population did not reproduce in significant numbers. Slave states relied on importing fresh slaves from Africa. Those slaves were provided by African rulers, through European middlemen. Long before the Europeans arrived in west Africa the trade was endemic, trans-Saharan routes carried enslaved black Africans to markets in Morocco, Algiers and Egypt. While slaves sold for high prices, and other local produce did not, the temptation to trade was irresistible. After 1830 the development of west African trade helped to close down the supply side, but only after the British replaced the slave markets with colonial administration. This effort had other costs; the advance of topical medicines struggled to keep British administrators alive in these areas before the 1870s.

The attack on the supply side had its limits. The Congo and Cameroon coasts remained beyond British control, and closely tied to the Brazilian slave market. In both cases cutting demand would be the key to ending the trade. This required a major diplomatic effort from London, the deployment of naval forces on the coasts of importing states and above all critical changes in internal political and economic conditions.

DEALING WITH DEMAND: BRAZIL

In the 1830s the British anti-slave trade patrol on the west African coast was small, under the direction of the commander in chief at the Cape of Good Hope, and largely equipped with unsuitable vessels. A handful of small warships primarily designed for sustained heavy weather cruising were never going to stop the sleek American built schooners that ran the trade, and they cruised well offshore, rather than close to the source of supply. Furthermore no British ships operated below the equator, an area closed off by the diplomatic situation. The British had no legal authority to search ships carrying slaves between the Portuguese colony of Angola, various Portuguese stations on the Congo coast and the strong Brazilian market. Further problems flowed from the requirement that ships were only lawful prize if seized with slaves on board. The "equipment" clause of the 1835 Anglo-Spanish treaty did not apply to Portuguese ships. This clause had removed the Spanish flag from the trade, only to see it replaced by that of Portugal.

While Portugal was reluctant to accept the "equipment" clause or extend the coverage of existing treaties below the equator Britain did not feel obliged to treat the Lisbon government with the same circumspection as France or the United States. Gradually the British and mixed commission courts loosened the interpretation of the treaties, allowing British ships to check the bona fides of Portuguese flagged vessels. In 1839 this new latitude began to bear fruit, more slavers were seized, and Portugal did not complain. At the same time it was clear that it would be essential to act on the Brazilian coast as well as the African, but the legal framework for such action was uncertain.

To make their campaign effective the British needed to extend their powers, either by negotiation, or unilaterally. Palmerston was prepared to use force, to seize all Portuguese slavers, leaving Lisbon to choose between acquiescence and war. He warned Lisbon that war would result in the seizure of all their colonies in Africa, India and China, the very thing that had alarmed the Portuguese for so long. Having been read a lesson about upholding the rights of other nations by Wellington, Palmerston secured a bill that covered the unilateral seizure of Portuguese ships in August 1839.[5] Portugal was forced to seek terms, the slave ships simply shifted to the Brazilian flag. This had been expected.

As Captain Joseph Denman RN observed Palmerston's act made it possible for the naval blockade to defeat the slave trade. Spanish, Portuguese and Brazilian ships could be searched north and south of the equator, and detained if they carried slaves, or slaving equipment. In addition the West Africa Squadron, effectively independent of the Cape from 1840 and reinforced to a total of 12–13 ships, including a steamer and some new, fast brigs, began to operate in African coastal waters. To ensure the officers and men were zealous they were given tonnage money on empty slavers, as well as head money on slaves. When Denman landed and destroyed the notorious barracoons at Gallinas it seemed the end was in sight – more slave depots were burnt, more local chiefs were signed up to British practice. This promising approach was halted when the slavers sued Denman for damages, and only revived after the case was finally resolved, in Denman's favour, in 1848.

The strategy of the campaign closely followed that employed against the Napoleonic empire: ships were seized at sea and condemned as lawful prize, ships in harbour were cut out, and coasts blockaded. The Brazilian and Cuban trades revived when a new foreign secretary, Lord Aberdeen (1841–46), ended the coastal raids, doubting their legality.

More significantly Aberdeen was quick to place the anti-slave trade effort in context. He had no intention of alienating Portugal, not for her own sake, but because the Tagus was "by far the most important spot in Europe for us outside our own Dominions": he knew that Britain needed to ensure this critical base was in the hands of a friendly minor power.[6] The key reason why Portugal was Britain's oldest ally, and why the Peninsular war had been fought, was to prevent the Tagus falling into French hands. British statesmen knew that Lisbon, the only secure, easily accessible deep water harbour between Brest and Cadiz, was an ideal base for attacks on British shipping. In the hands of an active enemy it would stretch the Royal Navy beyond breaking point.

In 1842 Portugal conceded the equipment clause, effectively removing its flag from the Brazilian trade. Ships sailing to Cuba shifted to the American flag, others ran without any registration, to avoid being handed over to Portuguese courts. The appearance of the American flag paralyzed the naval campaign, because Britain had a host of issues outstanding with the American government, from the Canadian frontier to the Mosquito Coast, and little desire for war when France would be quick to profit.[7] The American anti-slavery squadron proved ineffective.

Instead the British effort began to focus on the Brazilian trade south of the equator. Brazil was no threat to Britain, although her commerce was a useful element in the national economy, and she was isolated in South America, being the only empire, and the continent's only Portuguese-speaking state. By 1845 twenty-one warships were active on the African coast, including more fast "Symondite" brigs and seven steamers, the antidote to fast slaving schooners. The Brazilian government reacted to the increased pressure, both from the British and the slave interest inside the country, by closing the mixed commission in Rio de Janeiro and protesting against the interference in coastal shipping. The coffee plantations exerted a powerful hold on the national economy, and they depended on a constant supply of fresh slave labour. Unstable short-term governments and the growing authority of the young emperor further complicated the position. Offended by high-handed British action, the Brazilian government refused to extend the current treaties, and looked to the forthcoming renewal of trade treaties to exert leverage. An economic slump made matters worse. British imports were subject to no more than 15 per cent duty, while Brazilian "slave grown" sugar paid 250 per cent more duty in Britain than British West Indian "free grown" sugar.

Moves toward free trade in Britain, notably the Anti-Corn Law League, which sought to cheapen food in the interests of northern manufacturers, who could then lower wages, were given added urgency when those same manufacturers faced the loss of a market worth £3 million per annum. Little wonder some condemned the anti-slave patrol. By contrast the rump of the West Indian interest considered the Brazilian crops were unfair competition. In this debate there could only be one winner. Consumer interest ensured sugar duties were lowered. Both Palmerston and Sir Robert Peel, the Conservative prime minister, saw the duties as an opening to negotiate on the slave trade. The Brazilians did not. They were more interested in securing British support for their ongoing struggle with Argentina over Uruguay; but they would not compromise on the slave trade. Significantly the British were using naval force to open the River Paraná and Uruguay to trade, in large measure as a response to Chartism and domestic political pressure.[8]

In March 1845 Brazil unilaterally ended the treaty under which the Royal Navy had acted against the Brazilian flag in the slave trade. With no prospect of renewal Aberdeen followed Palmerston's precedent of 1839, taking unilateral action. Basing his policy on a clause in the 1826 treaty declaring any Brazilian ship engaged in the trade to be a pirate he could rely on common international law to seize and try such ships in British courts without the need for mixed commission courts. *The Times*,

Aberdeen's preferred mouthpiece, carried a clear warning of this policy in mid-May 1845.[9] The target audience was the Brazilian minister in London. The act was soon passed, and struck a massive blow to Brazilian self-esteem. In effect the national flag had been declared a worthless rag, and the rights of the state were null and void at sea. The law officers of the Crown were not convinced, but as one might expect their opinion was never made public.[10]

Nor was the act without teeth. By 1847 the west African station had 32 ships, seven steamers, including the pioneer screw propeller steamer *Rattler* which captured 8 Brazilian registered slavers in only eighteen months.[11] Between 1845 and 1850 over 400 ships were taken in the Brazil trade alone, but even this was not enough. The plantations were expanding and demand remained high.

The solution was obvious, close down both supply and demand ends of the trade. Unfortunately such a simple strategic approach faced a host of legal, diplomatic and operational problems. This was, as the great naval analyst Sir Julian Corbett famously observed, the deflection of strategy by politics. Palmerston wanted to send ships to the Brazilian coast, but could not move them from the African blockade, where the size of the squadron was determined by treaties with France and the United States, and the Navy had no spare ships in the fraught aftermath of the 1848 revolutions, the Turkish straits crisis and the Dom Pacifico incident.

RESOLUTION

In 1849 the end of the Rio Plata crisis released the ships of the South American station for operations on the coast of Brazil. The British *chargé d'affaires* in Rio, James Hudson, took the leading role. He believed an effective blockade of the Brazilian coast would end the trade.[12] When British warships arrived off Santos they prevented two infamous steam slavers, ships that had brought the trade to a new level of sophistication, from sailing. Commander-in-Chief Rear Admiral Barrington Reynolds' handful of ships, three steamers and two sloops, would be ineffective on such a vast coast without an intelligence advantage. Hudson had an agent within the slaving community; paying a percentage on all seizures in return for priceless intelligence on sailings, operators and markets.[13] This allowed a naval force that could be counted on the fingers of one hand to cripple a major industry. British diplomatic funds were also used to support abolitionist newspapers that chimed in with a growing sense of unease in Brazil at the sheer scale of the illegal industry, and of the poten-tially rebellious servile population. No-one had forgotten St. Domingue.[14]

Hudson persuaded Barrington to follow his orders to the letter, pressing the intelligence-led naval campaign into Brazilian waters, and even into fortified harbours. Hundreds of slavers were seized without protest, even though they were taken inside Brazil's three mile limit and even under the guns of national forts. One incident brought the campaign to a denouement. On 29 June 1850 on the steam sloop *HMS Cormorant*, Commander Herbert Schomberg, acting on intelligence, entered the River at Paranaguá, asking for the co-operation of the local fort. He found four slavers, one of which was promptly scuttled. When he towed out the other three the fort opened fire, and *Comorant* replied with vigour. One British sailor was killed and two wounded. Schomberg burnt two slavers in front of the fort, and sent the remaining ship to be condemned at St. Helena. Initially Brazilian passions ran high, British sailors were attacked in the streets of Rio, but the mood changed very quickly. The flow of information about slaving voyages reaching the British mission increased: Brazilians were denouncing the slavers.[15]

The incident at Paranaguá confirmed what Palmerston and Hudson had long suspected; Brazil "was virtually powerless to resist the British Navy and that any attempt to do so could only aggravate the situation". With the vital coastal and export trades at the mercy of five British warships the government declared that the slavers were not citizens – the old excuse of blaming foreigners, in this case the Portuguese.

Recognizing the need not to over-run the boundaries of prudence Hudson pulled the naval force out of fortified harbours, giving Brazil an opportunity to demonstrate its new-found zeal, while still seizing ships at sea. Fearing war with Britain, which could only be disastrous, a new Brazilian law made slavers liable to seizure in Brazilian waters, whether national or foreign, while the Brazilian navy and police began to take action against the trade in October 1850. France, usually happy to thwart British policy abroad, was quick to inform the Brazilians that on this issue they stood alone.[16]

Hudson's reward was promotion to envoy extraordinary. Full powers to negotiate a treaty with Brazil arrived in late July. Recalled in August 1851, he was appointed to the legation in Turin, where he earned further distinction.[17] Palmerston always rewarded those who had done good service.

For Palmerston, and his colleague Sir Francis Baring, first lord of the Admiralty, the naval campaign on the coast of Brazil had brought the long drawn-out saga of the Brazilian slave trade to a resolution within twelve months. So complete was the transformation that the British shared their key intelligence source with the Brazilian ministers, but they did not repeal that Aberdeen act. That was the ultimate sanction if Brazil reneged. By the end of 1851 the last flickering embers of the trade had been snuffed out. The danger of resumption passed long before Brazil became the last significant country to abolish slavery in 1888.

DEALING WITH DEMAND: CUBA

Just as the campaign to end the Brazilian trade was reaching a climax the limits of British power were demonstrated in Cuba, the last Caribbean slave market. Like Brazil the Cuban economy was heavily reliant on servile labour for plantation crops – sugar, coffee and tobacco. Unlike Brazil Cuba was at the centre of complex diplomatic and strategic issues, and these could not be resolved by the application of force against the government in Havana. Cuba was a Spanish colony, or more realistically *the* Spanish colony. Profits drawn from Cuba were vital to sustain the Spanish economy. Furthermore the dowager queen regent was a major player in the slave trade and the plantation economy, her money helping to keep the monarchy stable. The stability and generally liberal alignment of Spain was a significant British interest, critical to the maintenance of European stability, low defence estimates, and the concomitant cheap government that all nineteenth-century administrations sought. British ministers were well aware that the consequence of over-zealous action against the slave trade might be a Cuban rebellion, and Spain lurching back towards the absolutism that had only been defeated in the 1830s.

For the past thirty years the island had been the last major Spanish possession in the New World, a key contributor to Spain's economy, and the last hope of recovering her once great American empire. The Cuban economy was dominated by the export of sugar, which accounted for 84 per cent by value, with tobacco, cigars and coffee completing the list. Grown and processed on large, newly created plantations, sugar depended on advanced processing machinery and slave labour. The recent shift to large- scale sugar production required a major increase in slave labour, so the Spanish authorities persistently violated their treaty agreements with Britain to suppress the trade. Between 1800 and 1860 over half-a-million enslaved Africans were brought to Cuba, more than 300,000 of them after the trade became illegal. By 1850 41 per cent of the population were black, almost all of whom were slaves; 49 per cent were white and with the smaller mixed race group, were free.[18] Ironically the dramatic growth in Cuban sugar production was largely inspired by the British decision in 1845 to end the tariff barrier against sugar being produced in countries that still permitted slavery. This measure had been used to protect the British West Indian Islands market share after abolition. This clash of economic ideology and humanitarian concern would create bitter cross-currents in British politics, forcing Lord John Russell's government to fight for its survival in the House of Commons.

At the same time Cuba had long been coveted by the expansionist, aggressive United States. The Americans had recently despoiled Mexico of California, Texas and New Mexico, and their ambition seemed to recognise no limits. In 1848 the United States government offered to buy Cuba, and when this approach was rejected a series of filibustering expeditions were mounted from New Orleans, hoping to exploit local rebellions, overthrow the Spanish regime, and invite American annexation. This approach, already successful in Texas, was driven by southern politicians seeking to expand the slave owning element in the state, and find an outlet for their own servile population.

Whatever the commercial value of the island, it possessed enormous strategic importance. Havana was the finest harbour in the West Indies, and by far the most powerfully defended. In American hands it could close the Caribbean to British ships, and destroy West Indian trade. Successive British foreign secretaries had acted to forestall an American Cuba since Castlereagh first recognized the problem. Nor was Spain unaware of the threat: the rebuilding of the Spanish navy in the 1840s was driven by the need for improved communications with Cuba, while the threat of filibustering and local creole independence movements led Spain to station large forces in Cuba, and leave supreme authority in the hands of a military governor, the captain-general.[19]

British interests in Cuba were further complicated by the European situation. Palmerston's anxiety to abolish slavery was serious, as his astonishing action to destroy the Brazilian slave trade had demonstrated.[20] However, he could not follow the same principle in Cuba. Weak and divided as it was Spain was vital to the success of his liberal policies in Europe. Palmerston simply could not bully Spain over slavery, which the Spanish ministers knew was the key to the Cuban economy, and through that to the loyalty of the Cuban élite. Armed action against slavery would prompt a rebellion, American intervention, or the terrifying prospect of slave revolt and race war, leading to political and economic disaster on the scale first witnessed in St. Domingue in the 1790s. Palmerston accepted that the West Indies were not the best place to stop slave ships, stepping up activity on both sides of Africa instead. Even so, in June 1848 the Admiralty ordered the commander-in-chief in the West Indies, Admiral Lord Dundonald, to patrol off Cuba, to counter-act the sudden increase in slave imports, and sent an extra ship to facilitate the operation.[21]

The leading members of the Lord John Russell's government (1846–52) recognized the dilemma. British attempts to end the slave trade could drive Cuba into American hands, a development that would threaten the strategic basis of British power in the New World. The crisis arrived in September 1849, when the acting British consul-general in Havana, alarmed by reports of an impending American filibustering expedition, wrote to Commodore Thomas Bennett at Port Royal, Jamaica: "the period is very near at hand of this island being annexed to the United States". Bennett diverted the corvette *HMS Trincomalee* to Havana. The next spring the governor of the Bahamas stressed the danger of allowing Havana to fall into American hands: 'she would, in time of war obtain the complete control over the navigation of this vast gulf . . . they could shut us from the Gulf of Mexico".[22] With Lord Dundonald at Halifax, Nova Scotia, Bennett relied on local intelligence to change *Trincomalee*'s orders from Bermuda to Havana, taking a course south of Cuba.[23] Bennett was commended for using his initiative.[24] On 31 October 1849 *Trincomalee* put into Havana, saluting the Spanish captain general and admiral. She spent the next year, her last on the station, cruising on the Cuban coast. While many ships were seen, her main task was to maintain a strategic presence, and none was seized.

HMS Trincomalee was one of many Royal Navy ships to call at Havana over the next decade, concerned to protect British lives and property, and warn off American invasions, official or unofficial. Britain was highly unpopular with the leading elements in Cuban society, who were convinced by American claims that London controlled Madrid, and wanted to destroy the Cuban economy. Consequently visits to Havana were neither friendly nor relaxing. In addition the city was pervaded by an air of lassitude and decay, reflecting the enervating climate, endemic fevers and maladministration. It was not a place to remain if the ship's health and happiness were to be considered.[25]

Government policy came under sustained attack in Parliament, from economists, who wanted to end the attack on the slave trade, and West Indies landowners, who wanted protection for their interests. Palmerston and Russell made the question an issue of confidence, and won a clear majority in the House of Commons on 19 March 1850. This allowed them to push on with their programme of defending Cuba against American intervention, and it was this, rather than the suppression of the slave trade, that determined the deployment of British warships in Cuban waters.

Consequently the slave trade persisted. There had been a fall in demand in the mid-1840s, as old coffee estates were converted to sugar production, and slaves moved within Cuba, but by the late 1840s the trade was growing, partly through increased demand, and partly from increased supply after the closure of the larger Brazilian market. The 5–1 imbalance between male and female slaves, and the loss of 5 per cent of the slave population every year, ensured a steady demand, even without expansion. Although she would stop many suspicious vessels off the Cuban coast, mostly the American built schooners that were the standard slaving ship of the era, *Trincomalee* was too large, unhandy and costly for this service.[27] Her presence had more to do with Cuban security than the campaign against slavery.

Sugar, slaves and the Cuban trade, 1845–51[26]

	British Cuban sugar imports cwt	Slaving voyages	Locally-reported Cuban slave imports	FO estimates of Cuban slave imports
1845	197,000	6	950	1,300
1846	500,000	4	0	1,500
1847	875,000	4	0	1,000
1848	694,000	5	1,500	1,500
1849	664,000	20	6,575	8,700
1850	489,000	7	2,325	3,100
1851	811,000	7	3,687	5,000

In early 1850 Captain Warren landed part of his crew on the Cuban coast to conduct firing drill with field guns and muskets, and cut timber.[28] Landing and firing artillery without permission on the soil of a foreign state was insensitive at the best of times, but with the constant threat of filibuster invasions it was irresponsible and rather more than the Spanish authorities could tolerate. British protection was one thing, but to be insulted was quite another. Four months later Dundonald reported that he had received a Spanish complaint that *Trincomalee* had infringed their territorial rights. "I consider", he observed, "that Captain Warren acted with great want of caution, but as the Consul General is satisfied that no insult was intended, I trust no further notice will be taken of the affair."[29] Despite an official complaint from the Foreign Office Warren's career did not suffer.[30] Having passed on the Spanish complaint the Foreign Office did not pursue the matter: Palmerston doubtless thought it would do no harm to remind the Spaniards that their security against American threats was based on British power. As Sir Francis Baring, the first lord of the Admiralty, remarked the following year, "the interests of England are strongly concerned in America not having Cuba – whether Spain retain the island or not".[31]

The presence of *HMS Trincomalee* on the Cuban coast was significant. *Trincomalee* was too big and too slow to chase slave ships, usually sharp Baltimore-built schooners. Instead her patrol off Cuba was designed to deter American filibusters. Politicians from the American south, desperate to increase the number of slave-owning states in the union, supported illegal attempts to invade the Spanish island. While Britain opposed the slave trade Palmerston recognised that if he applied too much pressure Cuba might welcome an American invasion, while the loss of Cuba, the richest province of the empire, might bring down the shaky Spanish monarchy, seriously damaging British interests in Europe. Consequently *Trincomalee* was sent to patrol, because she could not catch slavers, but would prevent an invasion. To make matters even more complex free trade meant that Britain was buying much of its sugar from Cuba, where it was grown by slaves and processed by British steam powered machinery!

In such circumstances British naval power could not stop the Cuban slave trade: instead it ensured Cuba remained Spanish. While this outcome may have lacked the drama of the Brazilian intervention the outcome was highly significant for British strategic and commercial interests. Ultimately the resolution of the Cuban trade depended on larger issues, and these could only be resolved within the United States. Until then the Royal Navy and British diplomacy could only limit the trade in the New World, attack the supply side of the equation, and keep the Americans out of Cuba. *Trincomalee* played her part in that process.

CUTTING THE SUPPLY: AFRICA

The inability of Britain to stop American shipping carrying slaves to Cuba gave added emphasis to the work of the West African Patrol, a subject that has been treated at length by several authors.[32] However the key to success lay in the steady extension of colonial authority on the west African coast. Naval action alone could not stop the trade. However, the main slave supply sites were few in number, and well known. If they could be closely blockaded, destroyed, or ideally occupied by British authorities the slavers would be forced to use smaller, less well-developed bases, reducing the supply, while increasing the cost and risk of the operation. The destruction of the slave depots at Lagos in 1851 was a major blow, the annexation of Lagos in 1861 was critical. British pressure ensured Portugal limited the markets south of the equator. Local kings were drawn into client relationships, and tropical medicines enabled new trades and a new system to emerge that replaced human trafficking, but only because the Brazilian market had closed, and the Cuban was falling away.

CONCLUSION

Brazil was driven out of the slave trade by British naval and diplomatic pressure in the late 1840s, but Cuba was not. The lesson was obvious, ending the slave trade required a careful combination of diplomacy and force, tailored to specific situations. It had to deal with supply and demand before the scale of the trade could be reduced to a level where naval force could hope to be effective.

The American civil war 1861–65 ended the Atlantic trade. President Lincoln finally rendered existing American legislation effective, cutting the supply of shipping that had been carrying slaves (most ships running slaves into Cuba were American built and operated), and concluding an Anglo-American treaty giving the right of mutual search. This document, signed on 7 June 1862, marked a complete reversal of the American position. Lincoln's administration adopted British practice on naval blockades at the same time, to suppress the southern Confederacy. In addition Lincoln had an American slaver captain hung as a pirate, under existing American law, but only one. Without American ships and markets Cuba was too small a market to support the trade. In 1869 the West African Squadron was abolished because there were no slave ships to catch.[33] This fact, observed on the African coast, was easily explained: the Cuban slave market closed in the same year. The Royal Navy simply redeployed the ships and spent the next twenty years eradicating the Arab slave trade on the east African coast.[34]

Ultimately the transatlantic slave trade ended when there were no more slaves to carry, and no more slave states to buy them. If British government anti-slavery was always tempered by *Realpolitik*, and seen in a wider context than that of the passionate men and women who campaigned at home, it was nevertheless genuine and heartfelt. Sometimes morality has a place in diplomacy, but it is a currency too rare to be employed often, and too easily debased to be used in haste. When, at the end of a remarkable political career, Palmerston claimed that the abolition of the slave trade and the establishment of secure national defences were his proudest boasts he was referring to two sides of the same coin. Ultimately the British stand against the slave trade was only possible because the dominating power of the Royal Navy, the only strategic instrument with a truly global reach before 1945, made Britain a unique world power among regional players. For Palmerston, sea-power, based on an unrivalled battlefleet, was a flexible and irresistible instrument that could be used in many ways to advance his diplomatic aims.[35]

Notes

1 The standard account is Hugh G. Soulsby, *The Right of Search and the Slave Trade in Anglo-American Relations, 1814–1862* (Baltimore, MD: Johns Hopkins Press, 1933).

2 Leslie Bethell, *The Abolition of the Brazilian Slave Trade: Britain, Brazil and the Slave Trade Question, 1807–1869* (Cambridge: CUP, 1970), p. 190.

3 Donald L. Canney, *Africa Squadron: The U.S. Navy and the Slave Trade, 1842–1861* (Dulles Va: Potomac Books, 2006).

4 Kathleen M. Butler, *The Economics of Emancipation: Jamaica and Barbados, 1834–1843* (Chapel Hill: University of North Carolina Press, 1995).

5 Bethell, *Brazilian Slave Trade*, pp.155–66.

6 Ibid., pp. 186–7.

7 Kenneth Bourne, *Britain and the Balance of Power in North America, 1815–1908* (London: Longmans, 1967) examines the diplomatic and strategic issues between the two countries.

8 David McLean, "Trade, Politics and the Navy in Latin America: The British in the Paraná", *Journal of Imperial and Commonwealth History* vol. 35, no. 3 (2007), pp. 351–70.

9 Bethell, *Brazilian Slave Trade*, p. 257.

10 Ibid., p. 275

11 For the west African operations of this vessel, see Denis Griffiths, Andrew Lambert and Fred Walker, *Brunel's Ships* (London: Chatham Publishing, 1999), pp. 108–16.

12 Bethell, *Brazilian Slave Trade*, p. 307.

13 This agent had been recruited as far back as 1840. See The National Archives (TNA), FO 84/367, C. J. Hamilton Hamilton to Lord Aberdeen, Slave Trade despt. No. 17 and enclosure, 29 Nov. 1841. FO 84/408, Hamilton to Aberdeen, Slave Trade despt. No. 42, 20 Sept. 1842.

14 Bethell, *Brazilian Slave Trade*, pp. 310–12.

15 Christopher Lloyd, *The Navy and the Slave Trade: the suppression of the African slave trade in the nineteenth century* (London: Frank Cass, 1949), p. 145.

16 Bethell, *Brazilian Slave Trade*, p. 333, n. 2.

17 S. T. Bindoff, E. F. Malcolm Smith and C. K. Webster, *British Diplomatic Representatives, 1789–1852*, Camden Society, 3rd series, vol. 50 (London: Historical Society, 1934), pp. 31–2.

18 Luis Martinez-Fernández, *Fighting Slavery in the Caribbean: The life and times of a British Family in Nineteenth Century Havana* (Armonk, NY: M.E. Sharpe, 1998), pp. 12–20.

19 David Murray, *Odious Commerce: Britain, Spain and the Abolition of the Cuban Slave Trade* (Cambridge: CUP, 1980), pp. ix–x, 223. Martinez-Fernández, *Fighting Slavery*, p. 15. John H. Schroeder, *Shaping a Maritime Empire: The Commercial and Diplomatic Role of the American Navy, 1829–1861* (Westport, Conn: Greenwood Press, 1985), pp. 92–5.

20 Donald Southgate, *The Most English Minister: The Policies and Politics of Palmerston* (London: Macmillan, 1966), pp. 147–51.

21 TNA ADM 2/1607, f. 530,550, Admiralty to Admiral Lord Dundonald, 26 June 1848.

22 Murray, *Odious Commerce*, pp. 223–4.
23 Thomas Bennett, a captain of 1828 with considerable experience on the station, commanding the Leeward Islands Division.
24 ADM 2/1608, f. 132, Admiralty to Commodore Bennett, 3 Oct.1848.
25 Andrew Lambert, *Trincomalee: The Last of Nelson's Frigates* (London: Chatham Publishing, 2002).
26 Drawn from Murray, *Odious Commerce*, pp. 243–4.
27 Hurst Journal and Log Book.
28 Hurst confirms the details.
29 ADM 1/5602, Dundonald to Admiralty 3 May 1850 (rec. 27 May 1850).
30 ADM 2/1608, f. 505, Admiralty to Dundonald, 7 May1850.
31 C. J. Bartlett, *Great Britain and Sea Power 1815–1853* (Oxford: Clarendon Press, 1963), p. 275.
32 Lloyd is the best of these.
33 For the last years of the patrol, see Mrs Fred Egerton, *Admiral of the Fleet Sir Geoffrey Phipps Hornby* (Edinburgh: W. Blackwood, 1896), pp. 117–38.
34 The most recent study of the east African trade is Raymond Howell, *The Royal Navy and the Slave Trade* (London: Routledge, 1987).
35 Andrew Lambert, 'Palmerston and Sea Power', *Palmerston Studies II* (Southampton: University of Southampton, 2007), eds. David S. Brown and Miles Taylor, p. 61.

CHAPTER FOUR

Anti-Slavery Activists and Officials
"Influence", Lobbying and the Slave Trade, 1807–1850

DAVID TURLEY

As a reform movement sustained by recurrent phases of popular activism British anti-slavery had a long history that straddled decades of significant religious change and the emergence of new social forces. The longevity of the movement occurred because activists were able to develop forms of social and religious alliance that they then reconstituted over time as social, political and religious conditions changed. The character of the leadership of anti-slavery activism inevitably could not remain constant between the 1780s (or 1807) and the mid-nineteenth century and this had a number of consequences. Activists altered the balance of methods they employed according to what seemed the most urgent priorities in different periods.[1] Successive generations of anti-slavery leaders perceived their standing in relation to government in radically different ways and this too influenced their methods. In other words, activist leaders had to decide whether the issues they took up could best be advanced through "influence", "agitation" or a combination of methods drawing from both approaches.

This last point requires some expansion. Abolitionists concluded, after some internal debate, that fundamental changes in state policy in relation to the slave trade and slave labour in colonial economies necessitated propaganda and petitioning drives to stimulate "agitation". The purpose of this stirring of awareness and sentiment in the country was to frame debate on these public policies "by a loud, strong and solemn expression of the public opinion".[2] Activists also intended to build on the limits supposedly imposed on policy makers through the "agitation" of public opinion to exercise "influence" over them by means of memoranda, memorials and addresses, face-to-face meetings and indirect lobbying through the good offices of sympathetic members of both houses of Parliament. At the high points of anti-slavery mobilisation, when the objective was a fundamental change of policy, activists relied on a progressive interaction between "agitation" and "influence". One such period was in 1823 and the following years. Local organizing of petitioning for the gradual emancipation of the slaves gave backing to Fowell Buxton's House of Commons motion of May 1823 and his talks with ministers. The outcome was that Canning committed the government to a policy of "amelioration" that pointed in the unspecified future to emancipation once the enslaved were thought to have been sufficiently responsive to the "civilizing" project of activists and missionaries undertaken in various forms since the 1780s.[3] When "amelioration" was stymied by the West Indian legislatures' refusal to do much about it "agitation" resumed with demands arising for yet more radical action. The anti-slavery leadership eventually felt compelled to press for the more advanced objective of "immediate" emancipation both in public and in meetings with ministers and officials.

Other phases of the movement saw reformers concerned not with policy *change* but with monitoring, and seeking to keep officials up to the mark on, the implementation of policies. When the issue was the enforcement of British slave trade legislation, to which activists believed both they and the government were committed, and for which the government was directly operationally responsible, there was less room for "agitation" and instead a recognition of the need for "manoeuvring within". Abolitionists assumed this was even more the case in Britain's dealings with foreign powers over suppression of the international slave trade and the (possible) ending of slavery in foreign countries. In these instances what leverage activists felt they had depended largely, though not entirely, on influencing ministers, diplomats, officials and, occasionally, naval officers. "Agitation" was less likely not least because the issues seemed too distant easily to engage a public opinion already substantially convinced that Britain had done its Christian duty in 1806, 1807 and 1833 over the foreign and British slave trades to British territories and West Indian emancipation.

This essay focuses on lobbying by activists within the context of "influence", but with an awareness of the recurrent rise and fall of "agitation" in the background. It will take up the role of the African Institution in relation to the enforcement of British slave trade legislation. There will be some discussion of abolitionist attempts to shape British suppression policy towards the international transatlantic slave trade in the aftermath of the Napoleonic wars. The essay will conclude with consideration of how activists in Britain dealt with the slave trade and slavery in the Lone Star Republic of Texas. During the period of the *de facto* independence of Texas between its break away from Mexico and its annexation to the United States (1836–45) the issue was to prove especially revealing of the perils and futilities of *international* activist lobbying. Where appropriate, an argument about the response of ministers and officials to lobbying will be offered.

Activists of the Clapham sect of Anglican evangelicals celebrated the passage of the legislation of 1807 as a triumph of national virtue, "a truly providential success" in which abolitionists had been largely responsible for redeeming the nation "amidst the aboundings of iniquity".[4] The final phase of abolition had been achieved with relatively limited "agitation" and activists saw it largely as a result of collaboration between anti-slavery leaders and government ministers. The elder James Stephen was partic- ularly active in the process of abolition behind the scenes in the years up to 1807 as Wilberforce was the more public presence of the cause. In 1805 Stephen helped draft the Order in Council forbidding importation of slaves into the recently conquered Dutch colony of Guiana. In the following year he prepared for Grenville a draft bill to abolish the foreign slave trade to British territories and he presented a memorandum that became a basis of the 1807 measure.[5] It was not surprising that the assumption of the activists themselves underpinning the new national anti-slavery organisation created after abolition, the African Institution, was that activists were "insiders", virtual partners of ministers and offi- cials in overseeing the enforcement of British slave trade legislation. They conceived of themselves also as continuing to work with government to encourage amongst both British and African traders the expansion of "legitimate" commerce with Africa as an alternative to the slave trade.

Their claims to "insider" status derived from their sense of expertise both about the operations of the slave trade and their knowledge more generally of West African affairs. Considerable continuity existed between the evangelical reformers who had been active against the trade, administered or directed Sierra Leone through the Sierra Leone Company in the period (1791–1808) before the Crown assumed respon- sibility, and the active members of the African Institution committee. Eight of fourteen directors of the Sierra Leone Company in 1807–08 were on the committee of the African Institution and Zachary Macaulay was initially secretary of both organizations. He, Henry Thornton, the elder James Stephen and William Wilberforce, Claphamites all, were at the centre of a network of information, influence and patronage that, in the early years after 1807, appeared to make them indispensable to politi- cians and officials on slave trade matters. A network of correspondents in British and foreign ports provided evidence for the African Institution to recognize deficiencies in the slave trade laws as they applied to British subjects. Activists pressed the government to close the loopholes. Thus they brought to official attention the fitting out of ships for the slave trade under foreign flags in Liverpool and London. The African Institution drew information from subscribers who "frequent Lloyd's Coffee

House" on insurance business for such voyages and sent any such information to officials. Abolitionists also directly contacted naval officers involved in making a reality of the anti-slave trade laws, reminding them of the bounties to be gained from successful rounding up of slavers, a reward that the activists had promoted.[6]

On behalf of the African Institution in June 1810 Brougham in the Commons and Holland in the Lords pressed the government for action on information coming in of other infractions of the slave trade legislation. The activists helped draft the Slave Trade Felony Act (1811) and Brougham proposed it in Parliament. Their recommendations for the criminal penalties to be adopted – transportation for fourteen years or imprisonment for five – were incorporated into the legislation.[7] Macaulay and his colleagues apparently were shown official despatches from Governors Columbine (a subscriber to the African Institution) and Maxwell in Sierra Leone and responded with further enforcement suggestions to government. Columbine also communicated separately with the African Institution. The abolitionists claimed influence over the Admiralty's decision in 1812 to have naval patrols extend south as well as north of Cape Palmas, and particularly as far as the Bight of Benin.[8]

Activists' complementary concern to the naval suppression of the trade was the policy of developing "legitimate" trade in African goods. This was designed to meet the argument of British merchants trading to Africa that, with the loss of income from the slave trade, Africans were unable to pay for goods they wished to buy from British merchants. African Institution leaders thus focused on promoting conditions that would guarantee a level of imports of African goods into Britain that would produce an adequate return to Africans in the market for British products. They particularly wanted to equalize duties on African goods with those imposed on similar West Indian products. Using their good access to government they claimed some success when duties were modified on cotton, wool, ginger, coffee and palm oil in 1810.[9]

Prominent abolitionists thus behaved in their deployment of "influence" as a combination of non-official coadjutors and critical friends of government helping ministers and officials achieve their best intentions. Yet, whatever successes might be claimed for a relationship with government that operated largely behind the scenes, it ran a risk. "Influence" of this kind was only likely to be satisfactory to those with anti-slavery convictions, the majority of them by the very nature of the process excluded from any involvement, so long as they were content with the existing framework of policy. This gradually ceased to be the situation.

Concerned about the continuing international slave trade across the Atlantic activists pressed as early as 1813 for the insertion of a slave trade clause in a treaty with Sweden as a participant in the trade. When the clause was later added they saw this as a model for future treaties with any other powers who were also implicated in the traffic.[10] Once the Napoleonic wars ended abolitionists showed enthusiastic optimism over getting a general international agreement on suppression as a more rapid route to international virtue than pursuing bilateral treaties. They raised a brief but nationally extensive "agitation" in the form of a campaign in 1814 that produced many hundreds of petitions. The campaign was directed to reminding British representatives at the congresses of Paris and Vienna of the continuing strength of anti-slave trade sentiment and particularly to preventing the re-emergence of French slave commerce. Neither of these objectives was attained in 1814–15 although consultation with Castlereagh encouraged Foreign Office circulation of British representatives instructing them to raise suppression with the governments to which they were accredited. Abolitionists also approached Talleyrand and Tsar Alexander I without effect. Nor did success come in the following congresses, even with the enlistment in Paris and at Aix-la-Chapelle and Verona of Wellington who was seen, particularly by Macaulay and Clarkson, as rather more sympathetic than Castlereagh – and despite the lobbying of continental rulers by Thomas Clarkson, William Allen and Zachary Macaulay.[11]

Macaulay, in the hope of gaining some influence on French slave trade policy, cultivated close relations with a number of French political figures, including the Baron de Stael and the Duc de Broglie. The latter raised the issue of the French slave trade in the Senate though both were more identified with the moderate liberal opposition than the Restoration government. Macaulay's friend, Louis Dumont, a permanent official in the ministry of foreign affairs, provided information and contacts. In vain pursuit of more leverage on the French situation Macaulay also met figures as disparate as the old critic of slavery, the Abbé Grégoire, and the future chief minister, François Guizot.[12] The evidence suggests that there was some willingness to act on the part of the British government but too little awareness by activists that other states had powerful interests encouraging the maintenance or restoration of the trade and fostering suspicion of British motives. If this made a general ban impossible it also made enforceable bilateral treaties between Britain and other powers difficult to achieve. Drawn-out diplomatic negotiations (the ends of which were not disputed between diplomats and activists) preceded an unwillingness of officials of the other treaty powers consistently to enforce agreements when they were arrived at – no amount of abolitionist "influence" altered those facts. A framework of policy that focused on suppression did not in itself maintain activist enthusiasm when slave trading remained considerable. This was combined with a growing recognition, in relation to British abolition of the trade, of a disappointed expectation (despite James Stephen drafting a model Slave Registration Act for Trinidad and the islands ceded by France) that it would produce an improvement in the conditions of West Indian slaves. Time drained away support for the methods of the African Institution. It came to seem marginal and inactive in the ways that mattered as activists' attention shifted by the early 1820s to ending the institution of slavery both as necessary in itself and, ultimately, as the only sure way of reducing the trade in human beings.[13]

When activists came to deal with Texas in the later 1830s and early 1840s, and had to explore how best to work internationally on this issue, the social and religious character of British abolitionists had changed markedly from the early post-abolition years. How this younger generation of anti-slavery activists saw their situation and what they took from their recent experience sharply distinguished them from the generation of Wilberforce, the elder Stephen and even Buxton. The younger activists had participated in the campaign that brought emancipation in 1834 and the end to apprenticeship four years later. During this process Buxton and some of his associates were in frequent discussion about the evolution of policy with politicians and officials. But younger activists much more readily resorted to mass public meetings and public lectures and had organized vast numbers of petitions and several delegate conventions that implicitly questioned the moral, though not the constitutional, authority of Parliament. To these forms of "agitation" they attributed much of the success of the emancipation and anti-apprenticeship drives. Indeed, they tended to consider features of the emancipation legislation they disliked – the apprenticeship scheme and the large compensation of twenty million pounds to planters – as accommodations made by anti-slavery MPs to government ministers and officials with whom they had discussed policy without paying sufficient attention to mass opinion.[14] The method of using "influence" alone could be turned back upon activist parliamentary leaders and appear as part of the problem, and "agitation" seem to be the necessary means of giving "influence" both due weight and legitimacy.

One of the main reasons for this was that the younger element amongst the activist leadership saw themselves as "outsiders" somewhat distrustful of the remnants of the older generation of parliamentary abolitionists. They resorted to "agitation" as the natural mode of people who were, in Joseph Sturge's words, "not now in favour in High Quarters here". By this he meant not, at the beginning of the 1840s, that the British government had ceased to adopt an anti-slavery position, but that he and his like lacked access to ministers and officials on terms similar to those of the earlier generation. Parliamentary political leadership of the anti-slavery cause into the 1830s remained with the upper echelons of the

Anglican middle class, but the mass engagement in "agitation" had largely depended upon the activism of provincial evangelical and other militant Dissent. The death or retirement in the 1830s of virtually all the old figures produced an activist leadership more directly representative of this popular anti-slavery. By the criteria of position and experience they were correct to see themselves as "outsiders" compared with the earlier generation.[15]

The generation of Joseph Sturge and his associates did not give up on the face-to-face lobbying of decision-makers, but they were not sure that the method brought them "influence", at least unless they could also speak on behalf of large quasi-representative bodies. This was the context of the most crucial moments of lobbying during the Texas issue. The greater "distance" of this reform leadership from government ministers and officials increased their consciousness of the limited leverage they had on a question of international diplomacy like Texas. Their early experience in dealing with the Foreign Office when the issue was British recognition of Texan independence in the late 1830s seemed to confirm this.

British activists initially adopted the American anti-slavery view that the prime motive of proponents of the independence of Texas was the expansion of slavery in concert with the southern states of the United States. They believed the intended eventuality was annexation to the United States. Given the clear contrast with the situation when the province had been part of Mexico – an 1824 law forbidding the slave trade and the presidential decree of 1829 ordering the emancipation of slaves – the moral grounds for refusing recognition to Texas were powerful. The limited "agitation" of some public meetings and the issue of pamphlets emphasized that Britain's own record on emancipation must be the basis for rejection of approaches from the Texans for British recognition. This moral imperative had to be central to policy, an ethical argument only slightly qualified by optimistic forecasts of a growing commerce with Mexico that would be lost to Britain by recognition of Texan independence.

This absolutist position of 1839, however, left the activists exposed if the British government did decide to open negotiations with Texas on recognition. They had to have a clear view of suitable terms on which recognition would be acceptable or they would have no basis for bringing "influence" to bear on the Foreign Office. Sturge in particular, by the end of 1839, after correspondence with New York abolitionists, recognized the need for proposals as to how recognition could be the outcome of a process leading to the elimination of slavery in Texas. The activists may also have hoped for a productive outcome from any negotiations since Palmerston responded to an anti-slavery deputation in the autumn of 1839 that he was unwilling "to do anything by which the influence of Great Britain could become accessory to the extension or perpetuation of slavery". When he decided, in the autumn of 1840, to negotiate a commercial treaty with Texas, he is likely to have acted on the basis that Mexico did not have the strength to undermine the territorial integrity of the Lone Star Republic. He probably also desired not to lose any commercial advantages given that American and French recognition had already taken place. But since 1836 Palmerston had been clear that if Texas was able to confirm its independence Britain would negotiate a slave trade treaty with the new state. This may have been what he meant in his reply to the anti-slavery deputation. At any rate, in the negotiations with Texas he emphasized that he would not sign a treaty with any new state possessing a naval flag "unless such state would consent to conclude at the same time with Great Britain a Treaty for the suppression of the African Slave Trade". The Texans agreed since they saw recognition as a prerequisite for raising a loan on the London market and in mid-November 1840 such a treaty, with a right of search provision, was signed with a treaty of commerce and navigation and a convention on public debt.[16]

It is implausible to argue that the slave trade treaty with Texas marked a success for activist "influence". Britain had a settled policy on slave trade suppression and, in another aspect of that policy, Palmerston was a vigorous supporter of direct naval action against slave trade factories on the coast of west Africa at precisely the same time as the Foreign Office's dealings with Texas.[17] Moreover, the announcement of the conclusion of the agreements with Texas came as a surprise to the abolitionists who had not known that the negotiations were taking place. The initial reaction of the activists was hostile. The doctrine of the new generation of abolitionists was that only the ending of slavery itself guaranteed the cessation of the trade. In the particular case of Texas their resolutions at the World Anti-Slavery Convention in London in the summer preceding recognition showed their conviction that the important slave trade to Texas was not a seaborne trade but the flow across land boundaries from the southern United States. Foreign Office officials were unmoved by activists' denunciations arguing that refusal to sign a commercial treaty would not have led the Texans to abolish slavery and conclusion of a treaty would not now encourage them to maintain slavery.

Abolitionists' activity to get the British government to act against slavery in Texas and prevent its annexation to the United States indicates that they did not appreciate how the Foreign Office in the Peel administration under Aberdeen had adopted a shift in emphasis as compared with Palmerston's policies. Aberdeen thought of Texas as an element in a larger diplomatic situation involving Britain, the United States and

France and not simply as an issue in the international politics of slavery. British anti-slavery activists of the 1840s were not helped in their understanding of Aberdeen's policy in that, unlike the earlier generation of Claphamites, they had no close links with diplomats or officials and were in no position to come to any properly grounded independent judgement about the situation in Texas. They relied on their American colleagues for information about developments. The Americans in turn gave credence to reports brought back by the eccentric Massachusetts reformer, Stephen Pearl Andrews, who was not always able to distinguish between wish and fact. He provided optimistic accounts of anti-slavery sentiment in Texas, including to the General Anti-Slavery Convention in London in the summer of 1843 when international abolitionist zeal about Texas came to a head. Some reformers supposed therefore that encouragement from Britain would be sufficient to tip the balance amongst Texans in favour of a policy of emancipation with independence and convince them to shun any American offer of annexation. British activists were vulnerable to the American abolitionists' notion that British financial inducements to the Texans might be the key to getting the right outcome. It was hard for them to envisage any alternative since they lacked any independent knowledge of Texas and it was a "solution" that maintained their own relevance. They may also have been susceptible to a sense that, in talking about money, they were displaying a hard headed "realism" in pursuit of a noble objective and would therefore be taken seriously.

There was no question of Aberdeen departing from the settled British anti-slavery policy. But he was inclined to pursue the policy in less robust ways, or at least in ways less likely to antagonize other powers than had Palmerston. He ensured that naval officers were appropriately instructed. Any action against slavers "had to ensure us the good-will of other nations; and by proving to them our purity of intention and singleness of purpose, will lead them to reject the false and unworthy imputations which have been cast upon us by the national jealousy of some, and the interested motives of others".

On Texas Aberdeen indicated British preference for a free labour and independent Texas but, in line with his suppression policy, anti-slavery there had to be reconciled with his desire for better relations with France and with settling outstanding issues with the Americans. The successful negotiation of the Webster-Ashburton Treaty of 1842 on boundaries between British North America and the United States thus implicitly limited how far Aberdeen was prepared to go in opposing American policy in Texas.

His encouragement to Mexico, in collaboration with France, to recognize Texas as a basis for the Texans refusing annexation did not work but had the advantage, as a process, of helping improve Anglo-French relations. Texas was thus an occasion for the British government to express anti-slavery principle without anti-slavery being the prime objective of policy.

Anti-slavery activists as outsiders had little insight into these complexities and hoped that the government saw annexation, as they did, as the next stage in the potentially massive expansion of slavery that was a threat both to liberty more widely in the Americas and to British interests. This was the unpromising context of the two deputations of Anglo-American abolitionists from the second General Anti-Slavery Convention in the summer of 1843 to the Foreign Office to press for either a direct British loan or guarantees that would allow the Texans to raise private capital. The *quid pro quo* should be emancipation in Texas and a refusal of any American proposal of annexation. The activist view that finance could well be the key to getting what they wanted was not shared by either Aberdeen or (according to the anti-slavery banker Samuel Gurney) British bankers. Indeed, so fixed were they on their objective that few of the activists anticipated the danger that Aberdeen was alert to – the use of the British bogey in the United States to give the movement for annexation greater urgency.[18]

What conclusions can one draw from these various instances of activists' relations with officials and politicians? Policy *change* occurred at times when activists engaged in a combination of "agitation" and "influence", though that is not to say that is solely why policy changed. While there was more "agitation" preceding 1833 than 1807 specific anti-slavery activity was followed in both cases by the more general mobilisation involved in electing a new parliament. Change in the composition of the House of Commons was beneficial to the cause in both cases and was in part a tribute to the efficacy of "agitation", not in electing MPs, but in keeping anti-slavery on the election agenda. "Influence" on operational issues largely under the control of the British government and within an accepted framework of policy, was more effective earlier than later in the period. British anti-slavery policy assumed a settled character from about 1815 to the later 1840s. Activists believed it driven by a moral imperative though, as time passed, they had doubts about the efficacy and even the morality of the suppression policy in the form of naval patrols prepared to use force. There was also perhaps a growing sense amongst activists that the policy had become a constant but also almost reflexive rather than reflective of a priority that still had the power to displace other policy considerations.

Getting other powers to accede to effective enforcement of suppression was on the edge of British capacity unless force was used on foreign vessels or installations, as happened in relation to the Gallinas barracoons in West Africa at the beginning of the 1840s and Brazil in 1850. An illustration of the limits on anti-slavery policy short of force was Macaulay's fruitless efforts to replicate "insider" influence in relation to the French trade. Fear of the dramatic expansion of slavery represented by the possible annexation of Texas to the United States seemed to a different breed of activist to require a step change in policy. Yet these "outsider" activists had no experience of, and probably would have had little patience with, the range of factors and the practicalities to be considered in the making of policy. They wished to see Britain committed to more active international anti-slavery leadership through pursuing emancipation in Texas. Yet since this later generation of activists were external to any machinery of policy they were left seeking "influence" through wielding virtually only the moral imperative, an imperative more suited to be the centre piece of a campaign of "agitation" with which they were in truth more comfortable.

Notes

1   Across the first half of the nineteenth century activists focused, in chronological order of concern, on the abolition and its enforcement of foreign and British slave trades to British territories, suppression of the international slave trade, slave registration in British territories to measure the demographic impact of abolition, gradual and then immediate emancipation of colonial slaves, the ending of apprenticeship of former slaves and the universal emancipation of slaves.

2   David Turley, *The Culture of English Antislavery, 1780–1860* (London: Routledge, 1991), pp. 52, 54–5.

3   On the long running activist commitment to "civilizing" the victims of the trade and the slave system see David Turley, "British antislavery reassessed", *Rethinking the Age of Reform: Britain 1780–1850* (Cambridge: CUP, 2003), eds. Arthur Burns and Joanna Innes, esp. pp. 194–7, 198–9.

4   *Christian Observer*, 6, 2 Feb. 1807, p. 124.

5   See Patrick C. Lipscomb's succinct account of Stephen's activities in the *Oxford Dictionary of National Biography* (Oxford: OUP, 2004), eds. H. C. G. Matthew and Brian Harrison.

6   *Fourth Report of the African Institution, 1810*, London, 1814 ed., pp. 2–7.

7   *Fifth Report of the African Institution, 1811*, London, 1811, pp. 3–7; James Bandinel, *Some Account of the Trade in Slaves from Africa as connected with Europe and America* (London: Longman, Brown & Co., 1842), pp. 144–5.

8   *Fifth Report of the African Institution*, p. 37; *Sixth Report of the African Institution, 1812*, London, 1812, pp. 4–5.

9   *Third Report of the African Institution, 1809*, London, 1814 ed., pp. 12–13; *Fourth Report of the African Institution, 1810*, p. 15.

10 *Seventh Report of the African Institution, 1813*, London, 1813, pp. 14–15.

11 Huntington Library, San Marino, CA, Clarkson MSS., CN56, Thomas Clarkson, paper (c. 1815). Viscountess Knutsford, *Life and Letters of Zachary*

Macaulay by His Granddaughter (London: Arnold, 1900), pp. 313–14, 344–5. Betty Fladeland, "Abolitionist Pressures on the Concert of Europe, 1814–1822", *Journal of Modern History*, vol. 38 (1966), pp. 355–73.

12   Knutsford, *Zachary Macaulay*, pp. 356–60, 378, 409–14.

13   *Sixteenth Report of the African Institution, 1822*, London, 1822, pp. 43–5.

14   Turley, *Culture of English Antislavery*, pp. 62–3, 70–4.

15   Boston Public Library, Boston, MA, Phelps Papers, Joseph Sturge to Amos A. Phelps, 2 Oct. 1841. More generally see Alex Tyrrell, *Joseph Sturge and the Moral Radical Party in Early Victorian Britain* (London: Christopher Helm, 1987).

16   For a full diplomatic context for the recognition of Texas as an Anglo-American anti-slavery issue and references for the detailed story of abolitionist dealings with the Foreign Office see David Turley, "Relations between British and American Abolitionists from British Emancipation to the American Civil War", PhD thesis, University of Cambridge, 1969, chapter 2.

17   The naval attack on the Gallinas slave barracoons at this time was widely noted.

18   Turley, "British and American Abolitionists", chapter 3.

CHAPTER FIVE

"A Course of Unceasing Remonstrance"

British Diplomacy and the Suppression of the Slave Trade in the East, 1852–1898

T. G. OTTE

Slavery remains one of the most emotive and morally, and thus politically, charged issues in the history of mankind. As such it enjoys a high profile, especially so in public history. And yet it has proved remarkably resistant to thorough scholarly analysis. To assert that part of the debate surrounding slavery is flawed is not to denigrate the immense sufferings of its victims; nor is it meant to minimize the impact of this baneful practice on societies in Africa and elsewhere. On the contrary, it is aimed at correcting an element of imbalance in scholarly accounts of slavery as an historical phenomenon.

Not the least aspect of this imbalance is the almost exclusive focus on the Western-dominated Atlantic slave trade. There are, of course, studies of slavery and the slave trade in the Islamic world but, by comparison, they are few in numbers; nor is this dimension present in the public debate surrounding slavery.[1] Not infrequently, indeed, historical studies of the Arab and Ottoman worlds shy away from the subject, mostly in deference to assumed regional cultural or political sensitivities, often also in genuflection before current Western intellectual fads. And yet, "[t]o study the history of the Middle East without slavery would be as meaningful as to study the American South or the Roman Empire without slavery".[2] As for the efforts of mid- and late-Victorian foreign policy to suppress the slave trade in the East, its study, too, encounters a number of problems. For one thing, if slavery and the slave trade are given their due consideration, questions of definition inevitably arise. Indeed, it would be more appropriate to speak of different forms of slavery and multiple slave trades. In the Islamic world, as elsewhere, slaves were chattel, and thus under the complete domination of their owners, saleable or transferable at his will. Yet, there was considerable variety in the prac-

93

tice of slavery, reflecting local circumstances and variations in Islamic customs and law. In general, slavery was domestic rather than economic. As an integral part of the Muslim household, slaves thus fell under the law of personal status, the core of the *shari'a*.[3] To some extent, this provided slaves with a degree of protection against abuse as well as carefully defined routes of escape from their current status. It was, however, a law honoured as much, if not more so, in its breaches as in the observance. Nor did liberation mean being freed in a Western sense. Manumission left slaves and their progeny clients in perpetuity of their former owner and his successors. Concubines – by definition servile – were freed if they bore their master's child. But as women they remained in the immutable position of adult inferiors. Any attempt to challenge the practice of slavery, then, represented a challenge also to the personal authority of the Muslim male in the Muslim home, and was thus a threat to the Muslim polity and society. Assumptions, moreover, that slaves in the Islamic world, unlike those in the Americas, were not used as a source of agricultural labour are problematic. The plantations on the Arab-dominated east coast of Africa, for instance, were largely dependent on enslaved Africans imported from the interior of the continent.[4]

Finally, by and large, diplomatic historians have tended to ignore the slavery dimension of the international politics of the Near and Middle East in the nineteenth century. Yet, the suppression of the slave trade, though not its central plank, was nevertheless an integral part of British diplomacy in the region. Invariably, there were nuances of emphasis, depending on international circumstances and party political affiliations. Even so, this ethical dimension of British foreign policy enjoyed broad support among the political nation. In 1842, the Tory foreign secretary and future prime minister the Earl of Aberdeen, hailed the efforts to suppress the slave trade as this "new and vast branch of international relations".[5]

The moral motivation behind the policy was genuine enough. It was fuelled by sentiments of Christian charity, and inspired by the idea – hard-wired into the Victorian consciousness – of "progress". Lord Palmerston, in many respects the antithesis to Aberdeen, had always taken a strong interest in the anti-slave trade crusade. But he also reflected wider Victorian moral sensibilities and a sense of a civilizing, national mission in his condemnation of, for instance, the "barbarous practices" of the slave-trading native ruler of Dahomey.[6] There was little to be gained from "mealy mouthed" diplomatic notes on the subject: "It requires deep cutting[,] and often repeated[,] to eradicate the cancer of the Slave Trade."[7]

The sense of a national mission, divinely ordained, to extirpate the trade in humans was a frequently recurring trope in the political discourse of mid-Victorian Britain, suffused with assumptions of the country's supremacy among the nations of the world. It appealed more especially also to the nonconformist conscience, a potent political force in the wake of the first two franchise reforms. As one nonconformist journal noted, "it has been the special vocation of England to take the field against the slave trade in all parts of the world".[8] To some extent, then, official efforts to suppress the slave trade reflected the altered political realities at home. It served as a kind of political pressure valve, helping to reconcile radical reformism with parliamentary constitutionalism.[9]

Historians have rightly commented on the symbiotic relationship between humanitarianism and empire.[10] Without the latter, the former would have had no field of action. Had slavery not existed in a context in which British governments could plausibly exert their authority, domestic humanitarian activism would have lacked purpose and direction. In a similar fashion, it was also indicative of the constraints on British foreign policy. Efforts to suppress the slave trade were feasible only where Britain could make that authority felt, as was the case against marginal European Powers, such as Portugal and Spain, or an inferior naval power like the United States of America in the Atlantic slave trade. In the East, by contrast, British policy had to operate within quite different parameters. Here the weakness of the Near and Middle Eastern polities placed limits on Britain's ability to pursue a forceful anti-slave trade policy. Indeed, how to reconcile humanitarian inspiration with the imperatives of Britain's wider strategic interests remained the core problem for British diplomacy in the region.

∞

The slave trade in the Muslim world gained steadily in importance for policy-makers in London from the 1840s onwards. Two discrete developments in the 1860s provided the necessary impulse for the complete reorientation of British anti-slavery efforts to the Arab, Ottoman and Indian ocean regions. The North's victory in the American civil war was one; the other was the perceptible increase in the Arab-Swahili slave trade. At a conservative estimate, in the nineteenth century, around two million Africans were enslaved by Arab traders on slave-hunting expeditions in the interior of the continent, and taken from the coast of east Africa or along the overland caravan routes to the Barbary coast, Egypt, the Arab peninsula, the Persian gulf area and the remainder of the Ottoman empire.[11]

In general, the government in London was well informed about the extent of the Arab-dominated slave trade, its fluctuations as well as the variety of routes along which traders moved their human commodities.

95

Britain's extensive consular network saw to that. In the mid-1850s, Britain maintained no less than three consuls-general and forty-one consuls and vice-consuls in the Levant area, with an equally large number of consuls and agents around the Persian gulf and the Trucial coast, financed by the Indian government. As C.M. (later Sir Charles) Kennedy, a career Foreign Office clerk and future head of the Office's Commercial Department, then commissioned to investigate the Levant consular establishments, noted in 1871, consular intervention was frequently necessary in the Ottoman dominions "in very many instances not required in countries where society is constituted on the basis of European civilization". Extraterritorial jurisdiction over foreigners residing in the Turkish empire, but also Britain's commercial and political interests in the region, "render it imperative that Consulates should be more numerous, be placed nearer together, and be provided with a larger staff than is wanted in most other countries".[12] Given the Anglo-Russian competition for influence in the Near and Middle East, the Levantine consular network acted as a political early warning system. But it also provided London with observation posts for monitoring the slave trade and directing naval pressure against local authorities deemed to be lackadaisical in their attitude towards the trade or, indeed, found to be conniving in it.

No general slave trade instructions were issued to the Levant consuls beyond routine reminders of the legal prohibition for British subjects to be involved in slavery.[13] In practice, this gave consuls a considerable degree of freedom of action. Major George Frederick Herman, consul (from 1856 consul-general) at Tripoli, compiled annual statistical reports on the slave trade at the ports of Tripoli and Benghazi. These included not only data on the volume of the traffic in slaves. Herman also went to some considerable lengths to gather further intelligence, such as the average price per slave or the origins of the slaves.[14]

The Levant consular officials furnished London with information about and analysis of the nature of slavery in the Islamic world. For the most part, consular and diplomatic reporting tended to accept assumptions of the relative mildness of slavery in the Ottoman dominions. James Finn, the long-serving consul at Jerusalem, noted that:

> Slave-service is light in this country, where the habits of daily life are exceedingly simple, and never employed in rural labour. I know of several instances in which a Slave of a house is better educated, and as well fed and clothed as his master, riding the best horse, and carrying arms. Yet there are cases of cruelty to be heard in abundance among the Moslems.[15]

That slaves formed an integral part of especially the richer Muslim households was well understood by British consular representatives. The

Hon. F.W.A. (later Sir Frederick) Bruce, the agent and consul-general at
Cairo between 1853 and 1858, emphasized that "[b]lack Slaves and black
Eunuchs form an essential part of the establishment of every rich Turk,
and as they are supplied exclusively from the regions that border the
Upper Nile, every attempt will be made to render inoperative the
measures taken by Saïd Pasha [the Viceroy] for the abolition of the
traffic".[16] In Morocco, observed Britain's chargé d'affaires and later
minister-resident at Tangier, Sir John Drummond-Hay, slaves were "not
numerous". They were "well treated and cared for", and formed "part
of the family of the master". If ill-treated, they could demand to be sold
to another bidder. In general, he reported, slaves were "rarely employed
by their masters . . . for agricultural purposes, but both male and female
are generally retained as household servants". In stressing the mildness of
the prevailing regime there, Drummond-Hay, argued "that, if no immediate alteration can be brought about in the laws of Morocco as affecting
slavery, our coloured fellow creatures in Morocco are not suffering those
hardships and atrocious cruelties which have unfortunately been practised in other Mahommedan countries".[17]

The differences between Eastern and Atlantic slavery were a recurring
theme in the reports of Britain's consular and diplomatic representatives.
Sir Henry Lytton Bulwer, ambassador at Constantinople since 1858,
frequently emphasized the domestic character of slavery in the Ottoman
world. Their servile position offered slaves both material and legal protection. The institution of slavery, he noted, was "so deeply engrained into
the daily household habits that we may sometimes find both Master and
Slave uniting against our efforts. I say this, not to defend slavery which
presents greater evils indirectly and generally than it at times offers,
directly and in individual cases, advantages, but to explain how difficult
it is to deal with it."[18] Lieutenant-Colonel Charles Herbert, then acting
consul-general at Baghdad, drove the point home in an 1869 survey of
the slave traffic in the Persian gulf and Mesopotamia. Slaves were an integral part of a Muslim household, and both the institution of slavery and
the traffic in slaves were sanctioned by Islamic law. It was therefore his
"conviction that it will be found impossible to suppress the trade so long
as the country continues Mohammedan".[19]

Britain's consular network also produced intelligence on the patterns
and routes of the Arab slave trade. Bruce's successor at Cairo, R.G. (later
Sir Robert) Colquhoun, for instance, emphasized both official
connivance in the slave trade as well as external commercial stimuli. Its
protestations to the contrary notwithstanding, the Egyptian government
maintained, "at certain places, large barracoons, or depôts, where the
poor natives of the interior are collected for Government purposes". The
ranks of Egyptian regiments, Colquhoun observed, were mostly filled

with captured Nubians, while enslaved women and children were brought to Cairo "as house-servants in the harems". Conditions in the barracoons were "fearful"; small pox was rife, and the mortality rate among the captives was high. For every ten slaves who reached Cairo, "fifty have perhaps miserably perished in the transit, which has been described to me as worse than the middle passage in the Cuban slavers". The trade in slaves was fed by a regular traffic, controlled by Arabs in the Bahr-el-Gazal region, who carried out organized "razzias" on native tribes: "The plunder sought, consists of ivory tusks, cattle, and the vanquished individuals of the tribe."[20] British consuls understood the significance of the connection between the ivory trade and slave-hunting. As Colquhoun's successor as agent and consul-general at Cairo, General Edward Stanton, noted in 1865, "every Elephant's tusk that is brought to European Markets from this country has been procured by robbery and murder" carried out by Arab slave-hunters.[21] From the 1850s onwards, Europe's voracious appetite for ivory for a whole range of household and luxury goods, from combs and cane handles to billiard balls and piano keys, made ivory a precious commodity. But with the ever-increasing demand for ivory, the demand for slaves also increased. Captured Africans were forced to carry the tusks but then became saleable commodities themselves as soon as the caravans had reached their destinations.

The snatching and selling into slavery of children at Mecca during the annual Hajj season was "not an uncommon practice", observed the consul at Damascus, Edward Thomas Rogers. He and and his consular colleagues closely monitored the trade routes via Egypt and Gaza to Jerusalem, Beirut and Damascus.[22] Occasionally, consular intelligence gathering on the slave trade took on a somewhat "Greenmantle-ish" character. Thomas F. Reade, the acting consul-general at Cairo in the late 1860s, took an active interest in the matter. Disguised as an Arab, he visited several slave markets in the Egyptian capital and its environs in August 1867. At that time, he estimated around 5,000 slaves to be on sale in Cairo and another 2,000 at the Tantah fair outside the capital. Up to 15,000 enslaved Africans annually were brought down the Nile to be sold in Cairo, and this steady stream was kept up from "Jalabat, on the Abyssinian frontier, [where] an enormous Slave Mart is constantly open". From his Egyptian vantage point Reade had a much clearer picture of the brutality of the slave trade: "the cruelties and abominations perpetrated by the dealers and their Agents who supply the Egyptian Market, are not less atrocious than those ever committed by Slave Traders in any part of the world".[23]

Reade was no exception. Finn at Jerusalem took "every opportunity of inveighing against" slavery; Herman at Tripoli was well aware that he

had "it in my power to [secure the] . . . ready adherence to those enlightened views of Humanity" which inspired British efforts to suppress the
slave trade.[24] Most consuls in the Levant helped to secure the liberation
of slaves. Sidney Smith Saunders, consul at Prevesa in the 1850s, had been
authorized by Palmerston to purchase the freedom of slaves landed there
as part of the regular slave traffic from Candia (Iraklio) on Crete.[25] In the
late 1880s, Donald Andreas Cameron, the consul at Benghazi, even kept
a safe house for fugitive slaves, at no inconsiderable expense to himself.[26]
Manumission for escaped slaves could be obtained in a variety of ways.
Although domestic slavery in Turkey was generally acknowledged to be
light, ill-use was not infrequent. In such cases, personal contacts with
senior local officials and direct appeals to them on behalf of runaway slaves
frequently secured their manumission.[27]

In 1865, Bulwer, during a visit to Egypt on the eve of his retirement
from diplomacy, obtained the viceroy's agreement to place the current
ad hoc methods on a more regular footing. In future, consuls would
request a "letter of freedom" from the local police chief on behalf of the
fugitive slave. This certificate of manumission was then to be handed to
the latter in the presence of a member of the consular staff, and his name
entered in a register of slaves thus freed, kept at the consulate.[28] Although
this arrangement helped to systematize the process of manumission, it was
not without problems. Official sanction for the liberation of a runaway
slave through consular intervention, T.F. Reade observed three years
later in a lengthy memorandum, was easily enough obtained. But the
delivery of the required certificate was "almost invariably accompanied
by conditions which render it a very questionable matter whether the
social position of the recipient is at all bettered by the acquirement of such
a document". On the receipt of the certificate the newly manumitted
slaves were detained by the local police until someone could be found to
engage them as domestic servants. Moreover, freed slaves were not infrequently recaptured and resold, often with the connivance of the police.[29]

At the Foreign Office William Henry Wylde, the senior clerk and
head of the Slave Trade Department, and the assistant under-secretary
James Murray took up the problem of fugitive slaves seeking refuge in
British consular establishments in the Levant. Wylde had established for
himself a considerable degree of influence on slave trade matters within
the Foreign Office, far more than was usual for a clerk at that time.[30]
Although imbued with a strong sense of the righteousness of the anti-
slave trade cause, he nevertheless urged caution on the foreign secretary.
Britain did not "have any *well founded right* to interfere & require that
liberty shall be granted to every Slave that seeks the protection of a British
consulate". Following the sultan's *firman* of 1857 abolishing the trade in
slaves in the Ottoman empire, Britain's representatives were justified in

interceding on behalf of slaves illegally imported into the sultan's dominions. Even so Wylde considered it "not advisable that our Consular Agents in the East should become the Quixottic champions of every slave that may seek refuge in a British Consulate, and [consuls] . . . should be told to avoid as far as practicable interfering in the status of Domestic Slavery". Both Murray and the foreign secretary, Lord Edward Stanley, concurred with the senior clerk's observations. It was necessary, Murray averred, "to guard against any abuse of power by Brit[ish] Consular Officers in Egypt, however much their zeal in the cause of freeing Slaves might otherwise be considered laudable".[31] This, in fact, remained the official position of the Foreign Office. In 1872, Lord Granville, foreign secretary in the first Gladstone administration, impressed the need for circumspection upon the vice-consul at Damascus, William Kirby Green. Consular interference was justified "in cases where slaves are notoriously ill-used". At the same time, consuls "should not as a rule encourage slaves to look to them for interference or protection".[32]

Consular officers were the principal agents in Britain's efforts to suppress the slave trade in the Near and Middle East. Native officials, acting in cooperation with the consuls, however, were often found to be useful, necessary even. This provided an important variation within the overall pattern of British anti-slave trade policy, as was illustrated by the case of Mirza Mahmood Khan, the Persian slave trade commissioner at Bushir. Under the terms of an earlier Anglo-Persian agreement for the suppression of the slave trade British cruisers in the Persian gulf were allowed to intercept slavers sailing under the Persian flag. They were not allowed, however, to take the captured vessels as prizes, and, instead, had to hand them over to the Persian authorities. Without the close cooperation of Persian officials along the Gulf coast little progress was possible against the slave traders.

A number of circumstances hampered British efforts to suppress the traffic in slaves in the gulf region. One was the ill-defined Ottoman-Persian boundary around the Shatt-el-Arab waterway, which caused endless problems. Especially in the 1850s, moreover, the strength of Britain's naval presence in the gulf, furnished by the East India Company (EIC) until 1857, fluctuated in accordance with the defence requirements of India. During the 1853 war in Ava, for instance, the waters of the Gulf were practically denuded of EIC vessels, and the slave trade increased.[33] The other constraint was "the venality which marks the conduct of Persian functionaries of all ranks", noted William Taylour Thomson, the legation secretary at Tehran. With the shah's authority in the coastal provinces fragile at best, and officials underpaid, the temptation was great to connive in the activities of the slave traders in return for some financial consideration. To remedy this Thomson suggested a fixed annual gratuity to be paid to the commissioner at Bushir. This suggestion was supported by the outgoing minister at Tehran, Lieutenant-Colonel Justin Sheil, and swiftly approved by London.[34] It was clearly understood that this subsidy was dependent upon the commissioner fulfilling his duties. As Thomas Lawrence Ward, Wylde's predecessor at the head of the Slave Trade Department, minuted, "we only bind ourselves to pay it so long as the [British] Resident [at Bushir] is satisfied with the Conduct of the Commissioner, we shall retain in our hands . . . the Power of exercising an effectual control over this Commissioner in the Performance of his Duty". Control over the commissioner was one aim; the other was "to place him beyond the reach of corruption on the part of the Slave Dealers".[35]

The result was mixed. Mirza Mahmood Khan proved unreliable. Indeed, Captain Felix Jones, the British resident at Bushir, found him "in a state of derangement wholly unfit for the performance of any further duty".[36] In consequence, payment of the subsidy was suspended in 1859, not to be resumed until 1867. The allowance, indeed, was paid without the knowledge of the Persian government. Given its "doubtful character" – the Hon. Hussey Crespigny Vivian, briefly Wylde's successor in super-intending the Slave Trade Department, called it "a Secret Bribe" – it was removed from the accounts submitted for parliamentary scrutiny and the money was taken out of the secret service fund, which was under the control of the permanent under-secretary.[37] By 1876, the slave trade along the Persian coast was practically extinct, and the commissioner was withdrawn.[38]

∞

The case of the slave trade commissioner at Bushir illustrates the largely pragmatic nature of Britain's anti-slave trade policy in the East. Indeed, British efforts to suppress the trade in slaves reflected the fact that there was no single, uniform slave trade. While, in terms of volume, the import of African slaves, largely to serve menial purposes, formed the largest part of the traffic in slaves, the trade in white slaves, mostly females from the Caucasus region, played a more significant role. In the middle nineteenth century, Circassian and Georgian women, even under-age girls, were acquired in still substantial numbers for the harems of the senior officials and other members of the wealthy élites in the Ottoman empire – as concubines or as menials, two functions not always differentiated. Suppressing the African trade had the potential to affect the slave owners economically; restricting white slavery, by contrast, entailed a challenge to the sanctity of the Muslim home, and thus threatened to disrupt the social fabric of the Muslim world.

No doubt, diplomatic and consular reporting on the subject reflected some of the prurient nineteenth century Western fantasies about the Oriental decadence and the "lustful Turk". Even so, the sanctuary of the harem did much to blunt the humanitarian impulse that informed British policy. Turkey's relative international weakness during the Crimean war, and her dependence on Anglo-French military support, gave British diplomacy a degree of leverage. But there were clear limits as to what external pressure could achieve. Britain's ambassador, the otherwise bullish Stratford Canning, Viscount Stratford de Redcliffe, limned these constraints in the autumn of 1854. In the Islamic world in general, he pointed out, "the usages of society and the sanction of religion so fence round the practice of slavery, maintained by importation, that it is extremely difficult to obtain any mitigation, and still less a relinquishment of the practice". The "Great Elchi" was therefore reluctant to press the case on the Sublime Porte, lest "an unsuccessful attack may strengthen a bad cause".[39]

Even so, Stratford decided to remonstrate with the Turkish authorities to suppress the revived white slave trade, using Etienne Pisani, the *de facto* first dragoman at the embassy, as his intermediary. The war with Russia threatened "the very existence of the Turkish Empire". In continuing the trade, Turkey asked her allies to assist in "outrages which . . . they repudiate with unutterable abhorrence". Although he acknowledged the distinction between Eastern and transatlantic slavery, Stratford sought to exploit Turkey's exposed position during the war:

> Unlike the Negro in America, the Slave in Turkey is rather a domestic servant than a field-drudge or beast of burthen. He is not ostensibly ill-treated. If a male, he will rise occasionally to posts of profit and honour; if a female, ease and every luxury may be her portion in the Harem of a Court favourite or assistant functionary. The degradation nevertheless remains; and the privation of liberty . . . is itself an intolerable evil. [. . .] In one respect there is no difference between Negro and Circassian slavery. Black or White, wherever slavery exists, the whole Society suffers.

The continued existence of slavery would undermine the health of Turkish society, "minister[ing] to those habits of expence [sic] and sensuality which undermine the strength of the empire". Stratford urged the Porte to adopt stringent measures against the "three stages of the traffick, to *purchase*, to *conveyance*, and to *sale*".[40]

For his part, the foreign secretary, the Earl of Clarendon, amplified the pressure on the Turkish government to remedy "a state of things so atrocious and disgusting". He impressed upon Stratford that the matter "engages the serious attention" of the British government: "The honour of England no less than the interests of humanity require that no effort should be spared at this moment for the suppression of slavery in the Ottoman dominions."[41]

Under the exigencies of the war such pressure bore fruit. In October 1854, the Sublime Porte issued an imperial *firman*, prohibiting the traffic in Circassian and Georgian slaves in the region around Batoum.[42] Gratifying though this was, it marked little more than a transitory success for British diplomacy. The Porte resisted Stratford's efforts in the spring of 1855 to negotiate a comprehensive anti-slave trade convention, instead offering further instructions to provincial governors in the sense of the *firman*. Indeed, as General Fenwick Williams discovered, the Turkish officers of the Kars Army were heavily involved in the traffic:

> Boys are preferred by these brutes, and the girls are sent as bribes to Constantinople; and until the Allied Consuls are authorized to demand restitution of these victims to Turkish sensuality . . . ; and until the Porte is bound by Treaty to send the culprits . . . to the Gallies . . . , this infamous traffic will flourish. . . . [The] abolitionary Firman simply adds mockery to crime and vice.[43]

Clarendon decided to persevere. Only "a course of unceasing Remonstrance" would force the Porte to accept "what is due to Humanity".[44] Privately, Clarendon was full of the "gloomiest anticipations" about Turkey's future. Progress, he thought, was possible "in spite of the Koran & Mussulman prejudices", were it not for the character of Sultan Abdul Mejid: "What remonstrances ag[ain]st apathy, sensuality & extravagance w[oul]d avail with a man who thinks himself all powerful & is surrounded by people . . . making him reject advice that [it] w[oul]d put him to personal inconvenience to follow?"[45]

The ambassador's representations nevertheless produced, in February 1857, another *firman*. It was progress of a kind, expressly prohibiting the trade in African slaves. But even in this respect, it was found to be somewhat vague. The "long established usage" of slavery, Stratford warned, meant that slavery itself would not come to an immediate end. The sultan's "doubtful authority in Arabia", moreover, made it unlikely that the *firman* would be enforced there.[46] The prime minister showed some understanding of the vagueness of the *firman*: "The Porte can hardly be asked to stigmatize so strongly a Practice so extensively countenanced by the Sultan's subjects."[47]

Crucially, the *firman* made no provisions for the suppression of the white slave trade. And here no further progress seemed possible. It could not be denied, Stratford observed, that the introduction of Circassians and Georgians, whether Christian or Mussulman, into this country for slavery or service, is favored by circumstances which make its prevention extremely difficult. In the Turkish domestic system such licence is at least an inveterate usage, sanctioned by religion, if not an absolute necessity. There is little to be said on the score of ill-treatment. Female Slaves from Circassia or Georgia become not infrequently the wives of opulent and powerful men.[48]

British anti-slave trade diplomacy in the East had run headlong into the immovable obstacle of the cultural and social practices of the Islamic world. Clarendon doubted whether any further remonstrances would yield any positive results. Moreover, he noted that "[t]he only complaint we have ever heard from the Circassians has been ag[ain]st our attempts to stop the traffic & I believe the young Ladies in general look forward with infinite satisfaction to Stamboul & that each believes she will be mother of a Sultan". For his part, Palmerston insisted that the traffic "demoralizes & degrades Circassia and Turkey alike". Yet he had to concede that it was "uphill work to urge morality on Principle upon Turk or Frenchman". Instead, it seemed more profitable, "with a view to accomplishing some good [,] to concentrate our efforts for the suppression of the African Slave Trade into Turkey".[49]

This shift of the focus of British policy marked a compromise between its humanitarian impulse and the realities of the East. Ultimately, Britain's strategic interest in maintaining the Turkish empire outweighed abolitionist ambitions. Stratford's successors did not turn a blind eye on the Circassian slave trade. But their representations lacked force; they had become almost a matter of routine and habit. In 1860, Bulwer raised the idea of extending the 1854 *firman* to cover the whole of Turkey's Caucasian frontier with the grand vizier, but readily accepted Ali Pasha's assertion that the ban had been issued only for the duration of the war. Indeed, he explained to the foreign secretary, Lord John Russell, that the position of a white slave in a Turkish household was "in some respect like that of an adopted child". Given the established position of slavery in Turkey, "so blent [sic] in with oriental manners", it was impossible to modify it from without.[50]

Although the Ottoman authorities took steps to prohibit the traffic of slaves among the Circassian immigrants in Turkey proper, Bulwer continued to counsel against pressing the Sublime Porte for further reforms. The extreme poverty of Circassian parents often forced them to sell their offspring, in the knowledge that they were "getting from poverty to comfort, . . . half servants, half playmates for [the owner's] own children". The whole question was "so engrafted into oriental manners" that it was best left alone. Bulwer's ready acceptance of the limitations placed on Britain's anti-slavery policy was compounded by an element of cynicism. Turkey's growing impoverishment would do more for the suppression of the slave trade than external political pressure. Moreover,

> the dispersion of the Circassians and their reduced and pitiable condition, which will probably affect the beauty of the race, are also likely to lead to the gradual abandonment of a custom, of which the debasing tendency can hardly be appreciated as long as the wives of the first men in the Empire have belonged to a class which we should consider stamped with degradation.

Russell concurred with Bulwer's analysis, and confirmed that his was a watching brief, but that he was "to do nothing more in [the] present state of affairs".[51]

Only once, in 1867, during preparations for the sultan's forthcoming visit to Britain, did the British government exert real pressure on the Porte in the matter of white slavery. But this was a matter of political expediency. As the Turkish ruler was to be lodged at Buckingham palace, Edmund Hammond, the permanent under-secretary at the Foreign Office, impressed upon Lord Lyons, Bulwer's successor at Constantinople, that "the usual habits of Orientalism" had to "be laid aside". More especially, the Sultan was not to bring his Harem or any other slaves as part of his entourage to London:

> It would shock the good people in this country to hear of the Sultan being surrounded by persons not proper to be mentioned in civilized society; and no small inconvenience might result if he was known to have slaves in his suite, for it would be impossible to answer for the conduct of the enthusiasts of Exeter Hall, with so fair an opportunity of displaying their zeal and doing mischief.[52]

By contrast, British post-Crimean diplomacy took a more active role in the suppression of the African slave trade with the Turkish empire. Here the Levant consuls fulfilled a dual function. On the one hand, they frequently ensured that *firmans* or vizirial letters relating more especially to the trans-Mediterranean traffic in slaves were properly circulated among the provincial governors. In 1858, for instance, John Elijah Blunt, then acting consul at Monastir, attributed the occasional landings of slaves along the Albanian coast to the failure of the government in Constantinople to inform the local authorities of prohibition of the trade, and supplied copies of the relevant documents to the pashas at Monastir and Durazzo.[53]

At Tripoli, Consul Herman was repeatedly stung into action by the "improbable audacity with which orders of the Central Government are evaded not to say mocked at in this remote province of the Empire".[54] Throughout his fourteen years at the post he made strong and frequent representations to the Ottoman governor to act upon the *firman* banning the trade in African slaves. In the late 1850s, Herman found him receptive to his suggestions, and very effective in his measures against the slave dealers. Even so, he warned that, given the immense profits to be derived from it, "no measure . . . will . . . for a length of time . . . arrest the traffic in slaves".[55] Herman's forebodings were prescient. By the end of the next decade, the then governor proved more recalcitrant, arguing that the Porte disapproved of the suppression of the trade, with the inevitable consequence that the traffic in slaves picked up again. Herman's successor, F.R. (later Sir Frank) Drummond-Hay had to report "that the usual atrocities attending the kidnapping and transport of Slaves . . . are practised with perfect impunity within this Regency".[56]

The weakness of Turkish authority in the remoter parts of the Ottoman empire was most acute in Arabia and along the shores of the Red sea. Here the seaborne slave traffic from Massowah and Suakin to Jedda on the Arabian coast was a constant source of concern for the Foreign Office. At Jedda, more especially, the sultan's writ did not run. One of the centres of resurgent Wahhabism, Jedda also proved difficult, dangerous even, as a consular observation post. The murder, in July 1858, of the British and French consuls and a number of other Europeans by a mob of fanatics, and the subsequent mutilation of their bodies, served as a warning. In retaliation, the town was shelled by *HMS Cyclops*, a steam frigate cruising off the Arabian coast. No doubt, "the massacre of a consul and a considerable number of Christians was not an every day proceeding", as the prime minister, the 14th earl of Derby, noted. Even so, this reflex exercise in gunboat diplomacy did not produce "the desired effect"; and there was the additional risk that the episode would be used as a pretext by France to project her naval power into the Red sea. [57]

Walter Plowden, one of Britain's consuls in the region, was in no doubt that the "[m]elancholy events . . . at [Jedda had been] caused principally by our efforts to suppress the traffic".[58] In the following year, indeed, the Kaimakan of Massowah threatened to unleash a massacre of Christians if Britain persisted in disrupting the Red sea slave trade. The foreign secretary took a firm line: "However strong may be the Mussulman feeling in some of the Turkish provinces in favour of the Slave Trade, the threat . . . is a matter of too great importance to be allowed to pass with impunity"; the governor had to be dismissed.[59] The situation at Jedda, however, remained volatile, and more was at stake than the safety of the British consul and other Europeans in the place, as

George Edward Stanley, the new consul there, argued in 1860. If an attempt were made "to put a stop altogether to the traffic in slaves . . . there will be a general insurrection among the Arabs, the consequences of which might be disastrous to the Ottoman authority".[60] Colquhoun, the agent and consul-general at Cairo, reinforced Stanley's argument. The suppression of the Red sea slave trade "must be the work of time, as we have to fight against custom consecrated from time immemorial, almost sanctioned by their religion, and, lastly, against a commerce which brings in an immense profit to all concerned in it – so great as to make it worth the trader's while to bribe largely the authorities charged to arrest the trade".[61]

Jedda and the other slave marts in the Hejaz were supplied from the western shores of the Red sea. The focus of British efforts to suppress the slave trade in the region therefore shifted to Egypt. On Russell's instructions, Colquhoun pressed the viceroy's government to take more effective measures against the traffic in slaves on the upper Nile and along the Red sea coast.[62] Egypt's increased importance for Britain's anti-slavery diplomacy resulted from a confluence of two different circumstances. One was the relative weakness of Britain's naval presence in the Red sea – "all naval men hate the slave trade service" there, as Palmerston had to admit.[63] The other, ironically, was the success of Consul Herman's persistence at Tripoli for, rather than extinguishing the trade, it diverted it to the western oases of Egypt.[64]

British policy in the matter was a mixture of the by now habitual remonstrances and conciliation. At Bulwer's suggestion, for instance, Russell supported the transfer of Massowah under Egyptian jurisdiction: "anxious as I am to vindicate its [the Porte's] supremacy where I can I am inclined to think that it is less able than the Viceroy to do anything against slavery in those distant parts which its arm hardly reaches".[65] Bulwer's reasoning seemed well founded in light of the viceroy's energetic measures especially in the upper Nile region. These, observed General Edward Stanton, Colquhoun's successor at Cairo, had "a most marked effect upon the Slave dealers, so much so that . . . no Slaves whatever have been brought down as Khartoum during the past 12 months".[66]

The burgeoning optimism of 1865 was short-lived. As so often in the East, vociferous official assurances were not matched by deeds. As Sir Henry Elliot, the ambassador at Constantinople from 1867 onwards, noted, the bulk of slaves traded throughout the Ottoman empire was despatched from Egypt: "The most effectual blow that can be struck against Slavery in Turkey must be dealt in Egypt."[67] But this was the problem, for, as Reade, the vice-consul at Alexandria, warned London, "no reliance whatever can be placed in the anti-slavery protestations of this Government".[68] The checks carried out by Egyptian steamers on the

Nile and at inspection posts along the river were "merely nominal", and local officials were complicit in the activities of the slave traders.[69] In the case of the traffic on the Nile, the absence of a permanent consular presence at Khartoum at the junction of the Blue and White Niles, a well known hub of the slave trade, further hampered British policy.[70]

It even transpired that the Azizieh Steamship Company, of which the viceroy (since 1866 styled khedive) was the majority share-holder, was heavily implicated in the transport of slaves in the Red sea and the eastern Mediterranean.[71] The information received in the summer of 1869 caused much soul-searching at the Foreign Office. There could be no doubt, reported Sir Philip Francis, consul-general and senior consular judge at Constantinople, that the 1857 *firman* was "habitually violated with the cognizance of the Turkish Government and the consent of the Egyptian Authorities and chiefly through the Steamvessels belonging to the Azizieh Company". The white slave trade was well established but clandestine, and sales largely pre-arranged and private rather than public.[72] As for the Cairo authorities, their communications on the subject of slavery were tailored to European views. Yet Francis "totally disbelieve[d] their professions and utterly distrust[ed] the genuineness of the means they propose" for the suppression of the slave trade. He discounted the issuing of certificates of manumission to any African landed in an Egyptian port. This had only one advantage, "that of enabling some port official to extort backsheesh [sic]". As senior Egyptian officials owned, purchased and sold slaves, they could hardly be expected to curb the trade. Francis's conclusion was harsh. The slave trade could only be suppressed, "if at all, from without by pursuing the extreme and objectionable course of European Powers interfering actually, practically, and with physical force in Egypt itself and doing what the Egyptian Government . . . will [not] itself do".[73]

This was the constant refrain of diplomatic and consular reporting from the Levant region. At the Foreign Office, Wylde, now head of the Consular and Slave Trade Department, pressed for a renewed effort to tackle the problem:

> It is very evident that if the traffic in slaves on board Egyptian steamers is to be put a stop to something more will have to be done than the occasional confiscations of some of the slaves.
>
> The Egyptian Authorities from the Khedive downwards, if they do not openly abet at any rate connive at the traffic in Slaves.

Wylde insisted that, "unless some serious notice is taken of these continued shipment[s] . . . it will be futile to attempt to stop the traffic".[74]

An opening came with Sir Bartle Frere's mission to Zanzibar in 1873.

En route to east Africa Frere was received by the khedive, who empha-sized his willingness to "put an end to the Slave Trade in Central Africa", provided he had Britain's "moral support". Even so, senior officials in London suspected that Ismaïl Pasha sought a bargain under which Britain would make concessions regarding Abyssinia, the Sudan and extra-terri-torial jurisdiction in return for Egyptian anti-slave trade measures.[75] The latter concession, indeed, remained one of the sticking points in the talks at Cairo. The Egyptian draft proposals, moreover, as Wylde pointed out, made no provisions for an actual ban of the import of slaves. Then there was the unresolved question of Britain's right to detain Egyptian vessels. Without the right to search vessels suspected of involvement in the slave trade, all measures for its suppression would remain ineffectual, argued Vivian, who had now left Whitehall for diplomacy as acting agent at Cairo.[76]

With the talks hanging fire, there were discernible signs of a sharp increase in slave imports into Egypt from Benghazi and Nubia as well as across the Red sea.[77] Concluding the projected Anglo-Egyptian slave trade convention thus became all the more pressing. Progress, however, depended on Britain increasing its leverage over the khedive. Egypt's mounting financial weakness, exacerbated by an ill-fated military expe-dition against the mainland possessions of the sultan of Zanzibar at the turn of 1875–6, provided the required fulcrum. The initiative came from within the Foreign Office. Lord Tenterden, the permanent under-secre-tary, argued that, given the khedive's difficulties, the moment was "a very favourable & desirable time for negotiating a Slave Trade Convention with Egypt".[78] Tenterden insisted that the matter had to be dealt with bilaterally: "We particularly want to keep the French & others from inter-fering with the Egyptians or the approaches to the Red Sea." An international anti-slave trade convention, as had been mooted in the parliament, "w[oul]d certainly be an invitation to them to come & meddle where we don't want them".[79]

There were also domestic political advantages to be gained from restarting the talks, as Tenterden spelt out to the Hon. Robert Bourke, the parliamentary under-secretary. It would, he predicted, "have a very good effect on public opinion in England", and divert attention from the row over the fugitive slaves circular of 31 July 1875 that had embarrassed the Disraeli government: "It is not a matter to go to sleep over."[80] Such exhortations notwithstanding, the negotiations were not concluded for another eighteen months. Still, the Anglo-Egyptian slave trade conven-tion of 4 August 1877 marked a turning-point in Britain's efforts to suppress the traffic in slaves in the Islamic world. At the very least, it provided an agreed framework for further measures to curb it.

Frere's conversation with the khedive had set in motion the talks that would ultimately lead to the 1877 convention. His mission to Zanzibar, of course, also produced a similar convention with the Sultan Sayyid Barghash-ibn-Said. Zanzibar was a key staging post in the Arab-Swahili slave trade between the interior of Africa and the Indian ocean and the Persian gulf. The sultan of Zanzibar himself had long been involved in this trade.[81] British influence along the east African coast had steadily increased in the course of the 1860s, and a determined effort was made by British diplomacy to win over the sultan.[82] Without the latter's cooperation, no advances were likely to be made against the slave traders in those waters. Certainly, the Royal Navy vessels on patrol duty there were a blunt instrument, as Wylde commented in early 1867.[83] Yet, in its dealings with the ruler of Zanzibar British anti-slave trade diplomacy had to operate within the by now accepted political and cultural confines. Wylde stressed

> that it would be as absurd as it would be futile on our part to attempt to interfere with the *status* of Slavery in [Zanzibar] or in any part of Africa not under British jurisdiction.
>
> What we want, and what we ought to confine our endeavours to, is the preventing [of] the export of Slaves from the Afr[ica]n Continent.[84]

The "total abolition of Slavery", Vivian confirmed later, was "quite impossible in a Mohammedan Country like Zanzibar".[85] The regional slave trade itself was extensive, as Henry A. Churchill, the political agent at Zanzibar, reported in 1868. The trade centred on the port of Kilwa to the south-east of the island of Zanzibar. According to Churchill, between 1862 and 1867 in excess of 97,000 slaves were exported from there, and of these almost 77,000 were brought to Zanzibar. The island was a preferred staging post for the traders because, once on the island, the enslaved Africans found it impossible to escape.[86] As for the sultan, as Wylde observed, his principal concern was financial. The slave trade brought in revenue, and any measures to suppress it required some form of financial recompense or subsidy for the sultan.[87] Britain's efforts in the slave trade matter had produced but "wretched results", as Vivian noted in 1871.[88] The international situation, however, was more propitious now than it had been a few years earlier. France, the only other power with regional interests – indeed, French planters on Réunion or Madagascar were involved in the slave traffic – was *hors de combat* after her defeat at the hands of Germany in 1870, and so in no position to interfere with Britain's dealings with the sultan of Zanzibar.[89] Frere's slave trade treaty of 5 June 1873 secured Britain the right to search and seize slavers intercepted in the waters around Zanzibar.[90] As such, it placed Britain's position in the region on a firmer footing; but it was also a further step towards turning the sultan of Zanzibar into a British client.

The two slave trade conventions of 1873 and 1877 marked important milestones in Britain's efforts to suppress the trade in the East. A convention of this kind had also been the object of British diplomacy at Constantinople for some time. But here, too, the right to search suspected slavers, regarded as vital by the Foreign Office, was the chief complication, so much so that Clarendon decided to mark time until circumstances were more favourable: "The object is of great importance but it may be purchased too dearly".[91]

At Constantinople, the British ambassador, Sir Henry Elliot, and his embassy secretary, Henry Page-Turner Barron, sought to de-emphasize the significance of the slave trade. Barron, for instance, reprimanded Drummond-Hay at Tripoli for his efforts to stir the provincial governor there into more energetic measures against slave dealers.[92] Elliot, for his part, sought to restrain the consul at Smyrna, Robert William Cumberbatch, a man very active in monitoring the movement of slaves in the eastern Mediterranean. Indeed, he went rather far in suggesting that the consul had been overzealous and alarmist.[93]

In general, Elliot argued that as slavery was a recognized institution in Turkey, and the private selling of slaves was thus not illegal: "It is no doubt an abominable institution & an odious practice, but I am aware of no right of ours to stop it."[94] Elliot was especially reluctant to tackle the issue of Circassian and Georgian female slaves. As their role was well established in the social fabric of the Turkish empire, external pressure would have no effect. Instead, Elliot advocated a gradualist approach; it would require "a complete revolution in the social organization" and "the development of a higher moral feeling" in Turkey to extinguish slavery. Any attempt to abolish the institution of slavery was doomed to failure, he asserted: "Anyone who now proposes such a thing, would have about as much chance of being listened to as if he had suggested it to the Southern States of America previous to the late war."[95] Even so, Elliot was by no means passive in slave trade matters. The "horrors of that infamous trade", the importation of eunuchs to Egypt, called forth his wrath, and he encouraged the Porte and the khedive to take steps to prevent the trade by imposing draconian punishments on the perpetrators.[96] But in line with Clarendon's earlier decisions, Elliot focused entirely on the African slave trade, and here he was remarkably successful. Aided by Etienne Pisani, he worked closely with the Turkish minister of police, Hassai Pasha, to secure the release of all Africans landed at Constantinople or other ports along the coast of Asia Minor.[97]

When, in early 1873, Elliot and Cumberbatch reported a new kind of trade in Circassians, now destined for Alexandria, there was divided counsel at the Foreign Office. Wylde, somewhat uncharacteristically, took a more restrained view. Pointing to Britain's own domestic problem with prostitution, he opined that "it behoves us to remove the moat [sic] out of our own eyes before we can make too much noise about the beam in our neighbour's eyes". This was rejected by Tenterden: "I do not think that because there may be immorality of one kind in England we sh[oul]d wink at evil of another kind which we may have any means of suppressing in Egypt."[98] Wylde swiftly fell into line, chastising Elliot's fabianism: "The state of things . . . is one which ought not to be passed over in silence. However much we might have been inclined to shut one's [sic] eyes to the so-called Circassian & Georgian Slave Trade . . . , yet a totally new state of things is depicted by Sir H. Elliot which . . . ought to be taken serious notice of."[99]

Lord Granville concurred, and eventually instructed Elliot to broach the subject of an Anglo-Turkish convention. Still, he conceded "that however desirable it would be to suppress domestic slavery, it would not be expedient to press the point as an indispensable condition of the agreement".[100] Progress, however, there was none. It required Turkey's near-bankruptcy in October 1875 for British diplomacy to renew its efforts. Even so, Elliot argued that "the repugnance of the Porte to enter into any such general Convention would be found insuperable".[101]

As before, it was the Foreign Office that kept up the pressure for an agreement. By the beginning of 1878, Turkey's precarious position in consequence of the Russo-Turkish war, made her more amenable to British diplomatic pressure. The marquis of Salisbury, the new foreign secretary, was prepared to settle for an exchange of notes on the subject, but yielded to representations from his senior officials, led by Wylde and Sir Julian Pauncefote, the legal under-secretary at the Foreign Office, who insisted on the need for a treaty.[102] Turkey's current weakness and the occasional support of the khedive notwithstanding, Elliot's successor, A.H. (later Sir Henry) Layard encountered difficulties in overcoming Sultan Abdülhamid II's reluctance to enter into a binding slave trade agreement. It was not until January 1880 that the convention was concluded.[103]

The Anglo-Turkish slave trade convention complemented the arrangements with Egypt and Zanzibar, though final ratification, "in regular Turkish manner", was delayed until March 1883.[104] It was no mean achievement, one that had eluded Clarendon and Stratford under more favourable circumstances. It boosted Britain's efforts to curb the traffic in slaves in the Mediterranean and the Red sea. It also strengthened the hand of Hugo Marinitch, the second dragoman at the Constantinople embassy, who played a prominent role in securing the release of African slaves.[105]

The convention did not, however, mark the end of slavery. Indeed, shortly after the signature of the 1880 convention, Layard warned that "[a]ny direct interference in it on our part would excite the suscepti-bilities of the whole Turkish people".[106] In essence, then, British diplomacy continued to run along Elliot's gradualist groove. There was no practicable alternative to it. By 1889, Marinitch and Sir William White, ambassador since 1885, reported that "the Slave Trade in the Ottoman Empire tends to diminish by degrees". But Marinitch warned against undue optimism: "we cannot expect to see it disappear at once in a country where . . . people, owing to their principles and habits, are interested in keeping it up for domestic purposes".[107] Marinitch's obser-vation underlined the ambiguous nature of Britain's anti-slavery policy in the East. There was, indeed, as Sir Villiers Lister, one of the assistant under-secretaries at the Foreign Office, noted, "something absurdly illogical ab[ou]t allowing slavery & forbidding S[lave] T[rade]. It is like permitting the consumption of meat while punishing butchers. However, we are anxious to put down both & are not bound to be log-ical."[108]

In this manner, the activities of the embassy were largely confined to refining the existing regime of monitoring and suppressing the slave trade in the East. White suggested further reforms – of a largely administrative kind – while his embassy secretary, E.D.V. (later Sir Edmund) Fane, kept up the pressure on the Sublime Porte to ensure that provincial governors complied with Turkey's obligations.[109]

While the 1883 Anglo-Turkish convention tended to reinforce the established piecemeal approach to the slave trade, the arrangement with Egypt produced grave, albeit unintended, consequences. Indeed, the initial positive assessment of the workings of the convention soon gave way to a realization that the suppression of the slave trade fuelled the flames of the nascent Arabi revolt against the khedive, which was supported by the Egyptian religious establishment.[110] After the defeat of Arabi Pasha, and with British troops stationed in Egypt, E.B. (later Sir Edward) Malet, Vivian's successor as agent at Cairo, suggested that further measures to curb slavery were feasible, always provided that the military situation was satisfactory.[111] For his part, Granville was deter-mined to exploit British control of Egypt in order to implement more vigorous reforms. His approach was informed by the precepts of classic Victorian economic liberalism. The khedive's earlier failure to suppress the slave trade was "to be found in the first principles of political economy", he averred. For as long as there was a demand for slaves, the supply of them would continue; "the so-called religious prejudices of the richer classes of the nation" were irrelevant. "The only way to extirpate the Slave Trade and to restore peace and prosperity to the districts wasted and depopulated by its attendant horrors is to abolish slavery forever throughout the Egyptian dominions."[112]

Granville's abolitionist policy was well-intentioned, but it was fraught with difficulties. At the Cairo agency, Sir Evelyn Baring, the future Lord Cromer, sought to curb the foreign secretary's zeal. Though paying lip-service to Granville's supply-and-demand argument, he emphasized the importance of deeply engrained cultural practices. Slavery was "recognised by Mohammedan religious law, which could not be abrogated by a mere declaration in a Decree or Convention". It would be unwise, he warned Granville, to legislate for its abolition: "The difficulties with which we have to contend in Egypt are sufficiently great without adding to them."[113] Indeed, he even discouraged Lister's indirect approach to discourage slavery by levying a tax on male slaves.[114]

Religious opposition to slavery reform in Egypt remained strong, and clerics frequently refused to sanction manumission especially of female slaves.[115] Even so, Baring's cautious approach prevailed. This was hardly surprising, for British efforts to curb the slave trade in and around Egypt after 1877 contributed to the most serious crisis of British imperial policy in the 1880s – the Mahdi uprising in the Sudan. British anti-slavery measures not only aroused the hostility of the slave traders and their private armies, they also disrupted the fabric of Muslim society, so rallied the Muslim Sudanese in general to the Mahdi's flag, and contributed to the collapse of Turco-Egyptian overlordship in the Sudan. British officials in the region readily accepted the nexus between the suppression of the slave trade and the potential fragility of Britain's position in Eastern Africa.[116] Indeed, slavery was not abolished in Egypt until November 1895.[117]

In the case of Zanzibar, the patron–client relationship with the sultan placed constraints of a different kind on British policy. When, in 1884, it transpired that the sultan had purchased slaves at Jedda, the Foreign Office was presented with an awkward situation. Earlier in the autumn, during the preparations for the 1884–5 Berlin conference, the Cabinet had emphasized the "importance of our not being forestalled by any European nation in the exercise of at least paramount influence" in Zanzibar's mainland possession; and Sir John Kirk, the British agent on Zanzibar, was instructed to obtain a "spontaneous declaration" from the sultan that he would not accept the protectorate of another European power.[118] The news of the sultan's purchases was therefore "a very mal à propos piece of information", observed Clement Lloyd Hill, then acting assistant clerk in the Slave Trade Department and future superintendent of the African Department: "We can't afford just at this moment to fall foul of the Sultan of Zanzibar." Under the circumstances it seemed more expedient to let the sultan's ships slip through the British cruisers in east African waters, and to protest later.[119]

1. James Bandinel (1783–1849)

Senior clerk in the Foreign Office and first head of the Slave Trade Department. Lithograph by John Callcott Horsley, reproduced courtesy of the National Portrait Gallery.

2. Sir Percy Anderson (1831–1896)

Slave Trade clerk in the Foreign Office, 1852–1854, and head of the Consular and African Department, 1883–1894. As assistant under-secretary of state, 1894–1896, he superintended the African and Consular Departments (FCO Photographic Collection, TNA).

4. *HMS Primrose* capturing a Spanish slaver *Velos Passahera* in the Bight of Benin, 6 September 1830

(Royal Naval Museum, Portsmouth).

3. William Henry Wylde (1819–1909)

Senior clerk in the Foreign Office and head of the Slave Trade Department, 1859–1861, and of the Consular and Slave Trade Department, 1872–1880 (FCO Photographic Collection, The National Archives (TNA)).

5. *HMS Black Joke* engaging the Spanish slaver *El Almirante* in the Bight of Benin, 1 February 1829

According to the inscription, the Spanish vessel was captured after a chase lasting thirty-one hours (Royal Naval Museum, Portsmouth).

6. *HMS Arab* chasing and capturing a Portuguese schooner with 372 Africans on board off the south coast of Cuba, 12 April 1856

(Royal Naval Museum, Portsmouth).

7 and 8. Freed Africans on board *HMS Daphne*, 1869

These photographs were sent to the Admiralty in March 1869 by Commodore Leopold Heath, then in command of the Royal Navy's East India Station, and responsible for combating the largely Arab-controlled east African slave trade. 'The wretched and emaciated condition of the slaves' was, according to Heath, 'due entirely to the avarice or carelessness of the Arab dealers.' (The National Archives, FO 84/1310).

9. Captured slave trader on board *HMS Sphinx* of the Royal Navy's East India Station, *circa* 1907–1909

(Royal Naval Museum, Portsmouth).

10. Escaped slaves on board *HMS Sphinx*, October 1907

According to a report by Commander Litchfield of 15 October 1907, *HMS Sphinx* received 'six fugitives' while cruising off the Batineh coast of Oman. They had escaped captivity and reached the ship by canoe (Royal Naval Museum, Portsmouth).

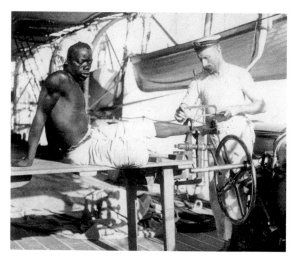

11. Ship's carpenter, *HMS Sphinx*, removing leg iron from an escaped slave, October 1907

(Royal Naval Museum, Portsmouth).

Such reluctance to tackle the last vestiges of the old slavery system was even more accentuated after the formal establishment of Britain's protectorate over Zanzibar in 1890. Its official nomenclature notwithstanding, the protectorate was more an aspiration than an established fact. As James Rennell Rodd (later Lord Rennell of Rodd), the acting agent in Zanzibar in 1893–4, reflected at the time, the position there "required the most delicate handling". The majority Arab population readily accepted the benefits of the British protectorate, but resisted attempts further to curb slavery, and the supervision of the illicit traffic in slaves took up a considerable part of the agency's work.[120] A.H. (later Sir Arthur) Hardinge, the agent after 1894, pursued a cautious policy. He stressed the more feudal aspects of the slavery regime, and suggested that, in order to avoid civil disturbances, the Arab plantation–owners had to be compensated for the release of their slaves. Privately, he vented his spleen at anti-slavery lobby groups at home:

they will read of all the horrors of "Uncle Tom's Cabin" & of the old slave caravans of Livingstone's time which we have suppressed throughout our centuries with the ordinary Mahomedan social system as it exists on the coast, where however it is dying very rapidly. However I care not myself for all the irritating bosh which is poured forth in press and on platforms on this subject, by the humorous spectacle of Bishop [Alfred] Tucker [Bishop of Mombasa] running in couples with [Sir Charles] Dilke [Radical MP], & the latter holding up his hands in hold horror at the "lack of moral fibre" evinced by our continued tolerance of [slavery].[121]

Hardinge was not alone in taking this view. At the Foreign Office, Francis Bertie, then an assistant under-secretary, similarly dismissed the representations made on the subject by philanthropic societies: "[They] do not have to govern countries full of Arabs with small military means. We must govern with the assistance of the Arabs and that aid will not be readily given unless we show a combination of justice and force."[122] The foreign secretary, Lord Salisbury, was equally seized of the importance of compensating the slave owners, but pinned his hopes on the civilizing influence of the railways then under construction. Without compensation, however, "we may have trouble".[123] His views in the matter were "old fashioned, . . . I see no justice in excluding people from the benefit of the eighth commandment because they have not adopted our very modern doctrine upon slavery".[124] Considerations of imperial administration and security ultimately prevailed. The legal abolition of slavery on Zanzibar, proclaimed on 6 April 1897, also granted financial compensation for the slave owners.[125]

∞

In the Islamic world British anti-slavery diplomacy encountered unique problems, quite different from those it had dealt with so successfully in the case of the transatlantic slave trade. It was a case of a "clash of cultures". In the face of deeply rooted cultural practices, sanctioned by religion, economic calculations, based on Victorian assumptions of the beneficent effects of legitimate trade, had little relevance. Nor could superior British power easily be brought to bear. If anything, the weakness of the polities in the Near and Middle East made it difficult to apply such pressure. The massacre at Jedda, moreover, served as a warning, one that was heeded by successive foreign secretaries. In the case of the Ottoman empire, Britain's ability to nudge the sultan in the desired direction was greatest whenever Turkey was faced with serious external threats, such as the Crimean and the Russo-Turkish wars. Once those threats receded, Britain's leverage was much diminished.

For much of the second half of the nineteenth century, the Foreign Office's Slave Trade Department kept up the pressure for more energetic measure for the suppression of the slave trade. Even so, the wearying effect of the slow grind of anti-slavery policy and the stubborn recalcitrance of the problem of slavery in the Arab and Ottoman world was considerable. The quasi-legal framework created by the conventions with Egypt, Turkey and Zanzibar seemed to furnish the best guarantee of success.

Britain's relative success in suppressing the slave trade in the East was the result of patient, piecemeal and persistent pressure – of Clarendon's '"course of unceasing remonstrance" in pursuit of humanitarian objectives. Nevertheless, the ethical impulse was always liable to be curbed by considerations of Britain's wider strategic foreign policy. As the internal debates about the projected abolition of slavery in Egypt demonstrated, in the more competitive international environment of the 1880s and 1890s, ultimately, imperial defence interests remained dominant. To that extent, the more restrained pursuit of an ethical foreign policy also reflected the relative diminution of British power.

Notes

I am grateful to G. R. Berridge for allowing me to consult the manuscript of his forthcoming study of the British embassy at Constantinople; to Geoffrey Hicks for making material from the Malmesbury Papers available to me; and to Laurence Guymer for saving me from an egregious error.

1   J. J. Ewald, "Slavery in Africa and the Slave Trades from Africa", *American Historical Review*, vol. 97, no. 2 (1996), p. 466. See also the pertinent observations on this in Jeremy Black, *The Slave Trade* (London: Social Affairs Unit, 2007), pp. 9–10.

2 Bernard Lewis, "In Defense of History", idem, *From Babel to Dragomans: Interpreting the Middle East* (Oxford: OUP, 2007), p. 9.

3 What follows is based on Bernard Lewis, *Race and Slavery in the Middle East: An Historical Enquiry* (Oxford: OUP, 1990), still the best treatment of the subject. See also J. Hunwick, "Islamic Law and Polemics over Race and Slavery in North and West Africa (16th–19th Century)", *Slavery in the Islamic Middle East* (Princeton, NJ: Markus Wiener, 1999), ed. Shaun Marmon, pp. 43–68; and Suzanne Miers, "Slavery: A Question of Definition", *The Structure of Slavery in the Indian Ocean and Asia* (London: Frank Cass, 2004), ed. G. Campbell, here pp. 4–5.

4 E. A. Alpers, "Flight from Freedom: Escape from Slavery among Bonded Africans in the Indian Ocean World, c. 1750–1962", *Structure of Slavery*, pp. 51–68, provides useful insight into this. On the ambiguities of religious law and practice see Humphrey J. Fisher and Allan G. B. Fisher, *Slavery in the History of Muslim Black Africa* (New York: NYU Press, 2001).

5 As quoted in G. S. Graham, *Great Britain and the Indian Ocean: A Study of Maritime Enterprise, 1810–1850* (Oxford: Clarendon Press, 1967), pp. 106–7. See also Muriel E. Chamberlain, *Lord Aberdeen: A Political Biography* (London: Longman, 1983), pp. 368–9.

6 The National Archives (TNA), Russell MSS., PRO 30/22/14C, Palmerston to Russell, 21 July 1862. For his earlier dealings with especially the Portuguese, see C. K. Webster, *The Foreign Policy of Palmerston, 1830–1841* (2 vols., London: G. Bell, 1951), vol. i, pp. 490–4. Also instructive is Roderick Braithwaite, *Palmerston and Africa: The Rio Nuñez Affair – Competition, Diplomacy and Justice* (London: British Academic Press, 1996).

7 TNA, FO 84/1141, minute by Palmerston, 16 Nov. 1861.

8 *Baptist Magazine* (Sept. 1873), as quoted in D. W. Bebbington, *The Nonconformist Conscience: Chapel and Politics, 1870–1914* (London: Allen & Unwin, 1982), p. 110. See also the comments by L. Colley, *Britons: Forging the Nation, 1707–1837* (London: Yale UP, 1994 (pb. ed.)), pp. 359–60.

9 For this consideration see J. Cell, "The Imperial Conscience", *The Conscience of the Victorian State* (Syracuse, NY: Syracuse UP, 1979), ed. Peter Marsh, pp. 184–5, though I do not accept his ideological premise.

10 Andrew Porter, "Trusteeship, Anti-Slavery, and Humanitarianism", *The Oxford History of the British Empire*, vol. iii, *The Nineteenth Century* (Oxford: OUP, 1999), ed. Andrew Porter, p. 204.

11 R. Segal, *Islam's Black Slaves: A history of Africa's Other Black Diaspora* (London: Farrar, Straus & Giroux, 2001), pp. 56, 154–5, 160–4, 166–74. See also R. Mauvy, *Les Siècles obscurs de l'Afrique Noire* (Paris: Fayard, 1970) for further statistics.

12 TNA, FO 366/1132, Kennedy to Granville, 10 Feb. 1871. For fuller discussions see: D. C. M. Platt, *The Cinderella Service: British Consuls since 1825* (London: Archon Books, 1971), pp. 125–63; G. R. Berridge, *British Diplomacy in Turkey, 1583 to the Present: A Study in the Evolution of the Resident Embassy* (Leiden: Martinus Nijhoff, forthcoming), ch. 4.

13 FO 84/1000, memo. by Wylde, 28 July 1856. The reference was to a circular of 31 Dec. 1843.

14 FO 84/919, 949, 974, 1000 and 1029, Herman to Malmesbury (Slave Trade no. 2), 18 Jan. 1853, to Clarendon (Slave Trade no. 2), 20 Jan. 1854 (Slave Trade no. 3), 22 Jan. 1855 (Slave Trade no. 3), 26 Jan. 1856 (Slave Trade no. 5), 28 March 1857.

15 FO 84/919, Finn to Clarendon (Slave Trade no. 1), 6 Dec. 1852.

16 FO 84/974, Bruce to Clarendon (Slave Trade no. 1), 17 Jan. 1855. Nubia was tributary to the Muslim empire since the 7th century. As Islamic law forbade enslavement or mutilation in Muslim territory, Nubia served as a convenient channel for the supply of domestic slaves and eunuchs.

17 FO 84/1029, Drummond-Hay to Clarendon (Slave Trade no. 1), 14 Oct. 1857.

18 FO 84/1246, Bulwer to Russell (no. 40), 15 April 1865.

19 FO 84/1305, Herbert to Clarendon (Slave Trade no. 12), 26 Nov. 1869.

20 FO 84/1204, quote from Colquhoun to Russell (Slave Trade no. 2), 17 Aug. 1863.

21 FO 84/1246, Stanton to Russell (Slave Trade no. 1), 26 Sept. 1865. The ivory connection was not limited to slave trade in Egypt, see P. E. Lovejoy, *Transformations in Slavery: A History of Slavery in Africa* (Cambridge: 2nd ed., CUP, 2000), p. 284.

22 FO 84/1246, Rogers to Clarendon (Slave Trade no. 1), 28 Nov. 1865. For Gaza as the gateway to the North see FO 84/919, Finn to Clarendon (Slave Trade no. 1), 6 Dec. 1852; and FO 84/1305, Moore [consul-general Jerusalem] to Clarendon (Slave Trade no. 1), 28 Oct. 1869.

23 FO 84/1277, Reade to Stanley (Slave Trade no. 1), 9 Aug. 1867. Reade secured the manumission of some 89 slaves between 1866 and 1868. See FO 84/1290, memo. by Reade, "List of Slaves freed by Tho[ma]s F. Reade, ... from 26 June 1866 to 19 June 1868", n.d.

24 FO 84/919, Finn to Clarendon (Slave Trade no. 1), 6 Dec. 1852; Herman to Clarendon (Slave Trade no. 5), 22 May 1853.

25 Ibid., Smith to Clarendon (Slave Trade no. 1), 5 Aug. 1853.

26 FO 84/1971, Cameron to Salisbury (Africa no. 1), 1 Jan. 1889.

27 For such instances see: FO 84/1060, Alison [chargé d'affaires, Constantinople] to Clarendon (Slave Trade no. 2), 19 Jan. 1858; FO 84/1204, Calvert [acting consul, Monastir] to Bulwer (Slave Trade no. 1), 6 Feb. 1863. A particularly egregious case was that of an African slave at Damascus who had been raped by her master's brother and then been tortured to induce a miscarriage. Consul Rogers, with whom she had sought refuge, secured her release, FO 84/1204, Rogers to Russell (Slave Trade no. 1), 17 July 1863.

28 FO 84/1246, Bulwer to Russell (no. 32), 23 March 1865.

29 FO 84/1290, memo. by Reade, 13 Aug. 1868. For later cases see: FO 84/1450, Jago [vice-consul, Damascus] to Elliot (Slave Trade no. 1), 18 Dec. 1876; FO 84/1570, Lister to Goschen (Slave Trade no. 24), 14 Sept. 1880.

30 Wylde was a strong advocate of an abolitionist policy, and following his retirement in 1880 played a prominent role in the activities of the British and Foreign Anti-Slavery Society. See *The Times* (10 Dec. 1886 and 28 April 1890). Despite his prominent role at the Foreign Office, Wylde remains an

unjustly obscure figure. For a survey of Wylde's official remit see Ray Jones, *The Nineteenth-Century Foreign Office: An Administrative History* (London: LSE, 1971), pp. 89–90.

31 FO 84/1290, minutes by Wylde, Murray and Stanley, 14 Aug. 1868. For Wylde's zeal see also A.H. Hardinge, *A Diplomatist in the East* (London: Jonathan Cape, 1928), p. 96.

32 FO 84/1354, Granville to Green (Slave Trade no. 2), 7 Aug. 1872, and minute by Wylde, 6 Aug. 1872. For similar instructions see FO 84/1412, Derby to Beyts [consul, Jedda] (Slave Trade no. 1), 11 Feb. 1875.

33 FO 84/919, Shiel to Malmesbury (Slave Trade nos. 1 and 2), 8 Jan. and 8 Feb. 1853. The latter deals with the Shatt-el-Arab borderline.

34 FO 84/919, Thomson to Clarendon (Slave Trade no. 6), 14 July 1853, and reply (Slave Trade no. 4), 30 Sept. 1853. See also FO 84/949, Thomson to Clarendon (Slave Trade no. 9), 20 Oct. 1854, for the weakness of the Tehran authorities.

35 Quotes from FO 84/949, minute by Ward, 1 May 1854, on Thomson to Clarendon (Slave Trade no. 3), 16 Feb. 1854; and FO 84/1000, memo. by Ward, 18 Feb. 1856.

36 FO 84/1144, Jones to Alison (no. 23), 5 July 1861. See also FO 84/1090, Doria to Wood (Slave Trade nos. 1 and 2), 26 July and 17 Oct. 1859.

37 For the internal discussions see: FO 84/1275, minutes by Wylde and Stanley, 19 Aug. 1867 and nd., on Alison to Stanley (Slave Trade no. 1), 8 June 1867; and FO 84/1341, minutes by Vivian and Clarendon, 19 and 21 Jan. 1870, and Hammond 22 March 1871 (quotes by Clarendon and Vivian).

38 FO 84/1450, Thomson to Derby (Slave Trade no. 2), 17 May 1876, and reply (Slave Trade no. 1), 22 June 1876.

39 FO 84/949, Stratford de Redcliffe to Clarendon (Slave Trade No. 1), 9 Sept. 1854. For contemporary perceptions see: A. Wheatcroft, *The Ottomans: Dissolving Images* (London: Penguin, 1995), pp. 208–30; also V. G. Kiernan, *The Lords of Mankind: European Attitudes to the Outside World in the Age of Imperialism* (London: Harmonsworth, 1969), pp. 131–8; and for a corrective Robert Irwin, *For the Lust of Knowing: The Orientalists and their Enemies* (London: Allen Lane, 2007 (pb. ed.)), pp. 141–88.

40 FO 84/949, Stratford de Redcliffe to Pisani, 27 Aug. 1854. For a discussion of Pisani's somewhat undefined position see G.R. Berridge, "Nation, Class, and Diplomacy: The Diminishing of the Dragomanate of the British Embassy in Constantinople, 1810–1914", *The Diplomats' World: A Cultural History of Diplomacy, 1815–1914* (Oxford: OUP, 2008), eds. M. Moesslang and T. Riotte, pp. 412–13.

41 FO 84/949, Clarendon to Stratford de Redcliffe (Slave Trade no. 2), 27 Sept. 1854.

42 Ibid., Clarendon to Stratford de Redcliffe (Slave Trade no. 4), 23 Oct. 1854.

43 FO 84/974, Williams to Clarendon (no. 37), 6 Feb. 1855. Herbert Maxwell, *The Life and Letters of George William Frederick, Fourth Earl of Clarendon* (2 vols., London: Edward Arnold, 1913) vol. ii, pp. 65–6. For Stratford's attempt to open talks for a convention, see FO 84/974, Stratford de Redcliffe to Clarendon (Slave Trade no. 2), 22 March 1855.

44 FO 84/1000, Clarendon to Stratford de Redcliffe (Slave Trade no. 11), 9 Oct. 1856.

45 TNA, FO 352/44/2, Stratford de Redcliffe MSS., Clarendon to Stratford de Redcliffe (private), 3 Oct. 1856.

46 FO 352/48/2, Stratford de Redcliffe MSS., Stratford de Redcliffe to Clarendon (Slave Trade no. 5), 31 Jan. 1857, FO 84/1028; also min. Ward, 18 Feb. 1857, ibid.; Clarendon to Stratford de Redcliffe (private), 13 Feb. 1857.

47 FO 84/1000, minute by Palmerston, 19 Feb. 1857.

48 FO 84/1028, Stratford de Redcliffe (Slave Trade no. 19), 21 Oct. 1857.

49 Ibid., minutes by Clarendon and Palmerston, 4 and 6 Nov. 1857. The 1856 Paris peace treaty (art. ix), moreover, gave Turkey immunity from outside interference in its internal affairs See Edward Hertslet (ed.), *The Map of Europe by Treaty, 1814–1875* (3 vols., London: Butterworths, 1875), vol. ii, no. 264, 1255.

50 FO 84/1120, Bulwer to Russell (Slave Trade no. 1), 12 Dec. 1860; also FO 84/1246 (Slave Trade no. 4), 10 Aug. 1865.

51 Quotes from FO 84/1225, Bulwer to Russell (Slave Trade no. 1), 31 Aug. 1864, and minute by Russell, nd. [c. 2 July 1865].

52 TNA, Hammond MSS., FO 391/13, Hammond to Lyons (private), 30 May and 2 June 1867 (quote from former); also Lord Newton, *Lord Lyons: A Record of British Diplomacy* (2 vols., London: Longmans, 1913), vol. i, pp. 171–3. Exeter Hall, off The Strand, was the principal venue for abolitionist and other Radical mass meetings.

53 FO 84/1060, Blunt to Alison (Slave Trade no. 2), 2 June 1858.

54 FO 84/1000, Herman to Clarendon (Slave Trade no. 14), 16 Nov. 1856.

55 FO 84/1090, Herman to Russell (Slave Trade no. 3), 7 Dec. 1859.

56 FO 84/1305, Drummond-Hay to Elliot (Slave Trade no. 1), 17 May 1869, and Clarendon to Elliot (Slave Trade no. 3), 22 June 1869.

57 Hampshire Record Office, Malmesbury MSS., 9M73/20/23, Derby to Malmesbury (private), 19 Aug. 1858. For the Jedda massacre and the subsequent bombardment, see *The Times* (15, 16 July and 20 Aug. 1858).

58 FO 84/1060, Plowden to Malmesbury (Slave Trade no. 3), 20 Nov. 1858.

59 FO 84/1090, Russell to Bulwer (Slave Trade no. 1), 23 July 1859. The Porte duly complied, v. ibid., vice versa (Slave Trade no. 2), 24 Aug. 1859.

60 FO 84/1120, Stanley to Bulwer, 13 March 1860 (copy). This remained very much the position of successive consuls at Jedda. See: FO 84/1305, Raby to Clarendon (Slave Trade, separate), 10 Dec. 1869; and FO 84/1571, Zorab to Salisbury (Slave Trade no. 3), 13 March 1879.

61 FO 84/1144, Colquhoun to Russell (Slave Trade no. 1), 18 Feb. 1861, and Stanley to Colquhoun, 17 April 1861 (copy) (quote from former).

62 FO 84/1204, Russell to Colquhoun (Slave Trade no. 2), 31 July 1863, and reply (Slave Trade no. 2), 17 Aug. 1863.

63 Russell MSS., PRO 30/22/15D, Palmerston to Russell (private), 8 Jan. 1865.

64 FO 84/1204, Herman to Russell (Slave Trade no. 3), 30 April 1863, FO 84/1204. FO 84/1225, Russell to Erskine (Slave Trade no. 1), 9 Feb. 1864.

65 FO 84/1246, Bulwer to Russell (no. 34), 10 April 1865, FO 84/1246.
Russell was nevertheless concerned that the effective suppression of the
trade might necessitate yielding to the Egyptian authorities the extraterritorial privileges enjoyed by Europeans in the Ottoman dominions, v. ibid.,
Russell to Colquhoun (Slave Trade no. 3), 9 June 1865.

66 FO 84/1246, Stanton to Russell (Slave Trade, no. 1), 26 Sept. 1865, and
reply (Slave Trade no. 3), 19 Oct. 1865.

67 FO 84/1315, Elliot to Clarendon (Slave Trade, no. 14), 3 Oct. 1869.

68 FO 84/1277, Reade to Stanley (Slave Trade, no. 2), 25 Aug. 1867.

69 FO 84/1260, Stanton to Clarendon (Slave Trade no. 1), 9 May 1866.

70 This was a recurring theme of consular reporting. See FO 84/1204,
Colquhoun to Russell (Slave Trade no. 2), 17 Aug. 1863; FO 84/1290,
Palgrave to Egerton (private), 5 June 1868; also FO 84/1597, minute by
Malet, 7 July 1881. Until 1863, John Petherick represented British interests
at Khartoum. However, there were suggestions that his own commercial
interests involved slave trading, or that his Maltese assistants were engaged
in it. See FO 84/1225, Petherick to Russell, 27 Jan. 1864; and FO 84/1246,
Bulwer to Russell (no. 2), 6 Jan. 1865. For the trade at Khartoum see A.
Moorehead, *The White Nile* (London: Hamish Hamilton, 1963), pp. 91–4.

71 FO 84/1225, Russell to Colquohoun (Slave Trade, no. 2), 26 Nov. 1864;
FO 84/1305, Clarendon to Elliot (Slave Trade nos. 8 and 14), 31 Aug. and
18 Oct. 1869. A Foreign Office circular of 31 Aug. 1869 instructed the
Levant consuls to report on the state of the slave trade in their districts and
the role of the khedive's company (ibid.). See also the reports by Eldridge
(Beirut), Holmes (Bosnia), Boom (Candia), and Taylor (Erzerum) in ibid.

72 FO 84/1305, Francis to Clarendon (Consular no. 95), 28 Sept. 1869. For
Francis see: Hammond MSS., FO 391/21, Elliot to Hammond (private), 26
July 1869; and E. Pears, *Forty Years at Constantinople:Recollections of Sir Edwin
Pears, 1873–1915* (London: Herbert Jenkins, 1916), pp. 50–1.

73 FO 84/1305, Francis to Clarendon (Slave Trade no. 1), 1 Dec. 1869.
According to Stanton, some 80% of the pashas in Egypt were involved in
the trade, to Clarendon (Slave Trade no. 5), 14 Oct. 1869.

74 FO 84/1354, minutes by Wylde, nd. and 27 July 1872, on Cumberbatch
[consul Smyrna] to Granville (Slave Trade nos. 12 and 22), 10 May and 17
July 1872. For similar comments on Egyptian connivance see FO 84/1324,
Elliot to Clarendon (Slave Trade no. 1), 12 May 1870.

75 FO 84/1354, Stanton to Granville (Slave Trade no. 13), 20 Dec. 1872, and
minutes by Buckley, 31 Dec. 1872, and Granville, nd. G.N. Sanderson,
*England, Europe and the Upper Nile, 1882–1899: A Study in the Partition of
Africa* (Edinburgh: Edinburgh UP, 1965), pp. 7–8.

76 FO 84/1371, Vivian to Granville (Slave Trade no. 12), 28 Nov. 1873. FO
84/1370, minutes by Wylde, 19 and 22 July 1873, on Elliot to Granville
(Slave Trade nos. 12 and 15), 12 and 22 July 1873.

77 FO 84/1397, memo. by Wylde, 5 July 1874, and Stanton to Derby (Slave
Trade no. 11), 3 Sept. 1874. FO 84/1412, Henderson [vice-consul
Benghazi] to Derby (Slave Trade nos. 1 and 5), 12 June and 24 Dec. 1875.
FO 84/1450, minute by Wylde, 25 Jan. 1876, on the latter despt. For the

Red Sea trade see ibid., Vivian (Slave Trade no. 5, confidential), 8 Dec. 1876.

78 FO 84/1425, minute by Tenterden, 24 Dec. 1875; memo. Wylde, 19 Dec. 1875. See also FO 84/1450, Derby to Stanton (Slave Trade no. 1), 14 Jan. 1876.

79 Liverpool Record Office, Derby MSS., 920 DER (15) 16/2/10, Tenterden to Derby (private), 28 Feb. 1876.

80 FO 84/1450, Tenterden to Bourke (private), 3 Feb. 1876. For the continued rumblings over the circular see: *The Times* (27 Jan. and 25 Feb. 1876); and Derby diary, 7 Oct. 1875, J. R. Vincent (ed.), *A Selection from the Diaries of Edward Henry Stanley, 15th Earl of Derby, 1869–1878* (Cambridge: CUP, 1994), p. 45.

81 FO 84/1000, Hamerton [consul Muscat] to Aberdeen, 21 May 1842 (copy). See also: R. Robinson and J. Gallagher, *Africa and the Victorians: The Official Mind of Imperialism* (London, Macmillan, 2nd edn. 1981), pp. 43–8; F. Cooper, "Islam and Cultural Hegemony: The Ideology of Slaveowners on the East African Coast", *The Ideology of Slavery in Africa* (London: Sage, 1981), ed. Paul E. Lovejoy, pp. 280–1.

82 FO 84/1279, Murray to Playfair [consul Zanzibar], 4 Jan. 1867; Stanley to Seward [acting consul] (Slave Trade no. 5), 21 Jan. 1867.

83 Ibid., minute by Wylde, 18 April 1867, on Seward to Stanley no. 46), 20 Feb. 1867.

84 Ibid., minute by Wylde, 14 May 1867, on Seward to Stanley (no. 81), nd.

85 FO 84/1344, Vivian to Kirk [agent and consul-general Zanzibar] (private and confidential), 12 Dec. 1871.

86 FO 84/1292, Churchill to Gonne [secretary to Bombay government] (no. 14/46), 4 March 1868, and to Stanley (no. 61), 21 Aug. 1868. Zanzibar was financed out of Indian funds, and, except for slave trade matters, the agent there was answerable to the Indian government.

87 Ibid., minute by Wylde, 28 May 1868, on Churchill to Stanley (no. 14), 14 April 1868.

88 FO 84/1344, Vivian to Kirk (private and confidential), 12 Dec. 1871.

89 FO 84/1344, minute by Enfield [parliamentary under-secretary], 24 March 1871; Granville to Gladstone, 3 and 6 Nov. and reply 7 Nov. 1873, in *The Gladstone—Granville Correspondence, 1868–1876* (Cambridge: CUP, reprint 1998), ed. A. Ramm, nos. 783–5.

90 *Slave Trade No. 2 (1874): Treaty between Her Majesty and the Sultan of Zanzibar for the Suppression of the Slave Trade, June, 5, 1873* (C. 889) (1874).

91 FO 84/1305, minute by Clarendon, 27 Aug. 1869, on memo. by Wylde, 24 Aug. 1869.

92 FO 84/1324, Barron to Clarendon (Slave Trade no. 1), 18 Jan. 1870.

93 FO 84/1305, Elliot to Clarendon (Slave Trade no. 9), 2 Sept. 1869. FO 84/1324, Elliot to Granville (Slave Trade no. 8), 18 Dec. 1870. FO 83/1354, Elliot to Granville (Slave Trade no. 1), 13 Aug. 1872. Cumberbatch refuted such suggestions, to Granville (Slave Trade no. 28), 6 Nov. 1872, ibid.

94 National Library of Scotland, Elliot MSS., MS 13069, Elliot to Hammond, 26 July 1870.

95 FO 84/1324, Elliot to Granville (Slave Trade no. 5), 16 Aug. 1870. Sir Robert Dalyell, the consul at Rustchuk, argued along similar, gradualist lines, to Clarendon (separate), 2 May 1879, ibid.

96 FO 84/1270, Elliot to Granville (Slave Trade no. 12), 12 July 1873.

97 FO 84/1341, Elliot to Granville (Slave Trade nos. 3, 5 and 6), 11 and 19 May and 2 July 1871.

98 FO 84/1370, minutes by Wylde and Tenterden, 26 and 28 Feb. 1873, on Cumberbatch to Granville (Slave Trade no. 1), 5 Feb. 1873.

99 Ibid., minute by Wylde, 27 March 1873, on Elliot to Granville (Slave Trade no 4), 3 March 1873.

100 Ibid., Granville to Elliot, tel. (Slave Trade no. 8), 11 July 1873.

101 FO 84/1450, Elliot to Derby (Slave Trade no. 1), 12 Jan. 1876.

102 FO 84/1510, minute by Pauncefote, nd., on Layard to Salisbury, tel. (no. 1027), 23 Nov. 1878.

103 FO 84/1570, Layard to Salisbury (Slave Trade nos. 29 and 31), 27 Aug. and 9 Sept. 1879; Layard to Salisbury, tel. (no. 49), 25 Jan. 1880. For the Khedive's support see FO 84/1543, Salisbury to Malet (Slave Trade no. 3), 28 Feb. 1879. On the sultan's role, see F. A. K. Yasamee, *Ottoman Diplomacy: Abdülhamid II and the Great Powers, 1878–1888* (Istanbul: Isis Press, 1996), pp. 41–52.

104 Public Record Office of Northern Ireland (Belfast), Dufferin and Ava MSS., D/1071/H/K/1/1, Plunkett to Dufferin (private), 10 May 1881. *Slave Trade No. 2 (1883): Declaration between Great Britain and Turkey, amending the convention of the 25th January, 1880, between Her Majesty and the Sultan for the Suppression of the Slave Trade, March, 3, 1883* (C. 3590) (1883). The drafts and related material can be found in FO 84/1658.

105 FO 84/1674, Dufferin to Granville (no. 5, Africa), and memo. by Marinitch, 30 July 1884.

106 FO 84/1570, Layard to Salisbury (Slave Trade no. 9), 15 Feb. 1880, and minute by Pauncefote, 4 Jan. 1881..

107 FO 84/1971, White to Salisbury (no. 13, Africa), 31 Aug. 1889, and memo. by Marinitch, 20 Aug. 1889.

108 Ibid., minute by Lister, nd. [c. 21 Sept. 1889].

109 Ibid.,White to Salisbury (no. 14, Africa), 9 Sept. 1889. FO 84/2227, Fane to Salisbury (no. 15, Africa), 15 Feb. 1892. See also S. Miers, "The Brussels Conference of 1889–1890: The Place of the Slave Trade in the Policies of Great Britain and Germany", *Britain and Germany in Africa: Imperial Rivalry and Colonial Rule* (New Haven and London: Yale UP, 1967), eds. Prosser Gifford and Wm. Roger Louis, pp. 82–118.

110 FO 84/1597, Malet to Granville (Slave Trade no. 20, confidential), 23 April 1881. For an initial, positive assessment see FO 84/1511, Lascelles [acting agent Cairo] to Salisbury (Slave Trade no. 37), 3 Sept. 1878, and memo. by Borg [legal vice-consul Cairo], "Return shewing the Number of Slaves manumitted", 23 Aug. 1878. Alfred C. Lyall, *The Life of the Marquis of Dufferin and Ava* (2 vols., London: John Murray, 1905), vol. ii, pp. 10–12.

111 FO 84/1618, Malet to Granville, tel., 22 Oct. 1882.

112 FO 84/1613, Granville to Dufferin (Slave Trade, Egypt no. 1), 3 Nov. 1882.

113 FO 84/1675, Baring to Granville (no. 1, Africa), 25 Feb. 1884.

114 FO 84/1675, Egerton [chargé d'affaires, Cairo] to Granville (no. 5, Africa), 5 Sept. 1884. For Lister's scheme, see minute by Lister, 5 March 1884, ibid. Baring was, however, by no means unreceptive to the anti-slavery cause. See Roger Owen, *Lord Cromer: Victorian Imperialist, Edwardian Proconsul* (Oxford: OUP, 2004), pp. 256–7.

115 FO 84/1721, Baring to Granville (no. 1, Africa), 12 Feb. 1885.

116 FO 84/1721, Egerton to Salisbury (no. 12, Africa), 25 Oct. 1885. For a fuller discussion of the connexion see: P. M. Holt, *The Mahdist State in the Sudan, 1881–1898: A Study of its Origins, Development and Overthrow* (Oxford: OUP, 2nd edn., 1970), pp. 32–43; G. R. Warburg, "Ideological and Practical Considerations regarding Slavery in the Mahdist State and the Anglo-Egyptian Sudan, 1881–1918", Lovejoy, *Ideology of Slavery*, pp. 249–52.

117 *Treaty Series No. 16: Convention between Great Britain and Egypt for the Suppression of Slavery and the Slave Trade, November 21, 1895* (C. 7929) (1896).

118 Quotes from FO 84/1676, memo. by Hill (confidential), 20 Oct. 1884, and Granville to Kirk (no. 80, secret), 27 Nov. 1884. See also S. E. Crowe, *The Berlin West Africa Conference, 1884–1885* (Westport, CT: Negro Universities Press reprint, 1970), p. 112.

119 FO 84/1674, minute by Hill, nd., on Jago [consul Jedda] to Granville (no. 3, Africa, confidential), 9 Nov. 1884. Jago's later attempts to secure manumission for the slaves onboard the ship failed, v. ibid., Jago to Granville (no. 5, Africa), 14 Dec. 1884.

120 James Rennell Rodd (ed.), *The British Mission to Uganda in 1893, by the late Sir Gerald Portal, KCMG, CB* (London: Edward Arnold, 1894), pp. xxxviii-ix. See also: idem, *Social and Diplomatic Memories, 1884–1919* (3 vols., London: Edward Arnold, 1922–25), vol. i, pp. 287–92; and Rodd to Rosebery, 12 June 1893, in *Africa No. 6 (1893): Paper respecting the Traffic in Slaves in Zanzibar* (C. 7035) (1893).

121 Lambeth Palace Library, Riley MSS., MS 2344, Hardinge to Riley, 8 Sept. 1897. Hardinge's insistence on the necessity of compensation was understandable perhaps also in light of his family background; his mother's family had owned a sugar plantation in the West Indies. See Hardinge, *Diplomatist in the East*, p. 194. Dilke had insisted on his removal from Zanzibar, ibid., p. 195; for his reflections on slavery, ibid., pp. 80–215.

122 British Library, Bertie MSS., Add. Ms. 63013, minute by Bertie, 1 Sept. 1896.

123 British Library Oriental and India Office Collection, Curzon MSS., Mss.Eur. F.111/1A, minute by Salisbury, nd., on Curzon to Salisbury, 21 Aug. [1895]; Salisbury to Curzon, 30 Nov. 1896.

124 Gloucestershire County Record Office, St. Aldwyn MSS., PCC/69, Salisbury to Hicks Beach (private), 8 March 1897.

125 Hardinge, *Diplomatist in the East*, pp. 196–98.

CHAPTER SIX

The British "Official Mind" and Nineteenth-Century Islamic Debates over the Abolition of Slavery

WILLIAM GERVASE CLARENCE-SMITH

Long after the 1833 act of Parliament that decreed the end of slavery in British crown colonies, the institution lived on in Islamic zones in Britain's formal and informal empire. The British slowly extended formal abolition through their various possessions and spheres of influence, but never actually abolished slavery in those parts of the Arabian peninsula where protectorate treaties only concerned the slave trade.[1] Moreover, legal measures were only a first step, for it was quite another thing to achieve real freedom for the enslaved.[2]

Hesitant progress towards abolition reflected Islamic resistance, but it also sprang from deep disagreements within the British élite. Some diplomats and officials went so far as to manipulate Islamic beliefs and institutions to delay the imposition and enforcement of abolition, for they were fearful that tampering with servitude would cause rebellions and wars. To that extent, imperial powers paradoxically "became the defenders of slavery and the greatest single impediment to full emancipation".[3]

In most cases, however, the "men on the spot" reacted pragmatically, as they were underfunded, understaffed, and unfamiliar with local conditions. They conceived of an inherent and "fanatical" Islamic attachment to slavery, which, if crossed, risked fanning the flames of pan-Islamism. At the same time, they saw Muslim élites as "born rulers" and "descendants of a conquering and ruling race", and thus as excellent agents of indirect rule.[4] Such officials simply hoped that suppressing slave raiding and trading would suffice for slavery itself to die a "natural death".

At the other end of the spectrum, a few Britons immersed themselves in the holy texts of Islam, with the intention of fostering the religion's abolitionist potential. Crucially, they attempted to discover and popularize Islamic arguments that would render the cessation of slavery accept-able to believers. Research is least developed on this group, reflecting a strong, if misguided, belief among scholars that Islam had little or no abolitionist potential.[5]

Britain appears to have been most prone among the colonial powers to take the path of engaging in Islamic debates over slavery. In part, this reflected an unusual degree of interest in Islam in Britain itself, together with the precocious growth of a metropolitan Muslim community. There was an Ottoman-appointed British *shaykh al-Islam* from 1889, the Manx solicitor and convert William H. (Abdullah) Quilliam. Muslims and sympathizers with Islam in Britain thus became involved in passionate debates about Islamic servitude.[6]

Moreover, British "men on the spot" remained for long periods in one place overseas, and were thus able to gain a deep understanding of local cultures. That said, Germany followed the same model, without German officials developing any obvious appreciation of Islam's aboli-tionist potential.[7] Conversely, some French officials did appreciate Islamic arguments for ending slavery, despite being constantly moved around.[8]

The focus here is on such "men on the spot", most of whom had connections of some kind with the Foreign Office. In addition to career diplomats, there were part-time or retired diplomats, and men seconded to Foreign Office duties from other posts. A few cannot be called diplo-mats at all, but are included to illustrate how the "official mind" grappled with the question of Islam and slavery. The period under consideration is the "long nineteenth century", from 1793 to 1914, with occasional forays beyond this time frame.

ISLAM EXPLOITED TO STALL ABOLITION

The dangers of provoking Muslims to violence by interfering with slavery cannot be denied. To take just one example, Sultan Ahmad of Pahang, in the Malay peninsula, refused to accept a British resident till 1887. The subsequent registration of slaves was one of the grievances that sparked off a rebellion from 1891 to 1895, portrayed by later nationalists as a rising "to safeguard Malay tradition".[9] The rebels declared their struggle a holy war in 1894, and enslaved opponents.[10]

Sarawak provided an example of prudence concerning slavery proper, coupled with vigorous action against slave raiding. Sir James Brooke (1803–68), the first "white raja", placed himself within Britain's informal sphere of influence, and the Foreign Office signed a protectorate treaty with Sir Charles Johnson Brooke (1829–1917) in 1888.[11] James Brooke cooperated with British forces in the suppression of slave raiding by land and sea, despite parliamentary protests at his methods, but left slavery itself well alone, contrary to Ooi's assertion.[12] Charles Brooke creatively manipulated local customary law (*adat*) and the decrees of rulers (*qanun*) to offset shari'a stipulations regarding slavery. Fearing the reactions of "Moslem aristocrats", he issued a cautious circular in 1868, introducing non-binding regulations. These were "not to be considered at present strictly as Law, but may simply afford assistance to those in charge of stations, and after a certain time may become *custom*". More traditions were invented in 1882, and Brooke toyed with the idea of complete abolition. In 1886, however, he merely declared that servitude had become "practically a thing of the past". Slavery was only legally ended under the third raja, Sir Vyner Brooke (1874–1963), in 1928.[13]

In the Islamic emirates of northern Nigeria, the policies of Sir Frederick Lugard, later Lord Lugard (1858–1945), provide a textbook case of indirect rule leading to prevarication over abolition.[14] Born of Anglican missionary parents in southern India, and trained at Sandhurst, Lugard fought many "small wars" in Asia and Africa against Muslim slavers, before becoming high commissioner in northern Nigeria in 1900.[15] Lugard never seems to have admitted to any abolitionist potential in Islam, and he portrayed slavery as the prime example of the degeneracy of rule by emirs in northern Nigeria.[16]

However, Lugard's abiding fear was that a rushed ending of slavery would pauperize and alienate the Muslim elite, rendering unworkable the "dual mandate" system of indirect rule, with which his name became associated.[17] He also feared that the economy would be disrupted by the emigration of former slaves.[18] Lugard therefore warned that slavery was "an institution sanctioned by the law of Islam, and property in slaves was as real as any other form of property among the Mohammedan population".[19] Although decreeing freedom for all those born after the first of April 1901, Lugard did nothing about concubines, allowing transactions in women of servile origins to continue.[20] He also left shari'a courts to regulate disputes concerning slaves.[21] Even administrative slavery was not finally repudiated by the emir of Kano until 1926.[22]

In the light of this checkered and controversial record in northern Nigeria, it might seem surprising that the Foreign Office proposed Lugard as Britain's delegate to the Temporary Slavery Commission of the League of Nations in 1924. However, Lugard rose to the challenge, and proved to be a generally effective champion of the League's attempts to end slavery around the world until his retirement in 1933. In particular, he played a key role in pushing through the League's Slavery Convention of 1926, still in force today.[23]

Egypt, under Foreign Office administration from 1882, was another clear example of the gap that existed between justifying British imperialism and actually implementing abolition. Sir Evelyn Baring (1841–1917), Earl of Cromer from 1901, ruled Egypt with a rod of iron from 1883 to 1907, although officially he was merely British agent and consul-general.[24] He castigated Islam as a "complete failure", in part because it accepted slavery, which he put forward as a factor vindicating British occupation.[25]

However, Baring was soon at loggerheads with the Anti-Slavery Society, which in 1885 published a pamphlet harshly critical of his performance. For Baring, it was essential not to aggravate either the "religious party" or the political élite by precipitate action, as these were groups essential for the functioning of Britain's "veiled protectorate".[26] He argued that since "Mahomedan religious law" recognized slavery, and "any measure likely to lead to a recrudescence of Mahomedan fanaticism [was] much to be deprecated", servitude was only to be gradually eliminated, by repressing imports and granting manumission on demand.[27] He did at least forbid the castration of servile eunuchs in Upper Egypt, although this merely displaced the activity to Darfur and Kordofan in the Sudan.[28]

Three high-ranking Egyptians, including the president of the legislative council, forced Baring's hand when they were arrested for buying slaves in 1894. Although they had been caught red-handed, the trial resulted in a single conviction, and revealed much support among the Egyptian élite for the legitimacy of buying slaves.[29] As late as 1894, Baring had argued that neither the khedive nor the legislative council possessed the authority to "tamper with the Islamic laws recognizing and regulating the practice".[30] After this well publicized scandal, however, the legislative council hurriedly passed abolitionist legislation in 1895–96. Even so, slaves could still "choose" to remain in servitude, and no penal sanctions were applied for owning slaves.[31]

The situation was similar in the Anglo-Egyptian Sudan, another Foreign Office responsibility. A year after his victory at Omdurman in 1898, Lord Horatio Kitchener (1850–1916) issued a memorandum discouraging interference in slavery, unless complaints were received. Although Kitchener rapidly moved on to new pastures, this document still governed official attitudes towards slavery as late as the 1940s.[32] Ending slave raiding and trading, together with the revocation of slave officials, were thought to be sufficient. Officials enthusiastically steeped themselves in Islam's holy law, but this had the effect of buttressing servitude. As Lovejoy comments: "Ironically, slavery became more 'Islamic' under the British regime than previously."[33] Allocated to reconstituted shari'a courts from 1902, bondage was bolstered by the astonishing decision to treat all female slaves as concubines, and thus as members of the family.[34] Indeed, in outlying areas such as northern Kordofan, the British left slavery to courts applying customary law rather than the shari'a. As late as the 1930s, the British turned a blind eye not only to slavery, but also to kidnapping and slave trading, in order to bolster indirect rule through Muslim notables in such areas.[35]

There were Britons who rowed against the tide in the Sudan. Initially, the principal thorn in the government's flesh was an energetic Scot, Captain A. M. McMurdo, who ran the Egyptian Slavery Repression Department. The Sudan administration took over this department in 1911, and abolished it in 1922, despite persistent reports of flagrant abuses, including persistent slave raiding and trading. Two young officials in Berber [Barbar], P. G. W. Diggle, an agricultural inspector, and T. P. Creed, Assistant District Commissioner, protested vigorously, but they were muzzled by their superiors. Diggle, the son of a radical evangelical bishop, resigned in disgust. He took his story to the Anti-Slavery Society in London, and the ensuing publicity deeply embarrassed the Foreign Office. Detailed information emerged on the "brutal excesses of slave-owners", and slaves were pictured as being legally worse off than donkeys. Although this scandal led to gradual reforms, British officials allied with traditional Islamic leaders to fight a sustained rearguard action against precipitate action.[36]

Abolition in Zanzibar and Pemba, under a loose Foreign Office protectorate, revealed another kind of conflict, pitting a cautious British diplomat against a reforming Muslim monarch. Sir Arthur Hardinge (1859–1933), British agent and consul in Zanzibar from 1894 to 1900, was a student of Islam, with previous diplomatic experience in Cairo and Istanbul. He belonged by instinct to the procrastinating party in the matter of slavery, on which he did not have strong personal views. Moreover, he was advised by Lord Salisbury to proceed with caution.[37]

Hardinge argued in 1895 that to speedily apply the principles of the Brussels General Act of 1890, to which the sultan of Zanzibar was a signatory, would be foolish and unjust: "To the Arab the holding of slaves is legal, sanctioned by his religion and the custom of his forefathers for ages." The Qur'an recognized both the institution of slavery and the right to enslave infidel captives, so that "arbitrary deprivation would be regarded . . . as manifest despoliation" by the ruling Arab élite.[38] Moreover, Hardinge later opined that "liberal and Europeanized Mohammedans" simply sought to curry favour with Britain by pretending that slavery was not a "fundamental principle of the social system of Islam".[39]

In 1897, however, the sultan abolished slavery on the islands of Zanzibar and Pemba. The Foreign Office was exhorting Hardinge to be seen to be acting in the matter of slavery, but the real change was the choice of a new sultan, Hamud b. Muhammad b. Sa'id (r. 1896–1902), after considerable problems experienced with his predecessor. At the time of his accession, Sultan Hamud owned no slaves, which the American consul attributed to poverty.[40] Personal conviction seems a more likely explanation, as even the poorest free family owned slaves in Zanzibar at this time, and the new sultan was far from impoverished.[41] Sultan Hamud was rather a pious Muslim, who performed the pilgrimage several times, and "worked hard to acquire knowledge of the rational and traditional sciences of Islam". A member of the Ibadi sect, as was usual among the Omani Arab élite, Hamud was greatly influenced by a great Algerian Ibadi reformer, Shaykh Muhammad b. Yusuf Attafayish (1820/21–1914). Calling on the sultan to follow the ways of reform and justice, Attafayish may have influenced his decision to abolish slavery.[42]

The preamble to Sultan Hamud's 1897 abolitionist decree was certainly couched in Islamic terms. It stated: "And whereas the Apostle Mohamed . . . has set before us as most praiseworthy the liberation of slaves, and We are Ourselves desirous of following his precepts, . . . "[43] While the sultan thus presented abolition as Islamic in nature, he also framed it as a generous personal act, and as one necessary to obtain free labour for the islands' clove and coconut plantations.[44] Ultimately, it remains unclear exactly what mix of factors led to this abolitionist episode, but scholars may well have underestimated the importance of Sultan Hamud's Islamic beliefs.

ISLAM EMPLOYED TO HASTEN ABOLITION IN COLONIAL SITUATIONS

Compared to the famous proconsuls who sought to delay abolition through their knowledge of Islam, those who followed the opposite tack were generally younger figures, and less socially established. For this reason, less is known about them, and some have escaped the attention of all but local historians.

John Richardson is the most obscure of all these men. In the opening years of the nineteenth century, he was district judge and magistrate in Bundelkhand, in central India. He was seemingly fired up by the British parliamentary decision of 1807 to abolish the Atlantic slave trade, praising William Wilberforce as a "benefactor of mankind", and citing Christian and "natural law" arguments against slavery, while also demonstrating the influence of political economy. In a strongly worded letter, dated March 1808, he urged the East India Company's high court in Calcutta to put an end to slavery. The registrar of the court sent the letter for comment to its Muslim muftis and Hindu pandits, who issued an opinion in 1809.

The muftis circumscribed the source of legitimate enslavement to infidels captured in lands not ruled by Muslims, and to those descended from such individuals, unless their mothers were recognized as concubines. They specifically rejected the sale, donation and inheritance of any other kinds of slaves, as well as kidnapping, self-enslavement, the sale of family members, and debt slavery. Strictly interpreted, this fatwa could have led to the immediate freeing of numerous slaves, and to the withering away of slavery over time.[45]

Although disappointed that maltreatment was rejected as grounds for obligatory manumission, Richardson considered the opinions of the Muslim muftis to be greatly superior to those of the Hindu pandits. In 1809, he thus boldly requested that Muslim law be applied exclusively in the matter of slavery in the Bengal Presidency, arguing that the Company was the heir to Mughal rule in terms of criminal law. The court waited till 1816 to forward this missive to the Governor-General, who, a year later, rejected such a radical and potentially destabilizing interpretation.[46]

Richardson's agitation was not in vain, however. In 1830 the appeal court in Calcutta confirmed the validity of the 1809 fatwa, which was more restrictive than the venerable and generally used Hidaya, an Inner Asian legal code.[47] The muftis of the Company's Madras court confirmed the ruling of their Calcutta colleagues in 1841.[48] All in all, slavery was gradually restricted in directly ruled parts of India before the legislation of 1843–44, which did not so much abolish slavery as refuse to recognize it as a legally enforceable status.[49] In addition, probing by Richardson and others seems to have helped to spark off an intense debate among Indian Muslims as to the status of servitude within Islam, a debate which took off from the 1870s.[50]

In Malaya, Sir William Edward Maxwell (1846–1897) was a prominent lawyer and scholar-administrator, from an Irish Protestant background but brought up in the country. He filled a number of senior legal and administrative positions in Malaya, before finishing his career as governor of the Gold Coast. He worked briefly on secondment to the Foreign Office in 1884, when he was sent to secure the release of survivors from a British ship, held captive in North Sumatra and threatened with enslavement.[51] The people of Aceh were at the time fighting with the Dutch, in part to preserve the legal status of slavery.[52] Isabella Bird portrayed Maxwell as a man who not only spoke the language of his charges fluently, but also "takes the trouble to understand them and enter into their ideas and feelings".[53] His son, Sir (William) George Maxwell (1871–1959), took over from Lord Lugard in 1933, as Britain's representative in the fight against slavery at the League of Nations.[54]

William Maxwell established that debt was the most common origin of servitude in Malaya, often leading to the permanent enslavement of unredeemed debtors, in flagrant contravention of Islamic legal principles. Maxwell thus cited the Qur'an to call for leniency in remitting debts. He further stressed that enslaving the whole family of a debtor was an unauthorized and illegal innovation in terms of Islamic law. A further blatant breach of the shari'a lay in the use of enslavement as a punishment for serious crimes.[55]

Taking up Islamic cudgels in the matter of enslavement had wider ramifications, for Maxwell was thereby siding with the ulama in their struggles to make the holy law of Islam prevail more firmly over customary law (adat). Islamic scholars had always granted a recognized position to customary law, whether codified or not, but without specifying where the line should be drawn.[56] The main indigenous law code, the Undang-undang Melaka, which influenced all other Malay codes and was carefully studied by Maxwell, mixed the provisions of shari'a, adat and rulers' decrees.[57] As Malays were wont to call upon the authority of adat to justify debt bondage, an assault on this practice in Islamic terms reinforced the position of the shari'a.[58]

ISLAM EMPLOYED TO HASTEN ABOLITION IN INDEPENDENT ISLAMIC STATES

The demise of slavery in independent Islamic states has traditionally been described as "one of the most typical examples of the transformation that the Muslim world has undergone, through European pressure or example".[59] For Adu Boahen, only the degree of pressure mattered: "The readiness with which the Sultan of Turkey and the Bey of Tunis granted the British Government's urgent requests, and the refusal of the Shah of Persia and the Sultan of Morocco, show quite clearly that the determining factor in these negotiations was not a ruler's religious convictions, but rather his political and bargaining power vis-à-vis the British Government."[60]

While there can be no doubt that slavery was a routine British justification for bullying independent Muslim monarchs, Boahen misses the internal dynamic leading to abolition, as suggested already in the case of quasi-independent Zanzibar. To take an even clearer example, Ahmad Bey of Tunisia was a ruler who made great play of Islamic considerations when he abolished slavery in 1846, two years earlier than his French neighbours in Algeria.[61] Indeed, the British consul worried that Ahmad was rushing his attack on slavery, having "come to a fixed resolution of putting a total end to it in his Dominions".[62]

Perhaps the earliest individual to encourage rulers to follow an abolitionist path, in accordance with the principles of Islam, was a quixotic

British admiral, Sir Sidney Smith (1764–1840). In 1798, as Napoleon threatened to conquer the Middle East, Sidney's brother Spencer happened to be Britain's minister plenipotentiary in Istanbul. Sidney was named "joint plenipotentiary" with his brother, and sent with a squadron to Palestine, where the Ottomans put him in charge of their forces. Sidney Smith became a national hero, in both Britain and Turkey, for stopping Napoleon's advance at the six-week siege of Acre in 1799. However, his career never really recovered from his subsequent blunder in signing the Convention of al-'Arish in 1800, which would have allowed French forces to be evacuated intact from Egypt. More generally, he gained a reputation as a wild and impractical dreamer.[63]

Smith certainly acquired a touching belief in his ability to influence his Muslim friends in the matter of servitude. He caused a sensation on his return to England by riding up Whitehall "attired in the Turkish dress", and developed a marked liking for Islamic culture. He founded the Knights Liberators of the Slaves of Africa in 1814, and, though debarred by the British government, he managed to participate actively in the Congress of Vienna by representing the exiled king of Sweden. As part of his attempts to make the congress focus on slavery, Smith wrote to the Ottoman sultan and to other leading figures in the empire in flowery language, calling on them to participate in the ending of servitude, both Black and White. Smith stressed that the humanitarian principles of the Qur'an were contrary to the existence of slavery, although it does not seem that he engaged in any close exegesis of the text. He further offered membership of his Knights Liberators to a highly-placed bey. No practical results came of these flamboyant efforts, but Smith had blazed a trail for others to follow.[64]

More learned in Islamic doctrine, and more successful in his efforts, was Sir Justin Sheil (1803–71), British minister in Tehran from 1842 to 1854. An Irish Catholic by origin, Sheil served in the Indian army, rising to the rank of captain in 1830. Three years later, he was sent to Persia, as second-in-command of a mission to oversee military reforms. He became fluent in Persian, and took a strong interest in local culture. Transferring to the diplomatic service, he became secretary to the British legation in Persia in 1836, and envoy and minister to the shah's court from 1844 to 1854.[65]

Sheil attempted to end slave imports into Persia, mainly by persuading the shah that Islam did not permit it. Muhammad Shah (r. 1834–48) was personally pious, and was much influenced by his Sufi shaykh and chief minister, Haji Mirza Aqasi, who seems to have pushed for reform in the matter of servitude.[66] Sheil further sought to influence the shah by stressing the progress accomplished by other prominent Muslim monarchs. This tactic backfired, however, for Muhammad Shah lambasted the Ottoman Sunni sultan as a schismatic, and the Omani sultan, of the Ibadi sect, as "a Kharijite, and as such little better than a kafir".[67]

In more specifically Shi'i terms, Sheil set out to prove to the shah that "the sacred law distinguished between slaves bought in commercial transactions and captives made in war.' The slaves imported by sea across the Gulf could in no sense be described as captives in a jihad. However the shah countered that, "buying women and men is based on the Shari'a of the last Prophet. I cannot say to my people that I am prohibiting something which is lawful". The shah also lamented that by abolishing the slave trade, "I would prevent five thousand people a year from becoming Muslims. This would be a great sin, and I would get a bad name." He further declared that "he could not be responsible for being the cause of preventing one human being from joining the true faith".[68] On a copy of a dispatch by Sheil, the shah apparently minuted, "It is against my religion. It is clear in the verses of the Qur'an."[69]

The debate moved out to a wider arena, as both Sheil and the shah sought the support of Shi'i scholars. In 1847, Sheil obtained an opinion from six Persian interpreters of the holy law. While confirming that infidels taken in war could be enslaved, the scholars agreed that a sound and well-known tradition attributed to the Prophet, to the effect that "the seller of men is the worst of men", meant that the slave trade was indeed an "abomination". Unfortunately for Sheil, the whole matter was then referred to the chief Shi'i *mujtahid*, residing in the holy city of Najaf, in Iraq. The latter agreed that slavery was generally "discouraged" (*makruh*) within Islam's fivefold ethical classification, and that the Hadith condemning "the seller of men" was valid. However, in a deft piece of casuistry, he asserted that the buyer of slaves was exempt from the censure proclaimed upon the seller.[70]

Despite the apparent victory of the slaving party, the shah issued a vaguely worded prohibition on importing slaves by sea, shortly before his death in 1848. Although poorly enforced by his successors, this was a symbolic first breach in Persian resistance to abolition.[71] Sheil's role in gaining this concession remains unclear, for the shah may have been chiefly influenced by Haji Mirza Aqasi, who was highly placed in the Nimatullahi Sufi order, which was later to play an important part in the reform and abolition of servitude in Shi'i Islam.[72] In any event, Sheil was unusual in his strenuous efforts to persuade the Persians to take measures against servitude, for his successors, at least up to 1875, were reported to have been far less active in this matter.[73]

Sir (Henry) Bartle Frere (1815–84) was more prominent than Sheil in British official circles. From an East Anglian family with a tradition of parliamentary service, he had made his career in the Bombay civil service. He was seconded to the Foreign Office in 1872–73, to travel to Zanzibar and negotiate the final abolition of the slave trade from east Africa.[74] From his long experience of western India, Frere had come to believe that "the gradual extinction of slavery involves nothing repugnant to the law of the Koran, as interpreted by the most learned men in the best times, and under the most orthodox and best Mahommedan rulers". Strangely, he also believed that Islam allowed enslavement for debt.[75] In reality, the latter was a notion accepted only in limited south Asian Muslim circles, and generally repudiated across the world of Islam.[76]

Frere found Sultan Barghash and his Arab council in a recalcitrant mood in Zanzibar. They argued that "the Koran sanctions slavery", while admitting that manumission was meritorious. Both the religious and the economic arguments were rehearsed at length.[77] As the Zanzibari élite remained uncooperative, Frere departed for India, leaving negotiations to Consul Kirk, who obtained the desired treaty by threatening a naval blockade.[78] Frere's career was ruined in 1879, when he was held responsible for the British defeat by the Zulus at Isandhlwana.[79]

On his way to Zanzibar, Frere had first gone to Cairo, where, in late 1872, he discussed slavery with Isma'il Pasha, khedive of Egypt (r. 1863–79). Frere put it to Isma'il that, "according to strict Koranic law most of the children sold as slaves in Cairo are not lawful slaves but simply stolen chattels". This was on the grounds that slave razzias were unlawful in the shari'a. Isma'il, who was fast becoming a bugbear for British abolitionists, prevaricated. He complained of opposition from local Muslims to any change in the laws governing slavery, adding, somewhat inconsequentially, that the institution went back to Pharaonic times.[80]

Whereas Frere was merely passing through Egypt, Sir John Scott (1841–1904) resided there for many years after 1872. He served as British judge on the court of international appeal in Alexandria from 1874 to 1882, moved to the high court in Bombay as puisne judge, and returned as judicial advisor to the khedive from 1891 to 1898.[81] When the British were threatening to occupy Egypt in 1882, Scott wrote an article in the *Anti-Slavery Reporter* in May. He averred that some "Mahomedan authorities" had declared that the Qur'an did not sanction slavery in 1877, when the British were persuading Isma'il Pasha to sign the Anglo-Egyptian Slave Trade Convention, setting up manumission bureaux. Scott backed the interpretation of these unnamed ulama, on the grounds that 47:4–5 was the only passage in the Qur'an that could be construed as allowing slavery, and even then only as one possibility for unransomed war captives. Moreover, 24:33 in the Qur'an urged the manumission of all who asked for it, and injunctions to manumit slaves as a pious deed recurred in several places in the text.[82]

Also active in Egypt at this time was Wilfrid Scawen Blunt (1840–1922). Impossibly handsome, and famed for his torrid love life, he is chiefly remembered today as a minor poet. He joined the diplomatic service as an attaché in 1858, and was posted all over Europe, and also to Buenos Aires, despite his lackadaisical attitude to his work. He ceased to be formally employed by the Foreign Office from the time of his marriage to Lady Anne Wentworth in 1869, but kept an impressive array of contacts in the service. Indulging in his wife's passion for Arabian horses, the couple travelled widely in the Middle East and India, buying horses for their stud-farm in England. They even found themselves arrested as spies by the Ottoman authorities in Iraq in 1878. In the process, Blunt, a more or less lapsed Catholic, developed a keen interest in Islam, and a great sympathy for its culture. His writings on reviving the Arab caliphate brought him to the attention of William Ewart Gladstone himself, whom he met in private for twenty minutes in 1880. However, Sir Charles Dilke and Lord Granville strongly contested Blunt's influence on the prime minister.[83]

Blunt's involvement in the issue of slavery was an unintended by-product of his forceful opposition to the British occupation of Egypt in 1882. Trying to ensure the success of Ahmad 'Urabi's military regime, Blunt urged that the ulama of al-Azhar, the foremost institution of learning in the Sunni world, be persuaded to issue an abolitionist fatwa.[84] However, he came up against the stubborn refusal of Shaykh Muhammad al-Anbabi, then in charge of al-Azhar, to do more than denounce abuses in the process of enslavement.[85] Quite unrealistically, Blunt dreamed up another scheme. An Arab caliph, from the tribe of the Prophet, should summon a general council of ulama in Mecca, which would issue an internationally binding prohibition on all forms of servitude.[86]

In a more practical vein, Blunt turned to his friend Muhammad 'Abduh (1849–1905), the greatest reformist Sunni scholar of the time, to whom he had been introduced by his Arabic teacher at al-Azhar.[87] In 1882, 'Abduh was working for 'Urabi Pasha's government, as director of the official journal and censor of the press. He sent Blunt a private letter, saying:

The present Ministry is trying hard to suppress domestic slavery. The Mohammedan religion offers no obstacle at all to this; nay, according to Mohammedan dogma, Moslems are not allowed to have slaves except taken from infidels at war with them. In fact they are captives or prisoners taken in legal warfare, or who belonged to infidel peoples not in friendly alliance with Mohammedan princes, not protected by treaties or covenants. But no Moslem is allowed to be taken as a slave. Moreover, if a person is an infidel, but belongs to a nation in peaceful treaty with a

136

Mohammedan prince, he cannot be taken as a slave. Hence the Mohammedan religion not only does not oppose abolishing slavery as it is in modern times, but radically condemns its continuance. Those learned gentlemen in England who hold a contrary opinion should come here and teach us, the sheykhs of the Azhar, the dogma of our faith. The whole Mohammedan world would be struck dumb when it learned that a Christian had taken upon him the task, in the greatest Mohammedan University in the world, of teaching its ulema, professors and theologians the dogmas of their religion, and how to comment on their Koran. A fetwa will in a few days be issued by the Sheykh el Islam to prove that the abolition of slavery is according to the spirit of the Koran, to Mohammedan tradition, and to Mohammedan dogma. The Egyptian government will endeavour to remove every obstacle in the way, and will not rest till slavery is extirpated from Egyptian territory.[88]

Doubt has been cast upon the veracity of this letter, which unfortunately only survives in English in Blunt's book, but Gabriel Baer considers it to contain "at least a grain of truth".[89]

The letter may well be genuine, for it manifests a glaring contradiction. In sticking stubbornly to the legality of enslavement in a just war, 'Abduh was gravely undermining the potential appeal of his missive to the British authorities. Had Blunt forged the letter, or just edited it, he would surely have taken out this passage. Indeed, Blunt himself pointed out this unfortunate problem, in a letter to the secretary-general of the Anti-Slavery Society.[90]

The long-term implications of this letter are also hard to gauge, although it long served to establish 'Abduh's credentials as an abolitionist. 'Abduh clearly remained to a certain extent a prisoner of the scholastic tradition in which he had been trained, at least at this stage in his career.[91] However, Riad Nourallah has shown that other documents exist, which suggest that 'Abduh became steadily more opposed to slavery, even if the writings of his disciple and successor, Muhammad Rashid Rida, have tended to obscure this fact.[92] 'Abduh returned from exile in 1888, making his peace with the British. Acting initially as judge, he was promoted to Grand Mufti of Egypt in 1899, a position in which he served until shortly before his death in 1905.[93] He thus probably played a part in the 1895–96 repudiation of slavery by Egypt's legislative council, discussed above.

As for Blunt, he fell out with Gladstone over the continuing occupation of Egypt, and became an ever more passionate supporter of the cause of Irish Home Rule, serving time in jail in 1888 for chairing a prohibited meeting in Ireland the previous year.[94] Although he ceased to be actively involved in the issue of slavery in the Middle East, he published his *Secret history of the English occupation of Egypt* in 1907. The frontispiece featured a delightful photograph of the recently deceased Muhammad 'Abduh, "my old Egyptian friend".[95]

CONCLUSION

The story of the manipulation of Islamic beliefs and institutions by British officials, with the intention of delaying emancipation, might appear to be a field relatively well-trodden by researchers. However, there are still aspects that need to be teased out. For example, it is unclear whether there was any detailed exegesis of Islamic texts to buttress Islamic conceptions of servitude, and, if so, how this was received by Muslims. The story also requires more publicity, for it neatly turns on its head the patronizing view of unwilling Muslims forced to accept abolition by upright Westerners.

The contrasting British stratagem, that of hastening abolition through an analysis of the emancipatory potential of Islamic beliefs, has been much more obviously neglected. Indeed, the stray examples presented here may well be the tip of an iceberg. This moves the spotlight to British personnel of a liberal and scholarly bent, often men of junior rank, whose efforts all too often remained unsung and unrewarded.

Moreover, the attention that such men paid to Islamic concepts of servitude underscores the significance of Muslim agency in the process of moving from legal to real emancipation. Too little work has been done on the ways in which Western notions of freedom had to be expressed in Islamic terms in order to become effective. More needs to be known about the efforts made to define and explain the suppression of slavery in ways that were acceptable to Muslims. Studying the Britons who engaged in such labours is one way to right the historiographical balance.

Notes

1   Suzanne Miers, *Slavery in the Twentieth Century: The Evolution of a Global Problem* (Walnut Creek: AltaMira, 2003), pp. 254–77, 300–16, 339–57.

2   William G. Clarence-Smith, *Islam and the abolition of slavery* (London: Hurst, 2006).

3   Paul E. Lovejoy, *Transformations in Slavery: a history of slavery in Africa* (Cambridge: CUP, 1983), p. 247.

4   Francis Robinson, "The British empire and the Muslim world", *The Oxford History of the British Empire*, vol. iv, *The Twentieth Century* (Oxford: OUP, 1999), eds. Judith Brown and Wm. Roger Louis, pp. 404–8.

5   Clarence-Smith, *Islam*.

6   Diane Robinson-Dunn, *The Harem, Slavery and British Imperial Culture: Anglo-Muslim relations in the late nineteenth century* (Manchester: MUP, 2006),

pp. 160–70. Gottlieb W. Leitner, Muhammadanism (Lahore: Muhammadan Tract and Book Depot, 2nd. edn, 1893). [Abdullah Quilliam], "Islam and Slavery", *The Islamic World*, vol. 3 (1985), no. 26, 54–6 (Eric Germain has indicated Quilliam as the probable author).

7 R. W. Beachey, *The Slave Trade of Eastern Africa* (London: Rex Collings, 1976), pp. 199–200 and 205. John Iliffe, *A Modern History of Tanganyika* (Cambridge: CUP, 1979), p. 95.

8 Georges Poulet, "Enquête sur la captivité en Afrique Occidentale Française", *Slavery and its Abolition in French West Africa* (Madison: University of Wisconsin, 1994), eds. P. E. Lovejoy and A. S. Kanya-Forstner, p. 40.

9 Barbara W. Andaya and Leonard Y. Andaya, *A History of Malaysia* (London: Macmillan, 1982), pp. 160–1 and 167–70.

10 W. Linehan, *A History of Pahang* (Kuala Lumpur: Malaysian Branch of the Royal Asiatic Society, 1973), pp. 140–2, 153 and 161–2.

11 *Oxford Dictionary of National Biography (ODNB)*, eds. H. C. G. Matthew and Brian Harrison (Oxford: OUP, 2004), vol. 7, pp. 876–8.

12 Ooi Keat Gin, *Of free trade and native interests: the Brookes and the economic development of Sarawak, 1841–1941* (Oxford: OUP, 1997), pp. 23–4. The 1842 laws, cited on pp. 355–6, in no sense abolished slavery.

13 Robert Pringle, *Rajahs and Rebels: the Ibans of Sarawak under Brooke rule, 1841–1941* (London: Macmillan, 1970), pp. 176–7.

14 Paul E. Lovejoy and Jan S. Hogendorn, *Slow death for slavery: the course of abolition in northern Nigeria, 1897–1936* (Cambridge: CUP, 1993).

15 *ODNB*, vol. 34, pp. 727–33.

16 Steven Pierce, *Farmers and the state in colonial Kano: land tenure and the legal tenure and the legal imagination* (Bloomington: Indiana UP, 2005), pp. 35–6 and 219.

17 Polly Hill, "From freedom to slavery; the case of farm slavery in Nigerian Hausaland", *Comparative Studies in Society and History*, vol. 18 (1976), no. 3, pp. 395–426.

18 Pierce, *Farmers and the state*, pp. 37–9.

19 Lovejoy , *Transformations*, p. 265.

20 Paul E. Lovejoy, "Concubinage and the status of women in early colonial northern Nigeria", *Journal of African History*, vol. 29 (1988), no. 2, pp. 245–66.

21 Allan Christelow, *Thus ruled Emir Abbas: selected cases from the records of the Emir Kano's judicial council* (East Lansing: Michigan State University, 1994), pp. 16, 62–4 and 113–16; Adamu M. Fika, *The Kano civil war and British over-rule, 1882–1940* (Ibadan: OUP, 1978), pp. 198–202.

22 Sean Stilwell, "'Amana' and 'Asiri': royal slave culture and the colonial regime in Kano, 1903–1926", *Slavery and Colonial Rule in Africa* (London: Frank Cass, 1999), eds. Suzanne Miers and Martin Klein, pp. 167–88.

23 Miers, *Slavery in the Twentieth Century*, pp. 103, 121–30, 217–18, 292.

24 *ODNB*, vol. 3, pp. 821–7.

25 Albert Hourani, *Arabic Though in the Liberal Age, 1798–1939* (London: OUP, 1970), p. 251.

26 Judith E. Tucker, *Women in nineteenth-century Egypt* (Cambridge: CUP, 1985), pp. 176–7.

27 Y. Hakan Erdem, *Slavery in the Ottoman Empire and its Demise, 1800–1909* (London: Macmillan, 1996), pp. 91–3.

28 Demetrius A. Zambaco, *Les eunuques d'aujourd'hui et ceux de jadis* (Paris: Masson et Cie., 1911), pp. 46 and 59.

29 Eve Trout Powell, "Indian Muslim modernists and the issue of slavery in Islam", *Slavery and South Asian History* (Bloomington: Indiana UP, 2003), eds. Indrani Chatterjee and Rucnard M. Eaton, pp. 150–5; Robinson-Dunn, *The Harem*, pp. 93–4.

30 Tucker, *Women*, p. 176.

31 Robinson-Dunn, *The Harem*, pp. 56 and 68 (n. 118); Gabriel Baer, "Slavery and its abolition", *Studies in the Social History of Modern Egypt* (Chicago: Chicago UP, 1969), ed. Gabriel Baer, pp. 181–9; Børge Fredriksen, *Slavery and its abolition in nineteenth-century Egypt* (thesis, University of Bergen, 1977), pp. 183–4.

32 S. Spencer *Trimingham, Islam in the Sudan* (London: Frank Cass, 1965 (reprint of 1949 edn.), p. 23; Beachey, *The Slave Trade of Eastern Africa*, pp. 144–7.

33 Lovejoy, *Transformations*, pp. 264–5.

34 Taj Hargey, *The suppression of the slave trade in the Sudan, 1898–1939* (DPhil thesis, Oxford University, 1981), pp. 419–53; Ahmad A. Sikainga, *Slaves into Workers: emancipation and labor in colonial Sudan* (Austin: University of Texas Press, 1996), p. 54–7.

35 Justin Willis, "Hukm: the creolization of authority in Condominium Sudan", *Journal of African History*, vol. 46 (2005), pp. 29–50.

36 Hargey, *Sudan*, pp. 268–85; Daly 1986: 235–6, 443–4.

37 Norman R. Bennett, *A History of the Arab State of Zanzibar* (London: Methuen, 1978), pp. 176–7; Hollingsworth 1953: 131–59.

38 Beachey, *The Slave Trade*, p. 295.

39 Arthur Hardinge, *A Diplomatist in the East* (London: Jonathan Cape, 1928), p. 355.

40 Bennett, *Arab State of Zanzibar*, p. 179.

41 M. Reda Bhacker, *Trade and Empire in Muscat and Zanzibar: roots of British domination* (London: Routledge, 1992), p. 132.

42 Philip Sadgrove, "From Wadi Mizab to Unguja: Zanzibar's scholarly links", *The transmission of learning in Islamic Africa* (Leiden: Brill, 2004), pp. 189–211.

43 R. W. Beachey, *A Collection of Documents on the Slave Trade of Eastern Africa* (London: Rex Collings, 1976), p. 125.

44 Hardinge, *Diplomatist*, p. 197; L. W. Hollingsworth, *Zanzibar under the Foreign Office, 1890–1913* (London: Macmillan, 1953), p. 217.

45 Amal K. Chattopadhyay, *Slavery in the Bengal Presidency, 1772–1843* (London: The Golden Eagle Publishing House, 1977), pp. 170–7; William Adam, *The Law and Custom of Slavery in British India* (Boston: Weeks, Jordan and Co., 1840), pp. 61, 64–7.

46 Chattopadhyay, *Slavery*, pp. 177–84; Adam, *Law and Custom*, pp. 196–207; Gyan Prakash, *Bonded Histories: genealogies of labor servitude in colonial India* (Cambridge: CUP, 1990), pp. 145–6.

47   D. R. Banaji, *Slavery in British India* (Bombay: D. B. Taraporevala Sons & Co., 1933), pp. 43–4.

48   Indrani Chatterjee, *Gender, Slavery and Law in Colonial India* (New Delhi: OUP, 1999), p. 213.

49   Chattopadhyay, *Slavery*, pp. 250–1.

50   Powell , "Indian Muslim modernists".

51   *ODNB*, vol. 37, p. 537; J. M. Gullick , "William Maxwell and the study of Malay society", *Journal of the Malaysian Branch of the Royal Asiatic Society*, vol. 64 (1991), no. 2, pp. 7–46.

52   Clarence-Smith, *Islam*, pp. 166–7.

53   Isabella L. Bird, *The Golden Chersonese and the way thither* (London: T. Fisher Unwin, 1883), pp. 285–6.

54   Miers, *Slavery in the Twentieth Century*, p. 217; Gullick, "William Maxwell", photo, p. 27.

55   W. E. Maxwell, "The law relating to slavery among the Malays", *Journal of the Straits Branch of the Royal Asiatic Society*, vol. 22 (1890), pp. 247–98. See also Hugh C. Clifford, *Malayan Monochromes* (London: John Murray, 1913), pp. 121–5; Mahmud bin Mat "The passing of slavery in East Pahang", *Malayan Historical Journal*, vol. 1 (1954), no. 1, pp. 8–10; Richard Winstedt (revised and updated by Tham Seong Chee), *The Malays: a cultural history* (Singapore: Graham Brash, 1981), pp. 54–5; Philip F. S. Loh, *The Malay States, 1877–1895: political change and social policy* (Kuala Lumpur, 1969), pp. 189–90.

56   Christelow, *Emir Abbas*, pp. 8–9.

57   Yok Fang Liaw, *Undang-undang Melaka: a critical edition* (The Hague: Nederlandsche Boek en Steendrukkkerij, 1976).

58   Maxwell, "The law relating to slavery among the Malays", pp. 247–8. See also on debt-bondage, Bird, "Golden Chersonese", pp. 370–5.

59   R. Brunschvig, "Abd", *Encyclopaedia of Islam* (Leiden: E. J. Brill, 1960), vol. 1, pp. 24–40.

60   A. Adu Boahen, *Britain, the Sahara and the Western Sudan, 1788–1961* (Oxford: Clarendon Press, 1964), p. 148.

61   L. Carl Brown, *The Tunisia of Ahmad Bey, 1837–1855* (Princeton: Princeton UP, 1974), pp. 322–5.

62   Erdem, *Slavery in the Ottoman Empire*, p. 48.

63   *ODNB*, vol. 51, pp. 304–8.

64   Tom Pocock, *Breaking the Chains: the Royal Navy's war on white slavery* (Annapolis: US Naval Institute Press, 2006), pp. 6–22.

65   *ODNB*, vol. 50, p. 171; Denis Wright, *The English among the Persians during the Qajar period, 1787–1921* (London: Heinemann, 1977), p. 22.

66   Vanessa A. Martin, *The Qajar Pact: bargaining, protest and the state in nineteenth-century Persia* (London: I. B. Tauris, 2005), pp. 159–60.

67   John B. Kelly, *Britain and the Persian Gulf, 1795–1880* (Oxford: Clarendon Press, 1968), pp. 594–5; Behnaz A. Mirzai, "The 1848 abolitionist farman: a step towards ending the slave trade in Iran", *Abolition and its aftermath in Indian Ocean Africa and Asia* (London: Routledge, 2005), ed. Gwyn Campbell, p. 96.

68 Kelly, *Persian Gulf*, pp. 594–6; Mirzai, "1848", p. 96.
69 Martin, *Qajar Pact*, p. 168 (n. 71).
70 Kelly, *Persian Gulf*, pp. 594–7; Mirzai, "1848", p. 97.
71 Kelly, *Persian Gulf*, pp. 599–604; Sheil, *Glimpses*, ch. 16; Heinz-Georg Migeod, *Die persische Gesellschaft unter Nasiru'd-Din Sah, 1848–1896* (London: Routledge, 1990), pp. 330–3.
72 Mirzai, "1848", pp. 97–9; Clarence-Smith, *Islam*, pp. 130–1, 169.
73 Joseph Cooper, *The Lost Continent, or Slavery and the Slave Trade in Africa 1875, with Observations on the Asiatic Slave-Trade carried on under the name of the Labour Traffic* (London: Frank Cass, 1968 (reprint of 1875 edn.)), p. 116.
74 *ODNB*, vol. 20, pp. 979–84.
75 Bartle Frere, "Correspondence respecting Sir Bartle Frere's mission to the East Coast of Africa, 1872–73', *Parliamentary Papers*, vol. 61 (C-820, 1973), pp. 14, 51–6.
76 Clarence-Smith, *Islam*, p. 74–8.
77 Frere, "Correspondence", pp. 51, 54–6.
78 Bennett, *Arab State of Zanzibar*, pp. 96–7.
79 *ODNB*, vol. 20, pp. 979–84.
80 Frere, "Correspondence", pp. 8–9.
81 *ODNB*, vol. 49, p. 430.
82 Beachey, *Documents on the Slave Trade*, p. 33.
83 Elizabeth Longford, *A Pilgrimage of Passion: the life of Wilfrid Scawen Blunt* (London: Weidenfeld and Nicolson, 1979); *ODNB*, vol. 6, pp. 357–9.
84 Wilfrid S. Blunt, *The Future of Islam* (London: RoutledgeCurzon, 2nd edition, 2002), edited and annotated by Riad Nourallah, pp. 149–50.
85 Baer, "Slavery and its abolition", p. 188; Erdem, *Slavery in the Ottoman Empire*, pp. 89–90.
86 Blunt, *Future of Islam*, pp. 149–50.
87 Longford, *Pilgrimage*, pp. 167, 173–8.
88 Wilfrid S. Blunt, *Secret History of the English Occupation of Egypt* (London: T. Fisher Unwin, 1907), pp. 244, 253–4.
89 Baer, "Slavery and its abolition", p. 188.
90 Eve M. Troutt Powell, *A different shade of colonialism: Egypt, Great Britain and the mastery of the Sudan* (Berkeley: University of California Press, 2003), p. 143.
91 Clarence-Smith, *Islam*, pp. 203–5.
92 Blunt, *Future of Islam*, p. 222 (n. 42 by Riad Nourallah); Riad Nourallah, personal communications.
93 Malise Ruthven, *Islam in the World* (London: Penguin, 2nd edn., 2000), pp. 300–3; Daniel Crecelius, "Non-ideological responses ofthe Egyptian ulama to modernization", *Scholars, Saints and Sufis: Muslim religious institutions in the Middle East since 1500* (Berkeley: University of California Press, 1972), ed. Nikki Keddie, pp. 167–209.
94 *ODNB*, vol. 6, p. 358.
95 Blunt, *Secret History*, frontispiece and p. vii.

CHAPTER SEVEN

The "Taint of Slavery"

The Colonial Office and the Regulation of Free Labour

MANDY BANTON

In 1837 Lord Glenelg, secretary of state for war and the colonies,[1] asked colonial governors to review legal codes to reflect changes in society resultant from the emancipation of enslaved people. He stressed that legislatures formulating labour law should avoid any system placing "the proprietary body in an invidious and apparently unfriendly relation towards those who are to live by the earnings of manual labour".[2] Glenelg and his permanent under-secretary Sir James Stephen were concerned to safeguard an inexperienced and, they believed, immobile wage-labour force, and were prepared "to curb the authority of the planters in the interests of the freedman's liberty".[3] They wished contract and vagrancy laws to be more lenient than those of England.

English labour law – the law of master and servant – had its basis in fourteenth century and Elizabethan codes, complicated by separate measures for individual trades and buttressed by provisions of the poor law. The labour contract was "a command under the guise of an agreement . . . the law of the status of those liable to be directed to work at wages fixed without their concurrence and liable to be punished for not accepting work on demand and for not doing it in accordance with the direction".[4] It was criminal law, enforced by the summary jurisdiction of justices of the peace and routinely imposing fines or imprisonment on defaulting employees, although rarely on employers. Although described in 1823 as "a great patchwork of legislation only imperfectly known", its essentials were familiar and in the 1830s it was not yet a political issue. By this period there already existed throughout the empire a variety of statutes based on English law, or the colonists' understanding of that law, which had evolved through a process of transmission, borrowing and adaptation.[5] In the Americas legislation dating from as early as the seventeenth century initially controlled European indentured and convict labour, and was distinct from laws regulating enslaved people. By 1664, for example, Jamaica had both an act "for the better ordering and governing of Negro slaves", and another, "for the good governing of servants".[6]

Colonial master and servant laws often covered the regulation of apprentices. "Apprenticeship" may be perceived as a respected training for a craft or trade, but, as Joan Lane has shown, traditional apprenticeship in England "had failed by the nineteenth century when it was used as a device of the Poor Law officials to be rid of large numbers of pauper children who were to be indentured beyond the parish to reduce the poor rate".[7] Similarly the need to avoid placing financial pressures on colonial authorities informed arrangements made for "slaves or natives of Africa"[8] seized from illegal traders or as prize of war[9] following British parliamentary abolition of the slave trade in 1807. They were not, as might be imagined, set at liberty but were, in the words of the act, "condemned as prize or forfeitures", and "provided for" by being enlisted as soldiers, sailors or marines, or bound as "apprentices" for up to fourteen years. The act ruled that indentures should be of the "same force and effect as if the party thereby bound as an Apprentice had himself or herself when of full age, upon good consideration, duly executed the same".[10] The king in council was empowered to make further arrangements "as may prevent such Negroes from becoming at any Time chargeable upon the Island in which they shall have been so bound Apprentices".[11] Early concerns that the "disposal" of liberated Africans might be open to abuse were confirmed in the 1820s when commissioners appointed "to ascertain the actual condition of all Negroes, who . . . have been apprenticed or otherwise disposed of" in the British West Indies found that few had been taught the trades detailed in their indentures, and many had been used to augment field gangs of enslaved people.[12] In Mauritius the Commissioners of Eastern Inquiry concluded that such "apprentices" were often worse off than slaves when assigned to slave owners, and reported allegations that some had been baptized with the names of deceased slaves and absorbed into the slave population.[13]

The entirely separate system of "apprenticeship" introduced by the 1833 Act for the Abolition of Slavery is well known and the subject of a considerable literature.[14] With the intention of "promoting the Industry and securing the good Conduct of the Persons so to be manumitted", it tied freed people to their former owners as wage labourers for a period of years.[15] While indicating the general nature of regulations required to support the system, the act left colonial governments to decide the detail so long as enactments were not "in anywise repugnant or contradictory to this present Act".[16] There is evidence that conditions for apprentices were often worse than those existing under slavery, which had been ameliorated in the 1820s and 1830s.

In Barbados, where there was little opportunity for apprentices to grow their own food, there was immediate concern for the welfare of young children. They were free if under the age of six when the act came into force, or born during the apprenticeship period, but no provision was made for their maintenance. The governor, Sir Lionel Smith, reported that 14,000 free children were living in a "destitute condition"; he complained that the legislature had refused to alter the law compelling apprenticed labourers to allow their free children to be apprenticed if they could not support them; and he forwarded reports noting "ill-feeling" of planters towards such children. He objected to the apprenticing of children, whose indentures would continue until they reached the age of 21, considering it a modified form of slavery.[17] In 1836, however, Smith's successor censured women who refused to apprentice their children, and the following year he refuted claims of the abolitionist Thomas Fowell Buxton that planters were attempting to force the apprenticeship of free children, although he admitted that the assembly had rejected proposals to terminate indentures in 1840.[18] Elsewhere, for example in Trinidad and Jamaica, parents also refused to apprentice their children.[19]

In Antigua, where the intermediate period of apprenticeship was omitted, legislation was introduced in 1834 to secure the labour of former slaves by a system of house occupancy. "Wage levels fixed by the employer, labour discipline and good conduct standards were to be enforced by the threat of eviction."[20] A more stringent Special Contract Act enacted the same year was, however, disallowed by the secretary of state who "condemned it in principle as subverting the rights of free labour" and saw it as "setting a precedent for wage-work legislation throughout the British Caribbean".

Prior to termination of the apprenticeship system in 1838 colonies were, as noted above, asked to review their legal codes. Master and servant legislation was imposed on only the "new" dependencies of British Guiana, St. Lucia and Trinidad, but James Stephen expected other legislatures, including that of the Cape of Good Hope, to adhere to the spirit of the model drafted in London. Its main features were that only contracts of employment for work within the colony should be binding, and their duration should not exceed four weeks if made orally or one year if in writing; written contracts must be signed by each party before a stipendiary magistrate who was empowered to enforce contracts and impose penalties for breach, neglect or non-performance. Breaches of contract deemed to be punishable offences were limited to three: failure to perform stipulated work; negligent or improper performance of such work; and causing damage to the employer's property by negligence or "improper conduct". Penalties were recommended as " . . . a pecuniary penalty for the benefit of the master, not exceeding one month's wages, the commitment of the servant to prison, with or without hard labour, for any term not exceeding 14 days, or the dissolution of the contract of service".[21]

Stephen subsequently examined newly-enacted statutes closely, pinpointing each divergence from the model. He reported variations in a Bahamas law, noting that it limited compensation payable to a worker by a defaulting employer to the value of one month's wages – "a change of which I am unable to explain the motive, or to surmise the vindication".[22] He approved statutes from St. Vincent and Tobago, but recommended disallowance of St. Kitts legislation framed on principles at variance with those of the model. He complained that a Barbados act contained nine "important variations", including changes in rules regarding foreign contracts, the allowance of extensions of verbal contracts indefinitely, a limit on the amount of unpaid wages which might be claimed, and the provision that a worker voluntarily quitting his employment was not entitled to any crop grown on land occupied by him as part of his contract, or to compensation in lieu. He believed that it was "eminently impolitic" to pay wages in the form of the assignment of houses and land, stating, "the practice is of course popular with the planters and the assemblies, because the first and apparent tendency of it is to bring the workmen into a state of dependence on their employers, and to bind them to the estate by the bond of local attachment".[23]

In 1840 Stephen objected to a Grenada act which exempted European artisans, servants and labourers because, it was claimed, they did not need the same protection as "Africans" and employers required longer contracts in order to recoup recruiting costs. He noted:

> . . . the most serious objection to this Enactment is that it establishes one of those distinctions in point of Law between the European and African Races from which so much evil flowed in former times . . . if a new course of legislation shall begin in which any distinctions of the kind are admitted, an opening will be made for a return to that system of Caste to which may be traced so large a proportion of the Calamities which the history of the West Indies records . . . [24]

Two years later Stephen examined a Jamaica act incorporating clauses of English law dating back to the sixteenth century. He stressed the extreme difficulty everywhere of legislating between masters and servants, and particularly in the Caribbean, but noted that the act had been in force for a year and no criticism of it had reached him. "There are", he wrote "so many vigilant eyes, and . . . censure is never spared if the slightest provocation for it is given."[25] Although it was difficult to condemn provisions which derived from English statutes still in force, he believed that "nothing is more certain than that a law may lose all its value from transplantation from its native soil".

There was much early revision of laws allowed by the Colonial Office but disliked by colonial legislatures, which were often dominated by employers. Only one year after its 1839 statute had been approved Tobago repealed provisions that contracts should be limited to one year and be valid only if for work within the colony. Stephen complained that this rescinded safeguards on which the British government had most firmly insisted, and noted that although the governor and attorney general had considered the enactment "indefensible" it had been passed by the assembly because their UK agent had convinced them that it would be allowed by the secretary of state.[26] Tensions between governors and legislatures, and sometimes between governors and their officials, were common, and continued.

Master and servant law was not the only legislation to be revised or introduced from the late 1830s "to reflect changes in society". Laws were enacted to control vagrancy, to strengthen militia and police forces, to prevent labour migration, to prevent squatting on unoccupied land, and many more designed to control the free populations.

Following James Stephen's retirement in 1847 responsibility for the review of colonial legislation went to Sir Frederic Rogers who was equally conscientious in his attention to legal detail and believed in the "moral responsibility" of government.[27] Although, in 1853, he approved Bay Islands legislation allowing verbal contracts to be automatically renewed from month to month unless one party gave a week's notice, he also believed that workers were entitled to exploit labour shortages to drive up wages and secure improved conditions. In 1858 he examined a law requiring west Africans to accept work on demand, and at wages fixed by the employer, and advised the secretary of state to insist on its amendment. He wrote:

> It must be remembered in dealing with a question of this kind that there is a constant tendency in Legislatures composed of employers to frame laws which (they flatter themselves) will relieve them from the necessity of humouring and improving the labouring population, and enable them to treat that population as a mere means of production bound to employ itself for their benefit according to certain laws fixed with reference to the employers' profits.[28]

The Colonial Office did not, of course, work in isolation but was influenced by the wider concerns of British society. The liberal, humanitarian and anti-racist beliefs informing the work of James Stephen and others, and generally accepted within the office during the first half of the nineteenth century, were inevitably dealt a blow by the "ideological turning-point"[29] resultant upon the Indian Mutiny of 1857 and exacerbated by the Jamaican "rebellion" of 1865. Support for the rights of indigenous workers, as demonstrated unequivocally by Frederic Rogers as late as 1858, soon gave way to distrust of humanitarianism and an emphasis on economic concerns, as subsequent Colonial Office involvement in the development of labour legislation in Africa demonstrates.

In west Africa master and servant legislation, based on English law with some innovations, had been introduced in Sierra Leone in 1820, following disallowance of an 1816 statute described by Stephen as an "imitation of the old English law of frankpledge".[30] It was extended to the Gambia in 1825. The metropolitan debates of the 1830s were not relevant to west Africa, where Britain had made no attempt to outlaw "domestic" slavery, and it was not until 1877 that legislation was passed in the Gold Coast to supplement the emancipation scheme of 1874 by introducing "the idea of a limited service voluntarily entered into, yet obligatory during its continuance, and having for its object the mutual benefit of both contracting parties".[31] Officials in London were now concerned that emancipation might have adverse effects on the Gold Coast economy; any fall in the export of palm oil would lead to a drop in revenue and immediately counteract development plans. But they had confidence in the judgment of the acting chief magistrate, who had drafted the legislation: "Sir D[avid] Chalmers is a very careful man, fully alive to the objections, real and pseudo-humanitarian, against which it is necessary to guard in framing such a measure as this."[32] Although based on earlier west African legislation, the statute followed rather closely the 1867 and 1875 reforms of English master and servant law, which had decriminalized breach of contract, by requiring magistrates to use civil procedure before resorting to the penal provisions retained for "aggravated misconduct". It empowered the courts to adjust and set off claims, to direct fulfilment of the contract, or to rescind the contract.[33]

The Gold Coast statute might have provided an acceptable model for other British African dependencies, but far harsher legislation separately developed in the Cape of Good Hope was to dictate the development of master and servant law in southern, central and eastern Africa throughout the remainder of the nineteenth century and into the first three decades of the twentieth. The 1856 Cape "Act to Amend the Laws Regulating the Relative Rights and Duties of Masters, Servants and Apprentices" had, by a simple clerical error, not been examined in the Colonial Office.[34] It imposed imprisonment with or without hard labour for up to one month, or six weeks for a second conviction, on workers found guilty of "minor" breaches including failure to commence an agreed contract, unauthorized absence from the workplace, negligent performance of work, drunkenness, abusive language, insubordination and making a "brawl or disturbance". The period of imprisonment was increased to two months, or three for a second offence, for "major" breach, including damage or loss to the employer's property, assault, or desertion. Imprisonment might include solitary confinement or a "spare" diet. Conviction did not cancel a contract, the duration of which was extended by the period of imprisonment, and workers refusing to recommence work might be re-imprisoned. In addition, unlimited compensation for loss or damage to property might be awarded from future wages, effectively tying the worker to his employer.[35] The law had been drafted following local criticism of the inefficacy of an 1841 statute already harsher than the recommended Caribbean model and disliked by James Stephen for its heavy penalties, long contracts, administration by resident magistrates rather than specially appointed stipendiaries, and lists of "vague" offences, but allowed by the then secretary of state who accepted the governor's claim that no-one without intimate knowledge of local conditions could judge.

The 1856 Cape act served as a model for legislation introduced in the Transvaal in 1880 and Natal in 1894. Although officials in the Colonial Office then expressed concern about the harsh provisions enacted, the close and knowledgeable attention formerly provided by James Stephen and Frederic Rogers was no longer exercised, the work of legal advisers was restricted to commenting on the legal form rather than assessing policy implications, and officials agreed that there was an acceptable precedent. They assumed not only that the Cape act had been examined and approved, but also that it remained appropriate for extension to neighbouring territories so many years later. Cape master and servant laws of 1856 to 1889 were adopted by Southern Rhodesia in 1891, and extended to the Bechuanaland Protectorate and Swaziland in 1911 for the control of labourers recruited for the mines. Also in 1911, however, officials in London vetoed proposed Gold Coast legislation based on that of the Transvaal. In the Gold Coast the development of expatriate mining enterprises had led to an influx of personnel with experience of South African mining practices and a desire for South African solutions to labour "problems".[36] But the mining companies failed to convince Gold Coast officials and took their demands and draft legislation based on Transvaal law directly to the Colonial Office. Discussions among officials in London indicate uncertainty in a complex and, by now, little-known area, and the secretary of state, Lord Harcourt, commented, "I feel a little out of my depth in this mass of detail".[37] But W. D. Ellis provided a more detailed report than any made since Stephen and Rogers were in office and convinced his superiors that the proposals must be rejected. "I see", he stated, "no reason to make it any easier than it is at present for the

Mining Companies to tie down the labourers to the very unpleasant work at the mines."[38] Unusually he stressed the likelihood of a political attack on Harcourt given the Transvaal Chinese labour controversy[39] and growing concern about the use of Indian indentured labour.

Despite the failure of mining interests to influence Gold Coast law, in 1906 legislation drafted by the Colonists' Association had been enacted in the East Africa Protectorate (EAP, later Kenya).[40] Colonial Office officials were not aware of its genesis but understood it to be the work of the crown advocate, and they accepted uncritically a confused accompanying report which claimed to trace the derivation of each section from existing Gold Coast and Transvaal law. In fact it consistently misnumbered sections of the Gold Coast ordinance used, and attributed two new provisions to it. The most important, imposing up to three month's imprisonment for the offence of absconding without working off an advance of wages, appeared in neither Gold Coast nor Transvaal law. The crown advocate's report also obscured the existence of a new clause removing the Gold Coast requirement that civil process should be used in all but the most serious cases of breach of contract. Officials complained that the legislation should have been submitted in draft prior to enactment, but one tentatively suggested that it was probably necessary "in order to obtain reasonable service from the natives who are unused to the benefits and obligations of continuous labour".[41] Although another underlined the word "benefits" and added the marginal note "including imprisonment for offences which are in no sense criminal" there was no serious suggestion that the statute should be disallowed.

Unusually the Colonial Office, which had only recently assumed responsibility for the EAP,[42] did request reports on the operation of the law.[43] Although unfamiliar with the territory they appear never to have questioned the assumption – made throughout the empire – that colonized peoples must be made to work for Europeans. The common argument was that labour was required to ensure the economic and social development of the dependencies, but as Sydney Olivier was later to point out, the east African colonies had not been advertized "as countries in which the white man could take up his burden, but as profitable and delightful places of residence for young Englishmen with a little capital".[44] In 1908 the governor, J. Hayes Sadler, submitted reports on the operation of the law and admitted that although its main objects had been to ensure that employees understood their contractual obligations, did not undertake obligations which they did not fully understand, and were properly treated and paid, the administration of the law had not been to their advantage.[45] A. C. Hollis, secretary for native affairs, reported that " . . . magistrates, instead of using their discretionary powers, have frequently punished the servants summarily and sentenced them to be flogged, in which case the High Court cannot upset their decision".[46] He criticized the legality of three-year contracts and the payment of wages in kind; the "award" of three months' imprisonment for breach of contract; the lists of "major" and "minor" offences copied from the Transvaal ordinance; the addition of any period of imprisonment to the term of a contract; and the power given to magistrates to order workers to pay compensation for damage to property, with imprisonment in default. He particularly disliked the application of the law to children, and described cases of "small boys" employed to herd animals on one-year contracts with payment in arrears. "After eight or nine months", he observed, "the boys, who have no conception of time, think that their term of service is completed and then being dissatisfied either leave in disgust without their wages or steal what is really due to them with the result that they are prosecuted and imprisoned." He also reported deaths from starvation among workers returning home without rations at the end of a contract. Sadler, however, believed that instructions circulated by the principal judge now ensured that officials and magistrates understood their duties, and that any continuing problems arose primarily from the workers' ignorance of the law; they habitually deserted rather than taking their grievances to a magistrate. In 1867 the lord chancellor had stressed that revised English legislation must be made known to workers before its provisions could be fully used, but in East Africa Sadler saw no need to educate workers. Maladministration of the law persisted.

Revised EAP legislation submitted in 1909 was considered in London to be "a great advance"; a section on "care of servants" was "most useful for bringing to the notice of people who do not cease from troubling about native labour".[47] But officials disliked the increased penalty of imprisonment with hard labour for absence from work, and the reduction in fines imposed upon employers withholding wages. They did not, however, comment on the restriction of the ordinance to "Arab and Native" workers. Although earlier legislation was assumed to apply only to Africans, the formal classification in law of African workers as a special group underpinned claims that they could not be employed under more modern and equitable conditions developed for quite different peoples, and thus increased the difficulties in the years to come of reforming the law. We can imagine James Stephen's reaction given his 1840 statement, quoted above, that it was the distinction in law between Africans and Europeans that had led to so many evils.

In most West Indian dependencies in the mid-nineteenth century major or minor revisions of the laws were quickly made, although the Jamaican statute of 1841 remained unamended for a century. Particularly common were the allowance of long contracts and contracts entered into outside the colony in which the work was to be performed, and the limiting of compensation payable to employees. After the immediate post-emancipation period there was no guiding policy within the Colonial Office until the 1920s and 1930s, and legislation was allowed to develop piecemeal. Officials were generally confident that workers in British colonies were adequately safeguarded, but they remained alert to the potential dangers of allowing contracts for work outside the British empire. In 1878 and 1879 British West Indians were involved in labour riots in the Danish colony of St. Croix following the enactment of new labour law there, and 23 of them were sentenced to death, although subsequently reprieved following Foreign Office appeals to the Danish government.[48] The 23 came from Antigua, Trinidad, Jamaica, Barbados, St. Lucia and St. Kitts. In 1892 West Indian governors were asked to make foreign contracts unlawful, unless approved by a magistrate, in view of labour problems associated with the construction of the Panama canal, and three years later a similar request to west African governors stressed "there may be cases, such as that of the Congo Free State, where the labourers are ill-treated and the contracts are broken". In 1872, however, when a Royal Navy officer expressed concern about the "trafficking" of labour in west Africa, an official had admitted that government could not control the movement of labourers seeking improved prospects amongst the multinational interests of the coast. Although legislation to prevent migration or foreign recruitment was always presented as being for the protection of workers, it also restricted mobility. And in 1878 the British consul in Samoa complained that although the Pacific Islanders Protection Act dealt with recruitment, it did not regulate working conditions on estates owned by British subjects.

It was not until the second decade of the twentieth century that one of the sporadic criticisms of labour regulation reaching the Colonial Office informed policy. In October 1917 the governor of St. Kitts forwarded a letter from the St. Kitts Universal Benevolent Association (formerly the St. Kitts Trade and Labour Union but reconstituted following enactment of the Trade and Labour Unions Prohibition Ordinance of 1916) calling for repeal of master and servant legislation dating from 1849. "We feel", it stated, "that the Act has out-grown its usefulness, and should not be tolerated on the Statu[t]e Books of a civilized community, moreover it tends to keep our people in a state of serfdom that is detrimental to progress and British Policy."[49] Officials agreed with the governor that wartime circumstances allowed for no immediate action; they were doubtful that the association was devoting itself solely to the legitimate activities of a friendly society; and one went so far as to comment that the office should not "deal specially and in an isolated way with the St. Kitts Ordinance at the demands of disloyal agitators who are hampering recruiting and threatening violence".[50] But they knew that the Indian government had insisted on the removal of imprisonment as a penalty from various laws regulating Indian migrants and fully expected attacks on colonial labour law to increase. The establishment of the Ministry of Labour in 1916, and the ongoing advocacy for an international body, which was to culminate in the creation of the International Labour Organisation (ILO) in 1919, also warned Colonial Office ministers and officials that they could not enjoy sole authority indefinitely. So, after the war, West Indian governors were asked to reform laws by removing imprisonment as a penalty for breach of contract save in default of a fine, when it should not exceed one month (and the fine not exceed forty shillings), and ensuring that time was allowed for the payment of fines.[51]

The laws of Antigua, Dominica, Montserrat, St. Kitts, St. Lucia and St. Vincent were subsequently amended, although not necessarily in full. An Antigua act of 1922, for example, restricted fines but failed to allow time for payment. The governor of Barbados, whose predecessors had pressed for reform of the legislation in the 1870s and 1880s, claimed that the only penalty provided was the loss of one month's wages; in British Guiana and Trinidad partial implementation was agreed; Jamaica, which in addition to its 1841 act still had legislation in force dating from the reign of George III, promised to reform the law, but failed to do so. No further action was taken by the Colonial Office until 1927 when a Virgin Islands ordinance was disallowed, and the question of penal sanctions for breach of labour contracts in the West Indian colonies was reopened by an official who deprecated the lack of co-ordinated policy and advocated the use of civil law.[52] Dismissing objections from other colleagues, E. R. Darnley, head of the West Indian department, wrote: "It may be well not to push reforming zeal too far, but there are certain serious drawbacks about leaving on the Statute Books legislation reeking with the taint of slavery, and providing for insolence, misdemeanour, miscarriage, ill-behaviour and other obsolete and indefinable offences."[53] His words echo those of James Stephen who had stated in 1840 "much of the essence of slavery consisted, and must always consist, in the power of summary punishment for offences either wholly indefinite or defined merely by vague and general words".[54] Darnley spelt out required reforms and instigated an investigation of existing laws, ensuring that his staff examine statutes with care rather than unquestioningly accepting reports from colonial law officers. In 1930, for example, the Barbados claim that no penal sanctions remained was found to be incorrect; there were still provisions under which domestic servants could be imprisoned, with or without hard labour, and without the option of a fine, for such misdemeanours as "wilful negligence or improper conduct causing injury to property". Although taken from the 1837 model, they were no longer acceptable; in Darnley's words "Mary Jane" could be imprisoned for breaking the crockery. In Tanganyika, a League of Nations mandate, where legislation on the increasingly criticized Kenyan model had been introduced as late as 1924, similar provisions were used against workers who "allowed" monkeys and wild pigs to eat the tender new leaves of sisal plants.[55] Other unintended use of the law was reported: penalties for unauthorized absence from the workplace were frequently used against workers taking complaints to a magistrate, and in Northern Rhodesia workers dancing and playing music on their afternoon off were convicted of creating a "brawl or disturbance". Legislation designed to enforce individual contracts was also commonly used against group industrial action.

It is unlikely that Darnley's initiatives would have had wide influence within the Colonial Office whose geographical departments worked largely in isolation despite the nominal overall responsibility for labour issues remitted to the General Department. But in 1929 the newly appointed parliamentary under-secretary of state, Dr T. Drummond Shiels, demanded a general enquiry into the working of colonial master and servant law following receipt of James Maxton's complaint that such legislation constituted "a peculiar device for perpetuating the economic slavery of the people",[56] and amending legislation from North Borneo allowing corporal punishment for wilful breach of contract likely to "cause riot or danger to life or property".[57] Maxton was not the first Member of Parliament to complain; in 1919 Ben Spoor had suggested " . . . we will shortly need in this Empire of ours a new Wilberforce to combat the tendency towards what might be described by many people, not as ordinary working conditions, but as very real slavery".[58] By the late 1920s the Labour Party's Advisory Committee on Imperial Questions, chaired by Leonard Woolf, was formulating colonial labour policy, and the ILO was committed to a study of the use of long-term contracts enforced by penal sanctions. Organizations such as the Anti-Slavery and Aborigines Protection Society and the London Group on African Affairs lobbied the office, as did concerned individuals. In 1930 Shiels, with the reluctant agreement of the secretary of state,[59] asked governors to review labour conditions and the use of penal sanctions, and set up a Colonial Labour Committee (CLC).[60] Members agreed to look first at master and servant laws, which some felt "contain provisions which are relics of a stage of development almost approximating to slavery",[61] but widely differing local legislative provision was quickly revealed and it was decided that it was impossible to legislate uniformly for "(a) the more primitive peoples (e.g. those in Africa and the Western Pacific), and (b) the more civilized peoples (e.g. in Malaya and the West Indies)".[62] The laws of Africa (outside southern Africa which was now the responsibility of the Dominions Office) and the western Pacific should be examined first. This decision reversed Shiels's plan to start with the West Indies, where a considerable amount of groundwork had been done and progress seemed feasible, and may have been a deliberate attempt by officials to curb his enthusiasm.

Shiels's initiatives were short-lived. The CLC first met on 20 April 1931; the change of government in August of that year removed Shiels from office. Although recommendations for the abolition of penal sanctions in "the more primitive territories" were finalized and circulated to governors in January 1932, there was no pressure for implementation. The essentials of the recommendations were that existing powers of magistrates to arbitrate between employers and employed should be more widely used, officials should be appointed to represent workers, dismissal should be substituted for punishment in most minor cases, and offences such as wilful damage should be removed from labour law and dealt with under existing or revised criminal codes. Penal sanctions should be retained only for desertion by porters, guides and carers, which might endanger the employer or his family. Responses from west Africa were positive, but replies from governors in eastern and central Africa were delayed, negative and marked by arguments reflecting attitudes to the African worker and to "native mentality". It was variously claimed that the "moral education" of the African was not sufficiently advanced for him to understand the "sanctity" of a contract; that it was impossible to trace deserters or to recover damages from men with no property "except the clothes, if any, in which they stand"; that removal of penal sanctions from workers' contracts must be extended to employers, which would increase already widespread illegal punishment.[63] During the course of the committee's deliberations encouraging correspondence from Tanganyika had introduced members to a range of practical issues of which they might otherwise have been unaware, for example that desertion might be caused by offers of higher wages from other employers competing for scarce labour and that some employers avoided taking defaulting workers to a magistrate because of the distances – and thus expense – involved and favoured various methods of imposing their own discipline. Sir Donald Cameron, governor from 1925 to 1931, had encouraged officials to enquire into reasons for desertion and believed that labour regulation should be relaxed as a stable labour force emerged. He had secured amendment of the law by, *inter alia*, removing penal sanctions for workers entering into a second or subsequent contract with the same employer. J. F. N. Green, head of the Tanganyika Department, stressed that attractive conditions of employment had ensured a "minimum amount of trouble with workers", but that, "the retention of penal sanctions removed the incentive to a bad employer to improve the conditions under which his labourers work".[64] Cameron's successor, however, believed "there is little to be gained by raising questions of general principle which are apt to result in vague discussions and to excite controversy in the Legislative Council and press. Penal sanctions for breaches of contract are merely an expedient designed to meet the particular conditions existing in primitive countries . . . ".[65]

Despite the opinions of men such as Shiels, Cameron and Green the belief that "primitive" workers required more stringent regulation than their counterparts in more "advanced" colonial economies was still strongly held both in Africa and in the Colonial Office. It contrasts rather strangely with the conviction of James Stephen and his political masters that newly emancipated West Indian workers should be treated more leniently than their English counterparts. And despite the agreement within the office by 1931 that workers in the West Indies and Malaya were now "advanced", employers and officials in those regions would not necessarily have agreed. In 1936 the attorney general of British Honduras claimed: "It is extremely doubtful whether the majority of workers of this Colony can be said to be sufficiently evolved to understand the binding nature of contracts" – to which an official in London irritably responded, "I do not think the A.G. is 'sufficiently evolved' to appreciate the difference between civil contract and criminal law."[66] Such arguments fostered the assumption that employers wanted experienced staff; some did, but very many preferred a regular turnover of cheap, inexperienced labourers who did not know their rights and could easily be dismissed. Reading between the lines of the many statements on the subject it seems that the real distinction was between workers totally dependent on wage labour and those whose subsistence was guaranteed by a traditional socio–economic structure and who worked only to meet a short-term need. This was occasionally spelled out by colonial officials, for example by the acting secretary for native affairs in Fiji who stressed that there was no necessity for any Fijian to work for wages, but that "even a partial failure of the industries of this Colony would result in the abandonment of many of the measures taken by the Government to promote the health and welfare of the Fijians".[67]

Darnley had put his attempts to reform Caribbean law on hold while he waited for the outcome of the CLC's work, and he left the West Indian Department during 1931. No co-ordinated policy had been agreed and the General Department pushed work back to the geographical departments to be dealt with on a piecemeal basis. But in 1935 the ILO's Committee of Experts on Native Labour recommended the immediate abolition of penal sanctions to enforce labour contracts, and early the following year, when another MP described the Antigua legislation as "a hopelessly out-of-date law, only made use of by scoundrels",[68] R. V. Vernon, who had supported Shiels's initiatives, warned that "pretexts" for postponing reform must end: "These provisions in West Indian laws treating breaches of contracts as penal offences are of course an inheritance from the period immediately following the abolition of slavery. They are absolutely out of date now; cannot possibly be justified by the British Government at Geneva; and I think it is time to tell the West Indies to get rid of them once and for all . . . ".[69] Strikes on the Northern Rhodesian copperbelt in 1935 and disturbances in Trinidad two years later drew more attention to the lack of any coordinated labour policy, and during a 1937 Commons debate Arthur Creech Jones, Labour's principal spokesman on colonial affairs, complained about a new Kenya resident labour ordinance, noting "this system of labour servitude carries with it penal sanctions . . . We are following in this respect the wretched practice instituted in South Africa and Southern Rhodesia."[70] Taking advantage of this climate of opinion Vernon drafted a circular stressing the desirability of improvements in labour supervision, workmen's compensation, trade union recognition, minimum wage legislation, and the position of "the more lowly paid workers", and reminded governors that contracts and penal sanctions were soon to be discussed by the ILO.[71]

In late 1937 a tabled Commons motion urged the creation of a labour department within the Colonial Office,[72] a demand soon echoed by the Trades Union Congress and the West India Royal Commission. Many officials were appalled by the suggestion, and even more appalled when their secretary of state discussed the related issue of the appointment of a labour adviser with R. A. Butler, then parliamentary secretary at the Ministry of Labour. One expressed his "lurking suspicion that there are certain people in the Ministry of Labour who would rather like to see their department take an active part in questions relating to labour policy in the Empire".[73] Eventually a compromise was reached; a labour adviser was appointed in 1938, and a Social Services Department, responsible *inter alia* for labour matters, established the following year. The decision to appoint Major G. St. J. Orde Browne as labour adviser was taken with little enthusiasm, but there were few people with relevant experience and the salary approved by the Treasury was not generous. Orde Browne had been a labour officer in Tanganyika, and a member of the ILO's Committee of Experts on Native Labour, but there was doubt as to his suitability and unexplained concerns that "he [was] committed to a particular point of view". In fact, in 1934 he had apologized to the ILO if his statements on penal sanctions seemed "obstinate and reactionary", but stressed: "It is so very simple to be really up-to-date and progressive, and abolish penal sanctions with a fine gesture, and then substitute Vagrancy Acts, Pass Laws and all sorts of other ingenious schemes for bedevilling the unsophisticated savage who then finds himself the prey of a crowd of unscrupulous lawyers, in addition to his other oppressors."[74] He was not an obvious ally for the more "progressive" element within the Colonial Office.

In the meantime officials in London had been forced by increasing pressure from the ILO and mounting criticism at home to examine the empire-wide use of contracts of employment enforced by penal sanctions. Only then did they discover the extent to which a law described by the ILO as a "relic of slavery" was retained, and became aware of the existence of comparable provisions within legislation other than master and servant. For example, the Bermuda Poor Relief Act of 1834 provided that a worker failing to fulfil his contract might be imprisoned, municipal bylaws were operative in Georgetown, Guiana,[75] and in many dependencies pre-emancipation statutes remained unrepealed and in use. They also finally accepted that although the British government was responsible for the application of international conventions to dependent territories, they were often powerless to insist on amendment of colonial laws. The office, represented when appropriate on the British government delegation to International Labour Conferences, consequently delayed action by securing agreement that an initial convention, on written contracts only, should exclude the abolition of penal sanctions. It was not until 1939 that the Penal Sanctions (Indigenous Workers) Convention (No. 65) was finally agreed. It called for the abolition of penal sanctions, but for a limited range of offences only: refusal or failure of the worker to commence or perform the service stipulated in the contract; neglect of duty or lack of diligence; absence without permission or valid reason; and desertion. Application of the convention would thus allow retention within labour law of criminal penalties for such offences as drunkenness, abusive or insulting language, using an employer's property without permission, damage, loss or serious risk to the employer's property, failure to report the death or loss of an animal and the raft of other offences denounced by Stephen and Darnley as vague and indefinable. Furthermore it demanded immediate abolition only for juveniles; for adults it required only "progressive" abolition and imposed no time limits.

The convention could not come into effect until it was ratified by two member states. The timing could not have been more unfortunate; Harold Macmillan, as parliamentary under-secretary, objected to British ratification, commenting: "What other country is likely to ratify in existing circumstances? In the present state of the world, the whole thing seems to me rather unreal."[76] But Ernest Bevin and the previous secretary of state for the colonies, Lord Moyne, had already informed Parliament that Britain would ratify the convention, and this was done in January 1943. As Macmillan had predicted, no other state ratified in wartime; New Zealand became the second signatory in June 1948.

Ratification was one thing; application another. Governors had been asked to consider application as early as August 1939, but responses were generally negative and officials in London forecast that application would be impossible in Kenya, Northern Rhodesia, Nyasaland, Somaliland, Tanganyika, Uganda, Zanzibar, Sierra Leone, the Seychelles, British Honduras, Jamaica, Fiji, the British Solomon Islands, the Gilbert and Ellice Islands and Tonga, and unlikely in another thirteen dependencies. Despite the efforts of Colonial Office officials, and particularly the enthusiastic J. G. Hibbert, little progress could be made, although penalties for juvenile workers were removed in some colonies. At the same time the realities of war imposed other measures under emergency legislation which did not need Colonial Office approval, particularly conscription of civilian workers (in effect forced labour), closer regulation of workers in essential services, and the outlawing of strikes and lockouts.[77] In 1946 the ILO drew attention to the danger of wartime measures being extended unjustifiably, as they had been after the First World War.[78] Arthur Creech Jones, now secretary of state, confirmed that the abolition of penal sanctions remained office policy, but they were still firmly in place in many territories. In Africa both employers and officials seemed to be particularly anxious to retain criminal penalties for use of abusive language. In 1945 a Kenya labour commissioner claimed that abusive language to female employers amounted almost to "common assault",[79] and in 1948 a United Nations visiting mission to Tanganyika was told, "the African command of satire and bitter invective transcends the comprehension of Europeans who have never been exposed to it".[80] There was also a rather curious determination to retain imprisonment; curious given the repeated claims that indigenous people cared nothing for a prison sentence since it carried no social stigma.

In 1951 the ILO found that although the 1939 convention had still been ratified only by the United Kingdom and New Zealand, Britain was far from being the leader. No penal sanctions for the limited range of offences specified in the convention now existed in French, Dutch, Italian, New Zealand or United States dependencies, and Australia was making progress in Papua New Guinea. They persisted in Kenya, Tanganyika, Zanzibar, Northern and Southern Rhodesia, Basutoland, Bechuanaland and Swaziland. West Indian colonies had, in general, amended their laws with only British Honduras retaining criminal penalties for desertion.[81]

A second penal sanctions convention, adopted in 1955, required total abolition of sanctions for the types of breach of contract specified in the 1939 convention within one year of the date of ratification by each member state. Knowing the impossibility of implementation, the Colonial Office – now with the support of the Ministry of Labour – advised the Cabinet against British ratification. Given the rapid movement towards decolonization the issue had also become largely academic; the convention was never ratified by the UK. Thus as late as 1974 an economist found that the majority of Rhodesian African workers were still controlled by a law hardly changed from the Cape model of 1856. He noted:

> So pervasive are the provisions, so stringent are their restraints on the employee and so heavily balanced in favour of the employer, that one can only surmise that the original architects of the legislation anticipated either the need to control considerable labour unrest, or sought to give legal ratification to an unequal bargain of employment struck between contractees whose political, social and economic status was inherently unequal.[82]

A proactive role in the introduction and development of colonial labour legislation was demonstrated by Colonial Office ministers and officials only in very particular circumstances: in the case of newly acquired British possessions; in support of emancipation schemes; and in response to international demands. Sporadic attempts by individuals to push reform of the law on to the agenda were short-lived as senior officials adopted a *laissez-faire* attitude, relied on inappropriate precedents, and made no attempt to take on the admittedly powerful colonial legislatures. Although James Stephen had complained in 1840 that "among all the duties which are to be discharged here, the most unwelcome has always been that of revising our Colonial Legislature . . . such a mass of uninteresting detail it would be difficult to bring together from any other quarter",[83] his meticulous work ensured a level of personal knowledge that was unequalled thereafter. By the 1930s the "mass of detail" had increased exponentially and although officials examined statutes they had little understanding of their operation, the development of case law, the attitudes of employers who often valued "vague" terms that could be manipulated to their advantage, or the extent to which remnants of former legislation – for example Roman Dutch law or the Indian codes initially applied in East Africa – remained in use.[84] Their resentment of any outside criticism and reliance on reports from colonial governors and legislatures blinded them to alternative and readily available expert knowledge until it was much too late to effect change.

Notes

1 Throughout this chapter the term "Colonial Office" is used to describe a government department which during the first half of the nineteenth

century was more properly known as the War and Colonial Department. The two functions of this department passed in 1854 to the newly-established War Office and Colonial Office. In 1907 the operational work of the Colonial Office was divided between a Crown Colonies Division and a Dominions Division, and the split was formalised in 1925 when the Dominions Office was set up. The Colonial Office then lost its responsibilities for, *inter alia*, South Africa, Southern Rhodesia, Basutoland, Bechuanaland and Swaziland.

2   The National Archives (TNA), CO 854/2, Lord Glenelg, circular despt., 6 Nov. 1837.

3   William A. Green, *British Slave Emancipation: The Sugar Colonies and the Great Experiment 1830–1865* (Oxford: OUP, 1976), p. 164.

4   Professor Sir Otto Kahn-Freund, "Blackstone's Neglected Child: the Contract of Employment", *The Law Quarterly Review*, vol. 93 (Oct. 1977), pp. 508–28.

5   For detailed background and case studies see Douglas Hay and Paul Craven (eds.), *Masters, Servants and Magistrates in Britain and the Empire, 1562–1955* (University of North Carolina Press, Chapel Hill and London: University of North Carolina Press, 2004).

6   Ibid., p. 23.

7   Joan Lane, *Apprenticeship in England, 1600–1914* (London: Routledge, 1996), p. 1.

8   The distinction is important; an African seized or purchased on the coast of Africa, and confined to a slave ship, was not – yet – a slave, but the act also covered people already enslaved who were illegally trafficked from place to place.

9   The 1807 act was set against the backdrop of the Napoleonic wars; slaves transported in enemy vessels, or employed as seamen or marines, were considered "prize" in the same way as other property and cargo.

10   47 Geo. III cap. 36, section 10, repeated in Order in Council, 16 March 1808 (in CO 854/1, ff. 16–17).

11   The Abolition of the Slave Trade Act (47 Geo III cap 36), section xvi.

12   The commissioners interviewed "apprentices", their masters and mistresses and local officials. Detailed manuscript reports are held at TNA (CO 318/81-98) and were printed for Parliament.

13   Anthony J. Barker, *Slavery and Antislavery in Mauritius, 1810–1833* (London: Macmillan, 1996), p. 41.

14   See for example: William L. Burn, *Emancipation and Apprenticeship in the British West Indies* (London: Jonathan Cape, London, 1937); Green, *British Slave Emancipation*; D. G. Hall, "The Apprenticeship System in Jamaica, 1834–1838", *Apprenticeship and Emancipation* (Mona, Jamaica: University of the West Indies, 1980), ed. Rex Nettleford; Roderick A. McDonald (ed.), *Between Slavery and Freedom: Special Magistrate John Anderson's Journal of St. Vincent during the Apprenticeship* (Philadelphia: University of Pennsylvania Press, 2001); Mary Turner, "The British Caribbean, 1823–1838", Hay and Craven, *Masters, Servants and Magistrates*.

15   Initially until August 1840 for praedial labourers, and August 1838 for non-

praedials, but in fact terminated for all in 1838.

16   3 & 4 Wm. IV, Cap. LXXIII, An Act for the Abolition of Slavery throughout the British Colonies; for promoting the Industry of the manumitted Slaves; and for compensating the Persons hitherto entitled to the Services of such Slaves, section xvi.

17   CO 28/113/65, Sir Lionel Smith to secretary of state, 25 Aug. 1834; CO 28/114/2, 8 Sept. 1934; CO 28/114/7, 30 Sept. 1834; CO 28/114/10, 1 Oct. 1834; CO 28/115/24, 28 Mar. 1835.

18   CO 28/118/36, Evan Murray John McGregor to secretary of state, 31 Dec. 1836; CO 119/52, 1 May 1837; CO 28/119/56, 9 May 1837; CO 28/119/78, 12 June 1837.

19   In Jamaica only nine free children who had been under the age of six on 1 August 1834 were allowed by their mothers to apprentice themselves. Hall, "Apprenticeship System", p. 12.

20   Turner, "The British Caribbean", p. 320.

21   Order in Council relating to Contracts of Service, 7 Sept. 1838, chapter iv, section 7.

22   CO 323/54, James Stephen to Lord John Russell, 23 Oct. 1839.

23   CO 323/55, James Stephen to Lord Normanby, 13 July 1840.

24   CO 323/55, Stephen to Russell, 11 April 1840.

25   CO 323/57, Stephen to Hope, 30 Dec. 1842.

26   CO 323/55, Stephen report on Tobago "Act to amend an Act entituled 'An Act for the adjusting and recovery of the wages of Servants in Husbandry, and of Artificers, Handicraftsmen and other Servants . . . '".

27   D. B. Swinfen, *Imperial Control of Colonial Legislation 1813–1865: A study of British Policy towards Colonial Legislative Powers* (Oxford: OUP, 1970), p. 30.

28   CO 323/86, F. Rogers, report on the Gambia Ordinance for the better regulation of artisans, sailors, labourers, and other servants, 21 Sept. 1858.

29   John M. MacKenzie, "Empire and Metropolitan Cultures", *The Oxford History of the British Empire,* vol. iii, *The Nineteenth Century* (Oxford: OUP, 1999), ed. A. N. Porter, pp. 270–93.

30   CO 323/40, report on Sierra Leone ordinances of 1816, 11 July 1817.

31   CO 96/115, report on the working of the Slave Emancipation Scheme, 6 Mar. 1875.

32   CO 96/122, R. Meade minute, 3 Feb. 1878.

33   M. K. Banton, "The Colonial Office, 1820–1955", Hay & Craven, *Masters, Servants and Magistrates*, pp. 268–9. For an examination of emancipation in the Gold Coast see Kwabena Opare-Akurang, "The Administration of the Abolition Laws, African Responses and Post-Proclamation Slavery in the Gold Coast, 1874–1940", *Slavery and Abolition*, vol. 19, no., 2 (1998), pp. 149–66.

34   An assistant junior clerk had forwarded a package of Cape acts to the library rather than referring them to his superiors for review. The Cape had achieved responsible government in 1853 and was no longer required to submit draft legislation to London prior to enactment. The secretary of state did, however, retain power of disallowance.

35   Banton, "The Colonial Office", p. 264.

36 Jeff Crisp, *The Story of an African Working Class: Ghanaian Miners' Struggles, 1870–1980* (London: Zed Books, 1984). Roger G. Thomas, "Forced Labour in British West Africa: the Case of the Northern Territories of the Gold Coast", *Journal of African History*, vol. 14, no. 1 (1973), pp. 79–103.

37 CO 96/513, Harcourt minute, 21 Feb. 1911.

38 CO 96/513, W. D. Ellis minute, 24 July 1911.

39 See Peter Richardson, *Chinese Mine Labour in the Transvaal* (London: Macmillan, 1982).

40 Anthony Clayton and Donald C. Savage, *Government and Labour in Kenya 1895–1963* (London: Frank Cass, 1974), p. 32. Formerly the Farmers' and Planters' Association, founded in 1903, the Colonists' Association was renamed and opened to other Europeans in 1904.

41 CO 533/16, H. J. Read minute, 12 October 1906.

42 An Anglo-German agreement of 1886 designated the area which was to become the EAP as part of a British sphere of influence: it was administered by the Imperial British East Africa Company from 1891 to 1895 when the Foreign Office assumed responsibility.

43 Reports on the administration of the Cape act of 1841 had been requested, but neither provided nor chased.

44 Sydney Olivier, *White Capital and Coloured Labour* (London: The Hogarth Press, 1929), p. 21.

45 CO 533/42, Sadler despt., 25 March 1908.

46 Ibid., "Report of Secretary for Native Affairs on the working of the Master and Servants Ordinance", 22 Oct. 1907.

47 CO 533/62, A.C.C. Parkinson minute, 3 Dec. 1909.

48 Correspondence in CO 318/273 and 274, and in various Foreign Office files including FO 22/435.

49 CO 152/356.

50 Ibid., G. Grindle minute, 1917.

51 CO 152/364, despt. to West Indies governors, 26 Sept. 1919.

52 CO 152/403/13, Sydney Caine minute, 29 June 1927.

53 CO 318/393/10, E. R. Darnley minute, 27 June 1928.

54 CO 323/51, Stephen to Lord Aberdeen, 16 Mar. 1835.

55 Anso Tambila, "A History of the Tanga Sisal Labour Force, 1936–1964", MA dissertation, Dar es Salaam, 1974.

56 CO 318/396/12, James Maxton MP to Lord Passfield, 24 Nov. 1929.

57 British North Borneo Ordinance No. 2 of 1929.

58 Parliamentary Debates, Commons, vol. 118, col. 2197.

59 The secretary of state was Lord Passfield, the former Sidney Webb. Many years later Leonard Woolf wrote, "Sidney was in politics curiously ambivalent . . . He was a progressive, even a revolutionary in some economic and social spheres; where the British Empire was concerned, he was a common or garden imperialist conservative". *Downhill all the Way: An Autobiography of the Years 1919 to 1939* (Oxford: OUP, 1980), p. 363.

60 Primarily an internal committee it included representatives of the Ministry of Labour and the Factories Department of the Home Office. Shiels also pressed for the inclusion of the general secretary of the Trades Union

Congress, a suggestion which alarmed even the most sympathetic officials and was dropped. External members did not attend after Shiels's departure from the office.

61 CO 323/1117/5, Shiels minute, 20 April 1931.

62 CO 888/1, CLC 4, Caine's paper on indentured labour, 19 Jan. 1931.

63 CO 323/1209/14, despts. from governors, 1932. It was not until 1952 that an official pointed out that, logically, if a deserter could not be traced neither could he be taken to court. CO 859/345, Sheila Ann Ogilvie minute, 19 Aug. 1952.

64 CO 323/1117/7, CLC minutes (5), 26 June 1931.

65 CO 323/1209/15, D. Jardine despt, 1 Mar. 1933.

66 CO 318/423/6, Vernon minute. 22 Dec. 1936.

67 CO 323/1117/6, CLC (22).

68 Ibid., report of meeting between Susan Lawrence MP and Sir Cosmo Parkinson, nd.

69 Ibid., Vernon minute, 24 April 1936.

70 Hansard, Commons, vol. 324, col. 1057–8.

71 CO 888/1, CLC 30, draft circular despt.

72 CO 866/29/1166, Pethick Lawrence motion, 8 Dec. 1937.

73 Ibid., Hibbert minute, 2 Feb. 1938.

74 Bodleian Library of Commonwealth and African Studies, Rhodes House, Oxford, Orde Browne Papers, Box 5/2, f. 26, Orde Browne to Weaver, 11 May 1934. Orde Browne's other viewpoints are spelled out in his monograph *The African Labourer* (London: Frank Cass, 1967).

75 Juanita de Barros, "Urban British Guiana, 1838–1924: Wharf Rats, Centipedes and Pork Knockers", Hay and Craven, *Masters, Servants and Magistrates*, pp. 323–37.

76 CO 859/52/4, Macmillan minute, 24 Feb. 1942.

77 M. K. Banton, "Colonial Office supervision of the introduction and revision of labour legislation in British Africa", PhD thesis, London, 1993.

78 For example in Kenya where penalties were increased, regulations concerning recruitment relaxed, and desertion made a cognisable offence. None of these revisions were withdrawn after the war and thus influenced the Tanganyika law introduced in the 1920s.

79 Kenya National Archives, L. Leg 1/15, labour commissioner to chief secretary, 4 December 1945.

80 CO 888/6, CLAC(49)19, "T.T. Government Comments on the Report of the U.N. Visiting Mission, 1948".

81 International Labour Organisation, *Labour Policies in the West Indies* (Geneva, 1952).

82 D. G. Clarke, *Domestic Workers in Rhodesia: The Economics of Masters and Servants* (Mambo Press: Salisbury, 1974).

83 Quoted in Swinfen, *Imperial Control*, p. 3.

84 In 1962 a Colonial Office official noted that he had no reference books on Roman Dutch law "which is the 'common law' of South Africa, Southern Rhodesia and the High Commission territories" and sought advice from the Institute of Advanced Legal Studies, University of London. CO 1048/271.

CHAPTER EIGHT

The Foreign Office and Forced Labour in Portuguese West Africa, 1894–1914

GLYN STONE

Before the First World War the subject of slavery and forced labour in Portuguese west Africa , notably in the islands of São Tomé and Príncipe[1] located in the gulf of Guinea close to the equator, attracted the attention of contemporary anti-slave campaigners and writers such as Henry Nevinson, the Reverend Charles Swan, John Harris, William Cadbury and Joseph Burtt.[2] Much later, historians of Portuguese colonialism such as Richard Hammond, James Duffy and William Gervase Clarence-Smith focused their attention in the late 1950s, 1960s and 1970s on slavery and forced labour in the Portuguese empire with a largely Portuguese perspective.[3] James Duffy, in particular, concentrated on slavery and forced labour in Portuguese west Africa in the nineteenth and early twentieth centuries in his book, *A Question of Slavery*, published in 1967, in which he paid some attention to the role of the Foreign Office, in particular the consular officials, as well as the British anti-slavery movement.[4] Nothing substantial has appeared since in English and after a forty year gap this current study aims to supplement and complement Duffy's research by a focused examination of successive foreign secretaries – Lord Kimberley, Lord Salisbury, Lord Lansdowne and Sir Edward Grey – and their officials and diplomats with regard to the prevalence and continuation of slavery and forced labour in Portuguese west Africa between 1894 and 1914.

The slave trade in Portugal was abolished in 1836, almost thirty years after Britain. In 1869 the children of slaves were declared free, and slavery was abolished officially in the Portuguese empire in 1876. Under the Anglo-Portuguese treaty of February 1884 both countries bound themselves "to use all possible means for the purpose of finally extinguishing slavery and the Slave Trade on the eastern and western coasts of Africa" and in 1890 Portugal, along with Britain, was one of seventeen countries which signed the Brussels general act for the repression of the African slave trade.[5] Yet, contrary to these agreements, the cocoa boom based on the plantations of São Tomé and Príncipe, which had commenced in the late 1880s and was to last well into the twentieth century, had already resulted in a considerable increase in the export of *serviçaes*, forced labourers. Indeed, between 1887 and 1897 the export of *serviçaes* averaged 2,500 a year and 4,000 a year during the ensuing decade.[6] According to Clarence-Smith, some 70,000 Africans were purchased for perpetual indenture in São Tomé and Príncipe between 1880 and 1908, most of whom came through Angolan ports from "a huge expanse of Central Africa", although a few were also imported from Dahomey, Gabon and China.[7]

The tendency of Portugal to sign treaties and then to avoid their consequences was not unfamiliar to the Foreign Office, but before 1894 it had for several years been disinclined to pursue the continuing existence of slavery in Portuguese west Africa, having been involved in controversial disputes concerning the boundaries between British and Portuguese territories across southern Africa. However, in 1894 in response to a question made in the House of Commons by Joseph Pease MP, and information subsequently provided by a retired Royal Navy captain, Algernon Littleton, the minister of state for foreign affairs, Sir Edward Grey, instituted an enquiry at Luanda in Portuguese Angola.[8] In his letter Littleton had claimed that while slavery had been abolished in Portuguese Africa it had been replaced by a system of contracted labour that was tantamount to slavery.

At the end of August William Brock, merchant and acting consul at Luanda, dismissed such claims pointing out that the essential difference between slavery and contracted labour was that "whereas the former is slavery pure and simple, the latter is hired labour under government supervision". To assume that they were one in the same was "to try to fit facts to a theory and to prejudice a good cause by taking for granted what is, to a great extent, hearsay". The *serviçaes* were, according to Brock, "well treated and cared for" and there was "no hardship in the way they are worked". He added that it was certain that the abolition of the present system would mean "absolute ruin to the island of San Thomé".[9] Brock's assessment, however, was not shared by the consul at Luanda, William Clayton Pickersgill, a former agent of the London Missionary Society. Based on his experience and contacts, he insisted that the system of contract labour in Portuguese west Africa was "simply a form of Slave Trade, however well the so-called immigrants may be treated on arrival: since it is evident that the process of collecting migrants directly encourages native chiefs to make wars and take prisoners whom they can dispose of at a profit".[10] In the Foreign Office it was recalled that the subject had previously been a constant source of correspondence with the Portuguese government and of publication in parliamentary Blue Books but also that slavery was nominally abolished in the Portuguese colonies. In January 1895, in discussing whether the government should intervene with the Portuguese authorities, the permanent under-secretary, Sir Thomas Sanderson, thought that "for the present we had better leave it alone" as did the Liberal foreign secretary, Lord Kimberley, who thought it "a very old difficulty".[11]

The matter was dismissed by the Foreign Office for two years until in March 1897 Pickersgill made a further critical report on labour conditions in São Tomé. According to the consul, the *serviçal's* fate was to be "taken from his home in the distant interior as a slave; as a slave he is purchased by white men for the labour market; the contract by which he is supposed to engage to work out his redemption is a sham; and he is kept in servitude to the end of his days". He could see no reason why the Portuguese government should not reform the system by forbidding further importations of *serviçaes* and by liberating gradually those who were already on the islands. However, the Foreign Office thought differently, recalling that when the subject was brought up in 1894 it was decided to take no notice and that decision still stood. Francis Bertie, superintending under-secretary to the African Department, insisted that it be left alone while the Conservative prime minister and foreign secretary, Lord Salisbury, in noting his comment, did not dissent.[12]

Five more years elapsed before the subject was again discussed in the Foreign Office in June 1902. On this occasion it was the claims of the Aborigines' Protection Society which compelled interest. The society drew attention to the "systems of slavery, under the name of forced labour, in operation in Angola" which, it claimed, was increasing alarmingly both in extent and severity and in violation of the provisions of the 6th and 9th articles of the Berlin general act of 1885.[13] Roger Casement, consul at Gomba in the Congo Free State, subsequently confirmed that the society's claims were "very largely borne out by fact", that the "so called contract labour existing in Angola whether it be for internal use or export to the islands of San Thomé and Principé is nothing else but a system of slavery having the sanction of legal forms". He insisted that "not one single native of the many thousand shipped to the cocoa plantations in San Thomé and Principé had been known to return to Angola".[14] The Foreign Office accepted that in Portuguese west Africa recruited labour were never released and never paid and that a *serviçal's* children were considered as "indentured labourers". Casement's report confirmed what was already known, that "the slave trade still exists in West Africa".[15] Further confirmation that repatriation was non-existent was received from Consul Arthur Nightingale at Luanda in January 1903 when he advised that contracts lasted for five years but that up to the present time the conditions had never been adhered to because of the assumption that "once a slave always a slave".[16]

Aware of the increasing criticism of their labour system in west Africa the Portuguese government issued a new decree on 29 January 1903 which purported to reform it. The British minister in Lisbon, Sir Martin Gosselin, confirmed that despite its elaborate provision for securing contracted labourers from Mozambique, Macão, Guinea and elsewhere the main source would continue to be Angola. Moreover, while article 58 of the decree laid down a "labour and repatriation fund" to be established in São Tomé and Príncipe under government control into which would be paid bonus funds destined for the *serviçaes*, it was to be feared that "the planters, in the future as in the past, will do their best to prevent repatriation" and unless a competent Portuguese officer was appointed with sufficient power there would be no repatriation.[17]

At this time, the Foreign Office was being pressed by the British and Foreign Anti-Slavery Society and by cocoa manufacturers, notably Cadbury of Birmingham and Fry of Bristol, to appoint a resident or agent to look after the interests of the labourers in São Tomé and Príncipe.[18] The officials in the Office realized that the task of persuading the Portuguese government to improve the condition and treatment of *serviçaes* would be difficult to say the least as the response of the Portuguese to the British and Foreign Anti-Slavery Society in February 1903 demonstrated. Allegations of the existence of slavery in Portuguese west Africa were refuted, the existing vigilance of the Portuguese authorities in west Africa stressed and the clear insistence made that the slave trade had been completely suppressed and now only existed "in the imagination of certain philanthropists".[19] The position, however, became more pressing with the news, communicated by Nightingale in May 1903, that the Portuguese authorities were taking advantage of prolonged drought in the Cape Verde islands to ship some inhabitants to São Tomé and Príncipe as *serviçaes*, 800 so far. Nightingale who had just arrived in Lisbon from the islands told Gosselin that "these unfortunate people reduced to the last state of want" could not possibly survive the climate of the equatorial islands and would inevitably succumb.[20] In these circumstances, the foreign secretary, Lord Lansdowne, warned the Portuguese minister at London, Marquis Luís de Soveral, that although no British subjects were involved and there was no direct ground for interference it was quite possible that the issue could be taken up in the British press and Parliament and an attempt made to create a feeling against Portugal similar to that aroused against the Congo Free State. He suggested that the Portuguese government might institute a formal enquiry both as to recruitment and treatment of labourers and to give Nightingale every facility on the occasions when he visited the islands.

Soveral confirmed that he would refer the suggestion of an enquiry to his government but he assured Lansdowne that the islands were "extremely rich and the climate conditions were upon the whole good".[21] The Portuguese government took the hint and suspended the shipment of labourers from Angola to São Tomé but "certain wealthy and influential people at Lisbon, owners of estates on San Thomé", according to Soveral, protested vigorously and attacked the authorities and as a result the export of labourers was resumed.[22]

For almost twelve months after Lansdowne's meeting with Soveral there was no sign of a formal enquiry but then in mid April 1904 it was announced that Dr Carlos Vaz, a medical officer, had been appointed by the governor-general of Angola, Custódio Borja, "to conduct enquiries and collect information as to the manner in which the emigration of natives was carried out, to report monthly and to communicate all cases of abuse and irregularity".[23] At the same time, Nightingale, who had yet to visit São Tomé and Príncipe, sent a despatch from Boma in the Congo which was highly critical of the Portuguese decree of 29 January 1903, regarding it as merely another elaborate set of regulations which like others before it did little or nothing to safeguard the interests of the *serviçaes*: "these elaborate decrees are nothing but a cloak to slave traffic".[24] The news of the death of Carlos Vaz in July 1904 without the announcement of a successor[25] served to further undermine Foreign Office confidence in Portuguese rule in west Africa. But there was still indecision as to whether to intervene at Lisbon and following further discussion in October 1904 it was agreed to defer any decision to intervene until Brock finally delivered his report and Nightingale had visited the islands.[26]

When, in January 1905, Borja gave prominence to the exportation of labour from Angola in his farewell speech as governor-general, Gosselin interpreted this as a sign that the Portuguese authorities were at last endeavouring to remedy the most flagrant abuses in the labour system and the African Department at the Foreign Office sought credit for this apparent change: "The Portuguese are waking up with regard to this Angolan slave trade. The various communications made to M. de Soveral have no doubt contributed to this".[27] In reality, there was little in the way of improvement, but the illusion that matters were improving in Angola was sustained by Brock's report at the end of June. This confirmed that the slave trade still existed but was falling into discredit; that the principal sources of supply were families whose members were sold by kinsmen under native laws generally for debt or for claims for damage arising out of tribal warfare; that raiding was diminishing; and that the Portuguese government was trying to stop it and would eventually succeed.[28] Brock, however, had not fulfilled his instructions to report on the effects of the decree of 29 January 1903 and with pressure being exerted by the Aborigines' Protection Society in the summer of 1905 the Foreign Office still lacked first hand reliable knowledge of the state of affairs in Portuguese west Africa and were therefore compelled to temporize, while Lansdowne turned down a request from the society to receive a deputation, pleading the number of engagements and pressure on his time.[29] Belatedly, and clearly not before time, Nightingale was reposted to Luanda as consul in autumn 1905 and instructed "to obtain full and reliable information in regard to the actual conditions of the labourers" by a visit to São Tomé and Príncipe.[30]

Nightingale commenced his visit to the islands on 24 November 1905 and remained there until 9 February 1906 and his report was completed in July and received in the Foreign Office on 20 August. Almost simultaneously, between August 1905 and February 1906 the well known campaigning British journalist, Henry Woods Nevinson, sometimes described by his critics, including the Portuguese and some officials in the Foreign Office, as a trouble-maker, international carpetbagger or hired hand for anti-slavery forces, wrote a series of monthly articles in *Harper's Magazine* which were subsequently reproduced in his book *A Modern Slavery,* published later in 1906. Nevinson's account of the traffic in contract labour from Angola to São Tomé, witnessed first hand, aroused international indignation and criticism of Portuguese colonial rule in west Africa which ignited the issue both in Britain and abroad.[31] The impact was immediate and following a visit to the Foreign Office by Nevinson and Henry Richard Fox-Bourne, secretary of the Aborigines' Protection Society, Sir Eric Barrington, superintending under-secretary to the African Department, was compelled to warn Soveral on 14 March that "the philanthropists were much excited and it would be very disagreeable if public opinion were aroused by the fact that the Portuguese Government were encouraging something painfully akin to the slave trade".[32] While awaiting the Nightingale Report, the Foreign Office were compelled to temporize anti-slavery pressure groups and MPs in the House of Commons who had commenced in July 1906 a concerted approach through parliamentary questions on the issue of labour in Portuguese west Africa that was to last through to 1914. In response to a question by Liberal MP Sir Gilbert Parker on 5 July as to what steps the government intended to take "to direct the attention of the Portuguese Government" to the alleged practices of slavery in São Tomé and Príncipe, the Liberal foreign secretary, Sir Edward Grey, who had succeeded Lansdowne at the end of 1905, referred to Nightingale's visit and to his expected report and he reiterated this again on 18 July.[33] On 30 July Fox Bourne wrote to Grey urging the Foreign Office to make representations to the Portuguese government to take effective measures to prevent the abuses which "were thought to have been put a stop to many years ago, but which, under specious disguises, have been more harmful than ever since the Slave Trade Conference of 1889–1890".[34]

Before Nightingale's report arrived at the Foreign Office news was received via the Admiralty of a visit to Príncipe on 17 June 1906 by the commanding officer of *HMS Dwarf* who reported: "The natives I saw employed on the plantations struck me as the most miserable looking beings I have ever seen in East or West Africa; large barracks are built for their accommodation, which certainly gives it the appearance of a slave compound".[35] Nightingale's report contradicted this impression. He had visited a considerable number of plantations both in São Tomé and Príncipe and considered that the labourers were both well treated and looked after and that in the main the new regulations were carried out. But, he also confirmed that the *serviçaes* were enlisted on the mainland without their wishes being consulted and that they were never repatriated; they were slaves in all but name. The considerable rise in the price of *serviçaes* during the previous twenty years, from about £5 for an adult male or female in the early 1880s to £25 currently, a sum more than a labourer could earn in four years, proved that in reality the *serviçal* was a slave and became the property of the person who contracted him "much the same as if he were a horse or some other marketable commodity". As Nightingale put it: "no sane man would pay such a fee for a contract unless he were certain of having the life-long services of the labourer". He concluded his report in agreement with the Aborigines' Protection Society that the real evil of the *serviçal* system was the manner in which the labourers were obtained on the mainland in Angola.[36]

Having read the report Grey decided that "no representations should be made to the Portuguese at present" and that "such portions of Consul Nightingale's report as relate to the present condition of affairs" might be communicated, though not for publication, to the Aborigines' Protection Society.[37] The society, having received the abridged report continued to urge the Foreign Office to make representations to the Portuguese government. In reply the Foreign Office insisted that the subject had received Grey's most careful attention and "it would not be lost sight of".[38] At the same time, further attention was called in Parliament to the *serviçal* question and demands made for the Nightingale report to be published. Grey, however, insisted that the report was not written in a form for publication and dealt with only part of the issue but that, generally, the conclusion was that the labourers on São Tomé and Príncipe were well treated. In addition, he admitted that it was doubtful "whether the provisions for repatriation under the new regulations have hitherto been made effective" and he insisted that the government intended to bring all the information they possessed to the notice of the Portuguese in the hope that they would take steps to remedy the evils of the existing system.[39] Despite the conciliatory tone adopted by the Portuguese foreign minister, Luís de Maglhães, Grey's answer was criticized in the Portuguese parliament where considerable resentment was shown at Britain's interference in the administrative service of Portugal.[40]

To ensure that the Portuguese got the message Sir Francis Villiers, British minister at Lisbon, was instructed on 22 November 1906 to reemphasize that the Nightingale report was not written originally for publication and that Grey considered it more courteous to place all the facts in their possession at the disposal of the Portuguese government before publishing any reports concerning the administration of their colonies.[41] Villiers passed on Grey's view to Maglhães on 7 December. The foreign minister expressed the view that the Nightingale report, which he had not seen, would contain nothing that would require his government to take action for there could be no doubt that "the natives were properly treated in the islands". As for the system of recruitment, he was adamant that no proof of the allegations had been furnished.[42]

At the end of 1906 the Foreign Office could be satisfied that it had treated the Portuguese slavery/forced labour issue with appropriate care and attention for a liberal democratic power needing to maintain cordial relations with its oldest ally, Portugal, while accommodating the demands of an increasingly critical public opinion in Parliament and anti-slavery pressure groups. But, as Grey and his officials recognized, the prospects of keeping a lid on the issue would diminish in the light of an expected report commissioned by the Cadbury company which had sent special commissioners to west Africa months previously to examine the conditions of recruitment and service of the contracted labourers.[43] In early January 1907 Villiers drew Maglhães's attention to the anticipated Cadbury report (or Burtt report after its author, Joseph Burtt) which would be laid before the Portuguese government and warned him that public attention on the issue of slavery and contracted labour in Britain was increasing and demanded some response from the British government. He warned the foreign minister that mere denial of the existence of abuses was insufficient and it was advisable for the Portuguese authorities to hold a searching enquiry in order to disprove the allegations or correct the abuses if they existed.[44] There was, however, throughout 1907, no sign of the Portuguese instituting an enquiry and the Foreign Office were not prepared to press the authorities in Lisbon before further evidence in the form of the Burtt report materialized. However, with the summer recess approaching, members of the Commons resumed asking questions about labour in the Portuguese islands and on 12 July Grey referred to the Burtt report and the willingness of the government to communicate it to the Portuguese government for their information provided the Cadbury company authorized it.[45]

In the event, because Burtt refused to compromise any of his informants, the original report was watered down, by the deletion of names and "the general failure to give chapter and verse for his allegations, to such an extent as seriously to diminish its whole value". It was recognized in the African Department that the whole system of labour seemed to be "an extraordinarily bad one and indistinguishable from slavery" but that it would hardly be seriously shaken by the Burtt report in its weakened form.[46] Nevertheless, in October a Portuguese translation of the revised report along with an English version was sent to the legation in London for communication to the Portuguese government and Villiers was instructed to emphasize that unless circumstances had altered since Burtt's visit in 1906 or the Portuguese intended "to remedy without delay" any abuses which had come to their attention, particularly with regard to the system of labour recruitment, the inevitable result of the publication of the report would be "an agitation which cannot but prove to be embarrassing both to His Majesty's Government and the Portuguese Government".[47]

Foreign Office pressure seemed to have an effect when in November the Portuguese foreign minister, Ayres d'Ornellas, told George Cadbury, who was visiting Lisbon on behalf of British cocoa manufacturers, that the Portuguese government "intended at once to make a thorough investigation of the whole subject [of labour] in Angola with the intention of replacing the present irresponsible recruiting agents by a proper Government system, as far as possible on the lines employed with success in Mozambique". In addition, Ornellas promised that the revised system of recruiting "would serve as a means of repatriation and make it practicable for the native to return to his home in the interior". When Villiers saw Ornellas's successor, Wenceslau de Lima, in early March 1908, he was assured that the government meant to carry out the intentions of their predecessors.[48] Indeed, in April a naval officer and former governor of the district of Benguela of the province of Cape Verde and of São Tomé and Príncipe, Lieutenant-Captain Francisco Paula Cid, was appointed to study the labour question and to acquire more precise and practicable knowledge of conditions before a revision of the regulations was attempted.[49]

It was clear that yet more time would now elapse while the Cid enquiry took place and following a further intervention by the Aborigines' Protection Society, to which the Foreign Office responded positively, Villiers saw Lima on 6 June and advised that steps should be taken while it proceeded "to remedy any shortcomings" in the administration of the existing regulations.[50] Prior to going on leave in July Villiers visited the Portuguese foreign minister again and laid stress on the need for some positive response by the Portuguese government. He warned Lima that if a similar campaign were commenced against Portugal as had taken place against the Congo Free State the result would be "exceedingly disagreeable for the Portuguese Government and also for His Majesty's Government". He advised that an assurance by the Portuguese government that their intentions to reform the labour system were being "actively and efficiently carried out" and that "no hesitation or delay was being interposed" would go far to mitigate criticism in Britain, including Parliament. Lima was not entirely convinced and expressed his concern that by acceding to this request his government might easily be accused of subservience to Britain.[51]

During the course of his conversation with the Portuguese foreign minister Villiers also disabused Lima of the notion that the movement agitating for changes in the Portuguese labour system was motivated by commercial and not philanthropic interests. Grey, however, suspected the motives of the cocoa manufacturers were at least partially commercial.[52] Whether the foreign secretary was being unduly suspicious the campaign against the Portuguese labour system was still attracting attention in Britain. Apart from the Aborigines' Protection Society, there was no lack of interest in Parliament. In February 1908 a former head of the African Department, now a Liberal MP, Sir Clement Hill, had requested a progress report on Foreign Office representations at Lisbon and the colonial secretary, Winston Churchill, standing in for Grey, had responded by emphasizing Portugal's intention to draw up fresh regulations placing "the recruitment of labourers for the plantations entirely and permanently under the control of Portuguese officials" and by adding that provision would also be made for repatriation.[53] In March the Liberal MP Sir Charles Dilke had enquired about the Portuguese intention to revise the regulations pertaining to indentured labour traffic to São Tomé and Príncipe and Grey had replied with a non-committal answer. Then, in June, the Liberal MP and populist politician, Horatio Bottomley, had queried whether the Foreign Office would make representations to the Portuguese government concerning the existence of slave labour on the cocoa plantations of São Tomé and Príncipe. On this occasion, Grey had stressed that the system in force on the plantations was contract labour not slave labour and that the Government were in communication with the Portuguese authorities with regard to the labour issue.[54] In July in response to further questioning by Dilke the Commons was assured that "the whole "serviçal" question" was engaging "the serious attention" of the government.[55]

In the autumn of 1909, with no indication that the Cid mission was being carried out effectively, there was a growing conviction in the

Foreign Office that an anti-slavery campaign was to be expected. For Grey as well as Walter Langley, superintending under-secretary to the African Department, the real evil was "the barbarous system or recruiting" and he anticipated that the completion of the Benguela railway through Angola would put a stop to it. Unfortunately, that might not be for some time and, meanwhile, it would be very useful if the Portuguese would provide information concerning recruitment.[56] Recognizing that *serviçaes* recruited under the 1903 regulations were reaching the end of their contracts, Villiers was instructed in October to obtain from the Portuguese authorities a statement of the number of *serviçaes* who had become entitled to repatriation and the number actually repatriated.[57] In addition, in a move to influence the Cid mission with regard to repatriation, Villiers was further instructed in late November to advise Lima that one result which the British government hoped for was "an arrangement whereby the return of natives might in some way be facilitated to their own homes and not merely from the islands to the mainland".[58]

Following a meeting at the Caxton Hall, on 4 December 1908, which discussed the issue of Portuguese labour in west Africa, a small deputation was received by Grey in the House of Commons on 10 December. The deputation, consisting of the editor of *The Spectator*, St Loe Strachey, the Liberal MP, Rudolph Lehmann, the Reverend Robert Horton, a dissenting minister, and Nevinson, were naturally critical and complained that the real evil lay in the recruitment process and they doubted the Portuguese, whose administration was extremely inefficient, had the capability to put a stop to it. Grey rejected the deputation's idea of British naval action and insisted that any action taken by the government must be of a diplomatic character, though he recognized that to be effective it was necessary for the British consul at Luanda to be allowed to observe and monitor the situation to determine whether "the final engagement of the labourers which takes place on the coast prior to embarkation was absolutely *bona fide* and voluntary".[59] Accordingly, Villiers was instructed at the end of December to request the presence of the British consul at Luanda to observe and monitor the recruitment process.[60]

As it happened, Villiers saw the new Portuguese prime minister, Campos Henriques, on 2 January 1909 and the latter indicated he would discuss the request with the minister of colonies.[61] But Villiers was not sanguine about the Portuguese government acceding to the request to provide facilities to enable the British consul to monitor the contracting process in Luanda. Acceding to such an arrangement was evidently distasteful to the Portuguese authorities who, he understood, found it derogatory and feared it would expose them to the charge in the Portuguese parliament and press that they were making "undue submission to a foreign power" and failing "to uphold Portuguese sovereign rights in the colonies".[62]

Meanwhile, William Cadbury in March 1909 concluded a visit to Angola, São Tomé and Príncipe which had lasted for five months and reported that no adequate steps had been taken by the Portuguese authorities to remedy the evils in the labour system. As a result Cadbury, Fry and Rowntree informed the Foreign Office that they had decided to make no further purchases of the cocoa produced in the islands.[63] Whether coincidentally or otherwise, Lima at the end of March suddenly informed Villiers that the Cid report had been received and contained proposals for improving the system of labour recruiting in Angola, including a strictly limited number of districts within which recruitment could take place that would be supervised and directly controlled by specially appointed officials responsible to the governor-general of Angola.[64] The Foreign Office response, encouraged by Grey, was to express their gratification at the intention of the Portuguese government to reform labour recruitment but to advise the merits of public scrutiny which would put an end "to all possible allegations reflecting on the freedom of contracts".[65]

Unfortunately, yet another government crisis in Portugal in April and May 1909 threatened progress on the labour issue as Soveral told Grey on 3 June 1909. The Portuguese minister revealed that his government now admitted the evil and would stop it.[66] As a first step it was decided in Lisbon that pending the introduction of new regulations which were nearing completion no further recruitment in Angola would be permitted and the new foreign minister, Colonel du Bocage, anticipated that the British government would recognize that previous assurances were being fully carried out and expressed the hope that "all ground for attack having been removed" the campaign against Portuguese rule in west Africa would cease.[67] Part of the anti-Portuguese campaign continued to be conducted in the House of Commons where Grey earlier in the year was confronted by a range of questions and comments, some of which were critical of the government and notably the Foreign Office. Indeed, on one occasion in March 1909 the Foreign Secretary was moved to remind the House that Angola and the cocoa islands were not British but Portuguese territories and that it was necessary to use diplomatic negotiation to bring about reform, including revision of Portuguese colonial labour regulations.[68]

Revised regulations were introduced in the summer of 1909 by the Portuguese government which on paper offered a range of improvements, including more effective regulation, the increase and systematisation of wages, the securing of repatriation for those who desired it, the reduction of the length of contracts at least for the time being and the temporary suspension of emigration.[69] Grey and the Foreign Office were not so sanguine, however, about the new regulations and declared intentions because as the foreign secretary observed repatriation was not to be obligatory and he regretted that although the renewal of contracts was to be effected in public, the actual engagement of labourers was not.[70] He put this point very strongly to the Portuguese foreign minister in November when he visited London insisting that from private sources it was beyond doubt that it had been the custom for natives "to be captured in the interior by people who were really slave-dealers" and that the captured natives were "then brought down to the coast and sent to work in the Portuguese islands". He insisted that this could "easily be stopped" if Portuguese officials held an enquiry into "the case of each group of natives who came down from the coast" in order to make sure that "the natives had come voluntarily and had been engaged voluntarily". Grey insisted further that if the enquiry was held in public "anyone could attend it and be satisfied that abuses were not being allowed". Finally, he emphasized the strength of feeling in Britain on the subject and "the certainty that abuses in the interior had been very great".[71]

In January 1910 the Foreign Office received a despatch from Consul Horatio Mackie at Luanda which reinforced their misgivings. He observed that regulations had been disregarded in the past and stressed that everything depended on compulsory repatriation. In this connection, Mackie revealed that 67,000 Angolan labourers had been shipped to São Tomé and Príncipe during the past twenty years, not including minors under the age of twelve or infants accompanying their parents, and no provision was made for their repatriation.[72] In an attempt to allay British concerns Villiers was told in January 1910 that the resumption of recruitment would not be permitted until there was assurance that due provision had been made for bringing the new regulations into effect.[73] Again, in February, Villiers learned that José Almeida, an official experienced in native affairs, had been appointed under special commission to superintend the labour regulations in Angola and instructed "to suppress any abuses which may come to his knowledge".[74]

But many in Parliament remained to be convinced and Grey was compelled to defend the Portuguese authorities in the Commons early in April 1910 when he stated that they had promised to reform slave traffic in Angola and had taken steps to suspend all recruiting except in a few restricted zones, had appointed a special commissioner to superintend in Angola the execution of the regulations and expressed their intention of reforming the labour system and dealing severely with any cases of irregularity.[75] It was clear that Grey occupied a difficult position and needed the Portuguese to take action rather than merely to make promises and write regulations. He told Soveral on 12 April that the best way of allaying suspicion both in Parliament and elsewhere, such as the recent news that recruiting in Mozambique had been discontinued but renewed in Angola, would be for the British consul at Luanda to make "a favourable report" as to the "facts of recruiting under the new regulations".[76] The foreign secretary returned to this theme in late June 1910 with the Portuguese minister, but Soveral insisted that it was unreasonable to demand compulsory repatriation because the labourers in São Tomé were "so well treated and the conditions there so much better than those in the places from which the labourers came that the latter often did not wish to go back". But he agreed with Grey when he said that it would be necessary "to make sure that the labourers had full opportunity to go back if they wished to do so" and he admitted that it was owing to British action that the question had been dealt with at all.[77] A month later in July 1910, when faced with further parliamentary criticism, Grey again defended his approach of bringing the Portuguese to accept labour reform through diplomatic means.[78]

The foreign secretary's faith in the Portuguese was to be sorely tested. While the Foreign Office learned in October 1910 that no *serviçaes* had embarked from Angola for São Tomé and Príncipe since the new regulation came into force in February, it was also clear that the repatriation system was scarcely operating with only thirty-nine repatriated during the same period.[79] As a result, Villiers was instructed at the beginning of November, following the recent overthrow of the Portuguese monarchy by republican forces,[80] to tell the Portuguese that in order to maintain cordial relations with Britain it was necessary to enable "His Majesty's Government to point to some decisive action by the Portuguese Government in the direction of reforming the system of contract labour employed in the Portuguese colonies". The new regulations were excellent in spirit but it was to their thorough enforcement that the British government looked and one excellent test would be the rate and method of repatriation.[81] When Villiers carried out his instructions on 19 November the Portuguese republican foreign minister, Bernardino Machado, acknowledged the serious character of the labour question and promised that special attention would be paid to the matter of repatriation.[82]

Words seemed to have been translated into action when Machado informed Villiers in February 1911 that in future workers could only be engaged in Angola for short periods of eighteen months at most, and they would not be able to be re-engaged during the following year even if they wished to, and efforts would be made to obtain work for those repatriated to Angola at the places where they landed. In communicating these instructions Villiers advised that they were provisional, had still to be approved by the council of ministers in Lisbon, and would meet with opposition and resistance from the plantation owners, resident in Portugal.[83] In the House of Commons, meanwhile, Grey continued to be confronted by a range of critical questions. In several exchanges during March 1911 he informed members that he understood recruitment to continue to be suspended and repatriation to be the subject of discussion before the Portuguese cabinet in Lisbon, while denying the need to make representations to the Portuguese on the basis of treaty provisions such as the Brussels act of 1890.[84] However, in late April he was able to inform the Anti-Slavery and Aborigines' Protection Society that according to the consul at Luanda, Francis Drummond-Hay, there was a distinct improvement concerning the slave traffic in Angola and he had been assured that the governor-general, António Guedes, was doing all he could to put an end to it and was appointing district governors and extra police in all parts of the colony.[85] Meanwhile, in mid-April the foreign secretary reiterated to the Portuguese minister that "British public opinion attached great importance to the recruitment of labour in Angola being carried out in free conditions" and that after the elections, which were to take place in Portugal in late May 1911, British public opinion would "recognise the Portuguese Government most willingly if the labour recruiting was entirely free".[86]

British recognition of the republican regime was finally granted after almost a year's delay in September 1911 though there was no marked improvement with regard to recruitment and repatriation in Angola. Previously, in May 1911, the provisional republican government had passed a decree modifying the regulations concerning native labour in the Portuguese colonies. It was intended to encourage shorter contracts and ease the process of repatriation. But as Drummond-Hay emphasized in mid-December 1911 the law of 13 May was "elastic enough to procure any given number of 'serviçaes'".[87] This was scarcely music to the ears of the Foreign Office who had also learned recently that contrary to Machado's claim of February 1911, that future contracts would be no longer than eighteen months, they were now to be for two years with a possibility of a further increase at a later date. Sir Arthur Hardinge, Britain's new minister in Lisbon, was instructed to raise this issue with the Portuguese foreign minister and also to insist that contracts be made in public, whether for engagement or re-engagement, a point to which the British government had always attached considerable importance.[88] When confronted by Hardinge on 16 March 1912 Augusto Vasconcelos stated that the Portuguese Republic wished "to be a humane and progressive force in the civilisation of Africa", but admitted that governors sent out to carry out the government's instructions had been "to a great extent paralysed by the power of the vested interests, European and native".[89]

The power of these interests was demonstrated on 30 March with the issue of a decree by the president of the republic, Manuel Castro, which increased the duration of contracts for labour in São Tomé and Príncipe from two to three years.[90]

At this time a leading article appeared in *The Spectator* which called into question the British alliance with Portugal. Largely based on a letter received from John Harris, the secretary of the recently merged Anti-Slavery and Aborigines' Protection Society, writing from the island of São Tomé, the article argued that contrary to the received wisdom that once on the islands the labourers were well treated their actual condition was akin to slavery, attended by "all the horrors that go with predial slavery – imprisonments, floggings, the separation of husbands and wives, of parents and children, misery, shame and cruelty". In these circumstances the British government should not, argued the article, renew the alliance with Portugal until they were satisfied that slavery did not exist in any part of the Portuguese colonies.[91] There was no intention of abandoning the alliance and Sir Eyre Crowe, superintending under-secretary of the African Department with responsibility for the Portuguese colonies in Africa, was disinclined to believe Harris, preferring instead the observations of Alexander Cumming who had written to the Foreign Office, having been until recently vice-consul at São Tomé. Cumming questioned Harris's sources, denied that flogging took place on the island except in isolated cases, expressed the conviction that the Portuguese were attempting to solve the repatriation problem and accused Harris and the editor of *The Spectator* of persecuting the Portuguese nation.[92] Crowe was equally unconvinced by an article on "Portuguese Slavery" written by Harris in the *Contemporary Review* of May 1912, which claimed a total shipment to São Tomé and Príncipe of over 63,000 slaves within the last twenty-five years; a human cargo, according to Harris, worth £2,500,000.[93] Grey continued to defend the Portuguese but remained uneasy in doing so. At the beginning of July 1912 in the House of Commons he refused to accept references to slavery insisting that the natives of São Tomé and Príncipe were not slaves but indentured labourers, yet he confessed to his officials that it was, nevertheless, "true in fact that before recruiting to Angola was stopped the labourers had practically all been captured by force and were not voluntary contract labourers".[94]

At the same time, the Portuguese government felt compelled to intervene in the unofficial debate taking place in Britain through the attendance of former Foreign Minister Machado and José d'Almada, first secretary in the Portuguese colonial office, at a meeting held under the auspices of the Anti-Slavery and Aborigines' Protection Society in the Westminster Palace Hotel, London, on 25 June 1912. Machado denied that slavery existed in the Portuguese islands; "labourers on the islands were paid and labour paid for was not slavery". On 2 July Almada had published in *The Times* a letter in which he vigorously defended the Portuguese position. The Foreign Office view was that Almada had made a very good defence as far as the plantations and recruitment were concerned but that he had not touched the repatriation question.[95] As if to answer it, the Portuguese minister at London, Manuel Texeira Gomes, on a visit to the Foreign Office on 2 July to reinforce the Almada letter, insisted that many of the labourers had no wish to be repatriated as they had no place to which they could go and no means of earning a living when they reached the mainland.[96]

Needless to say, the anti-slavery movement remained unconvinced. In a leading article on 29 June, reporting the meeting at the Westminster Palace Hotel, *The Spectator* roundly condemned the Portuguese connection, arguing that so long as the treaty of alliance with Portugal remained in force Britain was obliged to protect her and therefore incidentally to protect the institution of slavery. In a second article of 13 July *The Spectator* drew attention to the resolve of the Anti-Slavery and Aborigines' Protection Society to wage an unremitting campaign by keeping "the country continually informed as to what is happening" in order "to do its utmost to save Englishmen from the disgrace of holding themselves responsible for slavery".[97] As if on cue, a society deputation presented a detailed letter to Grey personally on 15 July in which, in order to speed up the repatriation process, they recommended the appointment of an international commission composed of Portuguese, British and Belgian representatives assisted by "men experienced in the tribal languages and cicatrices of the Angola, Congo and Rhodesian hinterlands". The commission to be empowered "to issue manumission papers to slaves demanding freedom; the process to be completed within six to twelve months to enable the planters to replace slave labour with *serviçal* labour from Mozambique and elsewhere and allow time to make arrangements for the return of the slaves".[98] In view of the increasing parliamentary and public pressure, the Foreign Office could not ignore the society's proposal even if they wanted to and the legation in Lisbon, the consulate at Luanda and the vice-consul in São Tomé were instructed to investigate and respond.[99]

Shortly before the deputation saw Grey the Foreign Office received on 10 July a favourable report of conditions on São Tomé from Drummond-Hay at Luanda who had spent eight days on the island followed by a visit to the Cabinda enclave. Drummond-Hay saw the acting governor and curator for the *serviçaes*, Ferreira dos Santos, who vehemently denied that corporal punishment was permitted. He told the consul that he was determined to carry out the law strictly concerning

repatriation in spite of the opposition of the managers of the *roças* (plantations) and he had already ensured the appointment of a resident doctor
on each of the principal estates. He made a most favourable impression
on Drummond-Hay as a serious man "who is earnestly endeavouring to
carry out the law". On visits to several plantations Drummond-Hay was
impressed by the treatment of the *serviçaes* using words such as "admirable
condition" to describe one *roças* and "most favourably impressed with all
I saw" to describe another. One doctor, a Dr Dias, assured him that he
had never seen any flogging or ill treatment of *serviçaes*. Drummond-Hay
himself questioned several *serviçaes* on another plantation and "they all
said their employers were good to them, and that they were
contented".[100]

Later in October 1912 the Foreign Office received a report from
Acting-Consul Robert Smallbones at Luanda which was somewhat less
favourable in that he admitted that slavery among the natives existed but
he had no evidence to show that it was "fostered by the authorities". He
confirmed that the actual repatriation of *serviçaes* was by no means satisfactory but he rejected the idea of an international commission on the
grounds that tribal identity would be impossible to confirm; that the
Portuguese would never accept powers of manumission being invested
in the commission because it would imply a state of slavery which they
denied existed; that it could be claimed that the *serviçaes* had been legally
recontracted and their arbitrary repatriation had no justification in law;
that the Portuguese could claim they were already doing all in their
power to accelerate repatriation within the limits of the law; and that the
policy of providing repatriated *serviçaes* with small holdings was now
about to be tried and should be given a fair trial before more "heroic
measures" were applied.[101]

Confronted with the increasing intensity of the anti-slavery movement, Grey and his Cabinet colleagues had taken the decision to issue a
parliamentary white paper (White Book) detailing correspondence on
the issue of "Contract Labour in Portuguese West Africa" which was laid
before the House of Commons in August 1912 and drew immediate criticism from *The Spectator* which declared on 17 August that "once and for
all this White Paper explodes the fiction that contract labour in the
Portuguese colonies of West Africa is not slavery" and warned that in the
autumn there would be an anti-slavery campaign and that "the
Government should be forced to commit themselves to some construc-
tive policy" namely, the international commission proposed by the
Anti-Slavery and Aborigines' Protection Society.[102] Grey was not
impressed and the society was informed on 14 October that he was
"unable to concur in the views expressed as to present conditions in
Portuguese West Africa" which were not borne out by British consular

sources. On 4 November in formally responding to its letter of 15 July the foreign secretary expressed no opinion concerning the proposed international commission but revealed his intention to lay a further collection of papers before Parliament as the most satisfactory way of dealing with the issue.[103] Despite the flurry of correspondence, there was clearly no meeting of minds between the Foreign Office and the society and the latter continued to insist that unless Portugal fulfilled its pledges to abolish without delay slavery and the slave trade "as now exposed in the recent White Book", Britain should withdraw from the alliance.[104]

While the Foreign Office, including Grey, would not concede to the anti-slavery movement's interpretation on contract labour or to its demands to consider ending the Anglo-Portuguese alliance, continuing pressure was put on the Portuguese to effectively carry out their declared reforms. In late November 1912 Hardinge was informed that under Grey's direction Crowe had spoken with Gomes on several occasions emphasizing "the importance attached by both His Majesty's Government and by public opinion in this country to the satisfactory regulation of the contract labour in the Portuguese colonies". The Portuguese minister had responded by insisting that the republican government had done more in two short years than was ever conceived of under the monarchical regime and was fully alive to their obligations and would steadily press forward the measures of reform which had been carefully planned and laid down in various laws and regulations.[105] Hardinge, for his part, had intervened in Lisbon to urge that there should be no interruption in the facilities for large scale repatriation which he understood would be resumed before the end of November.[106]

The dual Foreign Office approach of not conceding to the arguments and demands of the anti-slavery movement while continuing to apply diplomatic pressure on the Portuguese continued in 1913. The Anti-Slavery and Aborigines' Protection Society was told firmly in January that there was no prospect of summarily terminating the Anglo-Portuguese alliance. However, the government were ready to do all in their power to see that recruitment was carried out under proper conditions, that repatriation continued and that the labourers were treated fairly both in the islands and on their return to Angola. While in the main these conditions appeared to be satisfied, they had not hesitated to draw to Portugal's attention any infringements and they had found the Portuguese authorities ready to remove them. The Foreign Office view of the 30,000 labourers on São Tomé and Príncipe was that they were no longer in a condition of slavery in which manumission came into question. It was made abundantly clear to the society that Grey and his officials did not feel able to do more concerning repatriation other than to continue to press the Portuguese not to let the rate of repatriation slacken.[107]

The publication of a second White Book in February 1913 did not diminish criticisms and condemnations of Portuguese colonial rule; rather it provided the anti-slavery movement with more ammunition to fire at the government and particularly the Foreign Office.[108] In a stinging rebuke *The Spectator* on 8 March claimed that the contentions of the anti-slavery movement were vindicated by both white books, but more so by the second, and accused the Foreign Office of getting itself into "the intolerable and humiliating position of standing forth as the apologist of Portuguese slavery".[109] Further though milder criticism was directed against Grey and his officials in Parliament in March but the parliamentary under-secretary for foreign affairs, Francis Acland, in Grey's absence, was able to announce the appointment of two vice-consuls, one to spend some time on São Tomé and the rest at Fernando Po and the other at Benguela along with the consul at Luanda. The government intended, Acland argued, to watch the situation carefully, provide counsel and advice and encourage improvements rather than bring specific grievances to the notice of the Portuguese authorities who had been "so very definitely trying of late years to meet the criticisms and the points which we have made".[110] Two months later, at the end of May, Acland was compelled to defend the Portuguese again by refuting claims in the House of Commons that slave trading between the Angolan mainland and the islands still continued. He insisted that slave trading was a closed chapter and that repatriation was proceeding with over 600 labourers repatriated in January and February 1913 alone.[111]

It was certainly the case that during 1913 the criticisms of the anti-slavery movement, and particularly those of the Anti-Slavery and Aborigines' Protection Society, proved considerably irksome to the Foreign Office. On 13 February the society claimed that the Portuguese in delaying and prevaricating over repatriation were deliberately enacting a stratagem to keep the *serviçaes* on the islands at the bidding of the plantation owners.[112] Within two days the Foreign Office had vigorously refuted this claim and insisted that the actual conditions on the islands had improved during the last few years owing to the intervention of the Portuguese government.[113] Subsequently, in their correspondence and private discussion, the Foreign Office continued to adopt a critical attitude *vis-à-vis* the Anti-Slavery and Aborigines' Protection Society. In June, incensed by what was identified as a tendency on the part of the society to misinterpret official statements made in Parliament, Crowe advised that Grey should insist that he was not prepared to discuss such statements except in the confines of the House of Commons and the foreign secretary concurred.[114]

The anti-slavery movement had powerful allies in Parliament who could not be ignored, however, and in a debate in the House of Lords on 23 July 1913 the Foreign Office came in for a great deal of criticism. The earl of Mayo who initiated the debate charged that the second White Book published in February 1913 left the reader cold. He accused the Foreign Office of "explaining away the 40,000 slaves working in the cocoa plantations of St. Thomé and Principe" and of denying that "contract labour is not slavery at all". He demanded that either slave owning or slave trading should cease or that Britain should no longer be bound by treaty with Portugal. The archbishop of Canterbury was no less critical. He felt the reading of the second White Book as a whole "to be rather humiliating" and deplored the Foreign Office's "curiously cold view of the wrong which is being done". Lord Cromer, recalling his own experience of countering slavery in the Sudan, adopted a milder approach but insisted that it was a matter of will and that it was essential "to keep on insisting on the Portuguese Government putting pressure upon their own officials and keeping them steadily up to the mark". He was concerned that if the Portuguese called for assistance in time of war it would be extremely embarrassing to use British forces to support "a slave State". The former foreign secretary, Lord Lansdowne, used the same argument but with a different slant pointing to a situation in which Britain was confronted by her treaty obligations on the one hand and by a very strong and almost irresistible outburst of public opinion on the other; so difficult that "it might make it difficult for us to act up to them". Even Viscount Morley, secretary of state for India, was forced to admit that nobody denied that the conditions under which the labourers on the islands existed were "in effect bondage". At the same time, he insisted that the Portuguese authorities were doing their best to improve matters and that some of them were acting "extraordinarily courageously", including the governor-general of Angola, José Norton de Matos. He reminded the Lords that the government could not intervene directly in Portuguese affairs but what it could do, had done and was doing was "by counsel, advice, protest, and remonstrance, to induce the authorities who are responsible to take measures which will, at all events, ameliorate the mischief". As a statement of intent and policy it was an extremely accurate reflection of the position adopted by the Foreign Office.[115]

The House of Lords debate did nothing to move the Foreign Office in a different direction and nor did the continuing and insistent agitation of the Anti-Slavery and Aborigines' Protection Society. Crowe was adamant that the Office should resist "being dragged by the Society into an attitude towards the Portuguese authorities which would practically amount to a claim to exercise police supervision in their colonies".[116] He was equally critical of a series of articles by Lord Cromer in *The Spectator* during August 1913.[117] Later, at the end of 1913, he expressed a clearly held opinion that it was stretching the meaning of words unreasonably to apply the word "slavery" to the conditions existing in Angola and the islands of São Tomé and Príncipe.[118]

The prevailing view in the Foreign Office, that it was more productive to work closely with the Portuguese to achieve improvements, received a jolt in the autumn of 1913 when Smallbones reported that many of the *serviçaes* were working beyond their contracts and that it was not true that the authorities on São Tomé had made every effort to ensure the repatriation of those labourers who had completed their contracts. In May, June and July 2,189 *serviçaes* entered São Tomé and Príncipe whereas only 956 left these islands. Smallbones considered that the Portuguese plea that repatriation was being carried out as fast as available shipping permitted was "devoid of all foundation".[119] On 15 November following a further intervention at Lisbon by Hardinge's successor, Lancelot Carnegie, the Portuguese prime minister, Afonso Costa, announced that he was endeavouring to have made available more ships to speed up the process of repatriation and that he welcomed a proposal to appoint a British consul on the west coast of Africa, one of whose duties, he recognized, was to be the inspection of the labour conditions on the islands.[120] But there was still disquiet in the Foreign Office when it was learned later that month that recontracting on a large scale was taking place on the islands and from past experience this could only be achieved by some form of compulsion. As a result, Carnegie was instructed to stress the great importance which the British government attached to the steady repatriation of the *serviçaes* on the termination of their contracts.[121] When Carnegie carried out his instructions on 12 December António Macieira accepted that it was entirely in Portuguese interests that the proposed consul-general should have the fullest facilities on the islands for making accurate reports in order to confound the inaccurate ones supplied by the British anti-slavery movement. He was still preoccupied by "the necessity of avoiding any semblance of giving jurisdiction to a foreign official in Portuguese territory" but, having consulted his colleagues, he told Carnegie on 20 December that because of his conviction that the request was based solely on the British government's "friendly sentiments" and of their desire to see "an end to the campaign carried on against Portugal by the Anti-Slavery Society" it was in the interests of the Portuguese government to afford all necessary facilities to the proposed consular official.[122]

In early 1914 further consular reports were received at the Foreign Office which had been prepared by Lewis Bernays, the vice-consul attached to São Tomé, Príncipe and Fernando Po which indicated that an increasing number of *serviçaes*, whose contracts had terminated, still remained on the islands.[123] When Carnegie saw Prime Minister Bernardino Machado and the colonial minister, Lisboa de Lima, on 7

March he impressed on them the great importance of carrying out repatriation at a more rapid rate and on 20 March he impressed on Machado the desirability of codifying the existing laws and regulations.[124] Acting with unaccustomed speed the Portuguese instructed the governor of São Tomé to effect repatriations as quickly as possible at the termination of contracts, reorganized the functions of the curator's office to secure prompt repatriation and began the process of codifying labour regulations into a single, clear corpus.[125]

Yet, none of these improvements led to a substantial increase in repatriation during the remaining months before the outbreak of the First World War in August 1914. At the same time, the continuing anti-slavery campaign in Britain provoked a bitter response in Lisbon where on 7 July the Portuguese foreign minister, Freire d'Andrade, complained of the lack of credit given to his country for the improvements which had taken place on behalf of the labourers on the cocoa islands and could only conclude that there was a conspiracy "on the part of certain interested persons to ruin the planters, depreciate the value of their estates with the view of buying them cheaply, and of eventually cornering the cocoa market". When Carnegie did not rise to the alleged conspiracy but observed instead that much could be done to silence the campaign in England by increasing the slow rate of repatriation which was the principal object of criticism, Andrade countered by arguing that repatriation was being carried out on a far larger scale than the previous year and there was every reason to expect that most if not all the labourers brought to the islands before 1903 would be repatriated in about three years time.[126] This was scarcely a statement for congratulation and could be interpreted as feet dragging on the part of the Portuguese yet Grey stood up in Parliament on 10 July to express his belief that there had been a steady improvement in repatriation, and the reports he had seen recently had produced on his mind "the impression that, although a good deal remains to be done the Portuguese Government are really trying to remove the abuses that have existed".[127]

It remains true that the British government and in particular the Foreign Office had not succeeded by 1914 in bringing about a complete solution to the problem of slavery/forced labour in Portuguese west Africa. Issues such as repatriation, contracting and re-contracting remained to be resolved. Over a period of twenty years since 1894, and particularly with the advent of the Liberal government at the end of 1905, the Foreign Office endeavoured by means of diplomacy to bring about real improvements in recruiting, the treatment of *serviçaes* labourers and their repatriation. As demonstrated in successive white books the consular service in west Africa, though often undermanned, did sterling work in reporting conditions and developments pertaining to the labour question, including those on São Tomé and Príncipe while ministers such as Gosselin, Villiers, Hardinge and Carnegie exercised their diplomatic skills in pressing for reform at Lisbon without unduly alienating the Portuguese authorities. The clerks in the African Department of the Foreign Office, notably Hill, Edward Ashley Clarke and John Tilley supported by senior officials such as Villiers, Barrington, Langley and Crowe, sought to provide advice which on balance was probably more sympathetic to the Portuguese government than their anti-slavery adversaries. Of the two foreign secretaries most involved with the labour question, Lansdowne and Grey, it was the latter who felt the brunt of the anti-slavery agitation conducted by a number of organizations, most notably the Anti-Slavery and Aborigines' Protection Society, and their parliamentary and press allies who succeeded in keeping the issue of Portuguese labour in west Africa within the public view and in the public domain to the chagrin of the Portuguese government and occasionally the Foreign Office itself. It is a point of conjecture whether the intervention of the anti-slavery movement was entirely effective and decisive but there can be no doubt as to its influence on Anglo-Portuguese diplomacy during the period under review.

The three foreign secretaries before Grey – Kimberley, Salisbury and Lansdowne – approached the issue of slavery in São Tomé and Príncipe with a degree of indifference and they were certainly not prepared to disturb their relations with Portugal by intervening too forcefully at Lisbon to persuade the Portuguese authorities to end the traffic and exploitation of slaves even under the guise of forced labour. In the wider perspective of Britain's relations with Portugal, issues such as frontier claims and rectifications between Portuguese and British territories in southern Africa and the provision of Mozambican labour for the gold fields of South Africa, estimated in 1897 to constitute more than half of the labour force, carried greater significance.[128] As a result there was a disinclination to disturb Anglo-Portuguese relations any more than need be by raising the slavery issue. In addition, Portugal's support became essential to counter the Boer challenge in the Transvaal and the renewal of the Anglo-Portuguese treaty of alliance in 1899, by guaranteeing that support at a critical time, added to the disinclination to act on the slavery issue as did the absence of a concerted campaign against Portuguese rule in west Africa by anti-slavery bodies, otherwise distracted by events and developments in the Congo in the late 1890s and early 1900s.[129]

Grey himself was never entirely comfortable in defending the Portuguese authorities in the House of Commons on the labour issue though he made a number of positive statements in support when faced by the criticism of members on both sides of the House. In the confines of the Foreign Office and at Cabinet he occasionally revealed his reservations about the Portuguese colonial empire and was disinclined to defend it. In this he was influenced not only by the west African labour issue but by his knowledge of developments in other parts of the Portuguese empire, notably the prazo system in Mozambique and the "scandalous" conditions in the island colony of Macao centring on gambling and drugs. In December 1911 in a private letter to Sir George Goschen, British ambassador at Berlin, Grey referred to the Portuguese colonies as being "worst than derelict" so long as Portugal had them and he called them "sinks of iniquity".[130] Later, in July 1912 in the middle of protracted negotiations with Germany concerning a new agreement to replace the Anglo-German agreement of 1898,[131] which had envisaged in certain eventualities the partition of Portugal's colonies between the two powers, Grey told Cabinet that the administration of the Portuguese colonies was "hopelessly bad" and that "the scandals of Portuguese administration are such that public opinion would hardly support us in protecting the state of things that now exists in the Portuguese colonies". The position was "very uncomfortable if not inherently false" and Grey admitted that "it would be shameful to throw over the Portuguese alliance in order to facilitate a division of her African colonies between Germany and ourselves" but that it would also "be morally indefensible to protect the scandalous state of things that exist in the Portuguese colonies". Unfortunately, he concluded "the alliance gives us no discretion in the matter".[132]

It was the existence of the Anglo-Portuguese alliance with Britain's obligation to defend Portugal and her colonial possessions which encouraged the anti-slavery movement to believe that the Foreign Office had the means to force the Portuguese to end slavery and forced labour in their west African colonies once and for all by threatening to terminate or actually ending the alliance. The Foreign Office rejected this approach preferring to use their influence which was elevated by the existence of the alliance to apply diplomatic pressure. Under the terms of the ancient alliance, which had commenced in 1373 and which had been renewed as recently as 1899, the British government was obliged "to protect and defend the Portuguese colonies" but had always reserved the right to judge the circumstances when and whether to activate the alliance. The Anglo-German negotiations of 1912–1914 failed to produce an agreement which had it materialized would have terminated the Anglo-Portuguese alliance. Ironically, during the course of negotiations the Foreign Office had taken a disinterested stance with regard to São Tomé and Príncipe and had agreed not to put forward a claim to the islands.[133] The proposed Anglo-German agreement would have solved the issue of Portuguese slavery and forced labour in west Africa once and for all. Apart from the moral issues, an agreement was not signed because of concern at the growth of German colonial power in west Africa which was opposed by Britain's entente partner, France, and to the recognition of the significance of the Portuguese connection to British security and strategic interests. This salient fact was demonstrated in a powerfully argued memorandum written by Crowe in 1913 in defence of the alliance which, he argued, provided Britain with the *locus standi* to utilize and deny to an enemy the Atlantic islands – the Azores and Cape Verde islands – so vital to British Atlantic strategy that even Winston Churchill, a powerful critic of the republican regime in Lisbon, was forced to admit as first lord of the Admiralty that Portugal remained "an important factor in our naval strategy whatever form her government may be".[134] Without the alliance Britain's strategic position would be seriously weakened and put at risk and the price for preserving it was a British guarantee of the Portuguese empire in its entirety. The politics of grand strategy demanded that the Foreign Office adopt the diplomatic approach without the threat of force when seeking to resolve the issue of slavery/forced labour in Portuguese west Africa.

Notes

1   Throughout this chapter the Portuguese version São Tomé and Príncipe is used except where they appear in quotation marks when the original anglicised version is used. The same is the case for Luanda, the capital of Angola, except when Loanda is referred to within quotation marks or in the footnotes to denote the location of British diplomats and consuls.

2   Henry Nevinson, *A Modern Slavery* (London and New York: Harper & Bros., 1906). Charles Swan, *The Slavery of Today* (Glasgow: Pickering & Inglis, 1909). John Harris, *Portuguese Slavery: Britain's Dilemma* (London: Methuen, 1913). Joseph Burtt and William Cadbury, *Labour in Portuguese West Africa* (London: Routledge, 1909).

3   Richard J. Hammond, *Portugal and Africa, 1815–1910: A Study in Uneconomic Imperialism* (Stanford CA: Stanford UP, 1966). James Duffy, *Portuguese Africa* (Cambridge MA: Harvard UP, 1959). William Gervase Clarence-Smith, *Slaves, Peasants and Capitalists in Southern Angola, 1840–1926* (Cambridge: CUP, 1979).

4   James Duffy, *A Question of Slavery: Labour Politics in Portuguese Africa and the British Protest, 1850–1920* (Oxford: Clarendon Press, 1967).

5   For the Anglo-Portuguese treaty, see Roger Anstey, *Britain and the Congo in the Nineteenth Century* (Oxford: Clarendon Press, 1962), app. A, pp. 241–6. For the Brussels general act see Suzanne Miers, *Britain and the Ending of the Slave Trade* (London: Longman, 1975), app. I, pp. 346–63.

6   Clarence-Smith, *Slaves, Peasants and Capitalists*, p. 64.

7   William Gervase Clarence-Smith, "Labour conditions in the plantations of São Tomé and Príncipe, 1875–1914", *Slavery and Abolition*, vol. 14 (1993), p. 149.

8   *Hansard Parliamentary Debates*, fourth series, HC, vol. 25, cc. 285–6. The

National Archives (TNA), FO 63/1447. Pease to Grey, 5 June 1894; Littleton to Pease, 5 July 1894; Foreign Office (FO) to Pickersgill, 16 June 1894.

9 Ibid., Brock to Kimberley, 28 Aug. 1894.

10 Ibid., Pickersgill to Kimberley, 15 Dec. 1894.

11 Ibid., minutes by Sir Clement Hill (head, African Dept.), 12 Jan. 1895, Sanderson, n.d.; and Kimberley, n.d.

12 Ibid., Pickersgill to Salisbury,16 March 1897; minute by Bertie.

13 Ibid., Bourne to the Marquess of Lansdowne, 11 June 1902.

14 Ibid., Casement to Lansdowne, 17 Sept. 1902.

15 Ibid., FO minutes, 22 Oct.1902.

16 Ibid., Nightingale to Lansdowne, 12 Jan. 1903.

17 Ibid., Gosselin to Lansdowne, 7 Feb. 1903.

18 Ibid, Travers Buxton to Gosselin, 24 April 1903; Gosselin to Lansdowne, 5 May 1903.

19 Ibid., Soveral to the British and Foreign Anti-Slavery Society, 26 Feb.1903.

20 Ibid., Gosselin to Lansdowne, 6 May 1903.

21 Ibid., Lansdowne to Gosselin, 24 June 1903.

22 Ibid., Francis Hyde Villiers (superintending under-secretary, African Dept.) to Lansdowne, 24 Nov. 1903.

23 Ibid., Gosselin to Lansdowne, 1 May 1904.

24 Ibid., Nightingale to Lansdowne, 5 May 1904.

25 Ibid., Brock to Lansdowne, 23 July 1904.

26 Ibid., minutes by Edward Ashley Clarke (African Dept.), 11 Oct. 1904, and by Lansdowne confirming his agreement to defer intervention at Lisbon.

27 Ibid., Gosselin to Lansdowne, 16 Jan. 1905; minute by Clarke,13 Jan. 1905.

28 Ibid., Brock to Lansdowne, 30 June 1905.

29 Ibid., memo. by Edward Erskine (assistant head, African Dept.), 28 July 1905 and seen by Lansdowne; FO to Aborigines' Protection Society, 9 Aug. 1905; FO to editor, *Tropical Life*, 9 Aug. 1905.

30 Ibid., FO to Nightingale, 18 Oct. 1905. Lansdowne minuted on 16 Oct. that "I must meet Mr Nightingale" but there is no record in the file of such a meeting taking place.

31 Duffy, *A Question of Slavery*, pp. 186–90. Duffy, *Portuguese Africa*, pp. 159–61. For a recent detailed account of Nevinson's campaign against Portuguese slavery see Angela John, *War, Journalism and the Shaping of the Twentieth Century: The Life and Times of Henry W. Nevinson* (London: I. B. Tauris, 2006), pp. 42–59.

32 Duffy, *A Question of Slavery*, p. 191.

33 *Hansard Parliamentary Debates*, 4th series, HC, vols. 160 and 161, c. 229, c. 193.

34 TNA, FO 367/17, 26131/06, Fox Bourne to Grey, 30 July 1906.

35 FO 367/17, 27074/06, Admiralty to FO, 6 Aug. 1906.

36 FO 367/17, 28370/06, "Report on the Treatment of the 'Serviçaes' or Contract labourers in the Portuguese Islands known as the Province of São Thomé and Principe", 28 July 1906.

37 FO 367/17, 28370/06, minute by Grey, n.d., Aug. 1906; FO to Aborigines' Protection Society, 12 Sept. 1906.

38 FO 367/17, 32379/06, Bourne to FO, 24 Sept. 1906; Barrington to Fox-Bourne, 10 Oct. 1906.

39 *Hansard Parliamentary Debates*, 4th series, HC, vol. 163, c. 675.

40 FO 367/18, 38021/06, Villiers to Grey, 7 Nov.1906.

41 Ibid., Grey to Villiers, 22 Nov. 1906.

42 FO 367/18, 41793/06, Villiers to Grey, 7 Dec. 1906.

43 Ibid., Grey to Villiers, 29 Dec. 1906.

44 FO 367/46, 1099/07, Villiers to Grey, 5 Jan. 1907.

45 *Hansard Parliamentary Debates*, 4th series, HC, vol. 178, cc. 196–7. See also c. 916 and cc. 1189–90 and vol 179, c. 130.

46 FO 367/46, 29406/07, Lyell to Henry Beaumont (chargé d'affaires, Lisbon), 2 Sept. 1907.

47 FO 367/46, 33573/07, Grey to Villiers, 17 Oct. 1907.

48 FO367/86, 9057/08, Villiers to Grey, 7 March 1908.

49 FO 367/86, 12693/08, Walter Langley (superintending under-secretary African Dept.) to Fox Bourne, 28 April 1908.

50 FO 367/86, 15049/20538/08, Fox Bourne to FO, 1 May 1908; Grey to Villiers, 20 May 1908; Villiers to Grey, 8 June 1908.

51 FO 367/86, 24110/08,Villiers to Grey, 4 July 1908.

52 Ibid., minute by Grey, 13 July 1908.

53 *Hansard Parliamentary Debates*, 4th series, HC, vol. 183, c. 1408.

54 *Hansard Parliamentary Debates*, 4th series, HC, vol. 185, c. 1748 and vol. 190, cc. 1033–4.

55 *Hansard Parliamentary Debates*, 4th series, HC, vol. 193, c. 878.

56 FO 367/87, 33499/08, minutes by Langley and Grey, 28 Sept. 1908.

57 FO 367/87, 33499/08, Grey to Villiers, 10 Oct. 1908.

58 FO 367/87, 44211/08, Grey to Villiers, 27 Nov. 1908.

59 FO 367/87, 41211/08, minute by Clarke, 11 Dec. 1908.

60 Ibid., minute by Grey, n.d.; Grey to Villiers, 28 Dec. 1908.

61 FO 367/140, 1282/09, Villiers to Grey, 2 Jan. 1909.

62 FO 367/140, 11906/09, Villiers to Grey, 23 March 1909.

63 FO 367/140, 10102/09, Cadbury Bros. to FO, 15 March 1909.

64 FO 367/140, 13721/09, Villiers to Grey, 7 April 1909; FO to Cadbury Bros., 29 April 1909.

65 FO 367/140, 13721/09, minute by Grey, 15 April 1909; Grey to Villiers, 29 April 1909; Villiers to Grey, 1 June 1909.

66 FO 367/141, 20881/09, minute by Grey, 2 June 1909.

67 Villiers to Grey, 15 July 1909, "Correspondence respecting Contract Labour in Portuguese West Africa", August 1912. *Parliamentary Papers*, Africa No. 2, cmd. 6322, p. 1.

68 *Hansard Parliamentary Debates*, 5th series, HC, vol. 2, cc. 492–4, 898. See also vol. 1, cc. 1258–9.

69 FO 367/141, 35839/09, Hugh Gaisford (chargé d'affaires, Lisbon) to Grey, 10 Sept. 1909.

70 Ibid., Grey to Villiers, 16 October 1909.
71 FO 367/141, 43081/09, Grey to Gaisford, 22 Nov. 1909.
72 FO 367/186, 1505/10, Horatio Mackie (consul, Luanda) to Grey, 30 Nov.
73 FO 367/186, 1815/10, Villiers to Grey, 11 Jan. 1910. The news was tempered somewhat when a week later it was decided that from 1 February 1910 recruitment would be resumed in the one zone, Quillenges, Bailundo and Jinga de Ambbaca, in which control could be most effectively exercised. FO 367/186, 2423/10.
74 FO 367/186, 6973/10, Villiers to Grey, 22 Feb. 1910 enclosing memo. by the Portuguese foreign minister, 17 Feb.1910.
75 *Hansard Parliamentary Debates*, 5th series, HC, vol. 16, cc. 192–4. See also vol. 17, cc. 625–6.
76 FO 367/185, 12274/10, Grey to Villiers, 12 April 1910.
77 Ibid., Grey to Gaisford, 27 June 1910.
78 *Hansard Parliamentary Debates*, 5th series, HC, vol.19, cc. 1569–75, 1588–93.
79 FO 367/187, 36997/10, Francis Drummond-Hay (consul, Luanda) to Grey, 16 Sept. 1910.
80 For British responses to the overthrow of the Portuguese monarchy and the establishment of the republic, see John Vincent-Smith, "The Portuguese Republic and Britain", *Journal of Contemporary History*, vol. 10, 1975, pp. 707–28.
81 FO 367/187, 40016/10, Grey to Villiers, 3 Nov. 1910.
82 FO 367/187, 42686/10, Villiers to Grey, 19 Nov. 1910.
83 FO 367/234, 6391/11, Villiers to Grey, 17 Feb. 1911, and note from Bernardino Machado to Villiers, 14 Feb. 1911.
84 *Hansard Parliamentary Debates*, 5th series, HC, vol.22, cc. 354, 522 and 1002; vol. 23, cc. 212–13 and 1294–5.
85 FO 367/234, 14086/11, FO to secretary, Anti-Slavery and Aborigines' Protection Society, 25 April 1911.
86 FO 367/234, 14370/11, Grey to Villiers, 13 April 1911.
87 FO 367/285, 1323/12, Drummond-Hay to Grey, 14 Dec.1911.
88 FO 367/285, 7641/12, Grey to Hardinge, 7 March 1912.
89 FO 367/285, 12635/12, Hardinge to Grey, 19 March 1912.
90 Hardinge to Grey, 22 April 1912, "Correspondence respecting Contract Labour in Portuguese West Africa", August 1912. *Parliamentary Papers*, Africa No. 2, cmd. 6322, p. 96.
91 *The Spectator*, 23 March 1912, p. 465.
92 FO 367/285, 14381/18241/12, Crowe to Hardinge, 11 April 1912. Alexander Cumming to John Tilley (head, African Dept.), 28 April 1912.
93 FO 367/285, 19413/12, minutes by Crowe and Grey, 13 May 1912.
94 *Hansard Parliamentary Debates*, 5th series, HC, vol.40, cc. 928–9.
95 FO 367/285, 29638/12, minute by Langley, 16 July 1912.
96 FO 367/285, 28264/12, Grey to Hardinge, 18 July 1912.
97 *The Spectator*, 29 June 1912 and 13 July 1912, pp. 1032–3, 46–7.
98 FO 367/285, 30248/12, Anti-Slavery and Aborigines' Protection Society to Grey, 15 July 1912.
99 FO 367/285, 30248/12, FO to Anti-Slavery and Aborigines' Protection

Society, 6 Aug. 1912; Grey to Hardinge, 12 August 1912.

100 Drummond-Hay to Grey, 8 June 1912, "Correspondence respecting Contract Labour in Portuguese West Africa", August 1912. *Parliamentary Papers*, Africa No. 2, cmd. 6322, pp. 109–12.

101 FO 367/286, 43254/12, Smallbones to Grey, 26 Sept. 1912.

102 *The Spectator*, 17 Aug. 1912, pp. 225–7.

103 FO 367/286, 42326/45082/12, Crowe to Anti-Slavery and Aborigines' Protection Society, 14 Oct. 1912 and 4 Nov. 1912.

104 FO 367/286, 47707/12, Anti-Slavery and Aborigines' Protection Society to Grey, 8 Nov. 1912.

105 FO 367/287, 50715/12, Grey to Hardinge, 27 Nov. 1912.

106 FO 367/287, 51287/12, Hardinge to Grey, 23 Nov. 1912.

107 FO 367/334, 4929/13, Crowe to the Anti-Slavery and Aborigines' Protection Society, 31 Jan. 1913.

108 "Further Correspondence respecting Contract Labour in Portuguese West Africa", Feb. 1913, *Parliamentary Papers*, Africa No. 2 (1913) cmd. 6607.

109 *The Spectator*, 8 March 1913, pp. 389–90.

110 *Hansard Parliamentary Debates*, 5th series, HC, vol.50, cc. 1874–83.

111 *Hansard Parliamentary Debates*, 5th series, HC, vol.53, cc. 458–9.

112 FO 367/334, 6981/13, Anti-Slavery and Aborigines' Protection Society to FO, 13 Feb.1913.

113 Ibid., Crowe to Anti-Slavery and Aborigines' Protection Society, 15 Feb. 1913.

114 FO 367/335, 26055/13, minutes by Crowe and Grey, 24 June 1913.

115 *Hansard Parliamentary Debates*, 5th series, HL, vol.14, cc. 1283–1307.

116 FO 367/336, 39871/13, minute by Crowe, 30 Aug. 1913.

117 FO 367/336, 40955/13, minute by Crowe, 30 Aug. 1914. For Cromer's articles, see *The Spectator*, 16, 23 and 30 Aug. 1913, pp. 235–7, 268–70, 304–5.

118 FO 367/337, 56493/13, minute by Crowe, 22 Dec. 1913.

119 FO 367/336, 47570/13, Herbert Hall Hall (consul, Luanda) to Grey, 27 Sept. 1913 enclosing report from Smallbones to Hall Hall, 26 Sept. 1913.

120 FO 367/337, 52186/13, Carnegie to Grey, 11 Nov. 1913; 52767/13, Carnegie to Grey, 15 Nov. 1913.

121 FO 367/336, 47570/13, Grey to Carnegie, 25 Nov. 1913.

122 FO 367/337, 56923/56925/58235/13, Carnegie to Grey, 12, 13 and 20 Dec. 1913.

123 TNA, FO 371/1955, 6646/14, Hall to Grey, 23 Jan. 1914.

124 FO 371/1955, 11087/13148/14, Carnegie to Grey, 7 and 20 March 1914.

125 FO 371/1955, 15107/14, Carnegie to Grey, 30 March 1914.

126 FO 371/1956, 31658/14, Carnegie to Grey, 7 July 1914.

127 *Hansard Parliamentary Debates*, 5th series, HC, vol. 64, cc.1149–50. See also cc. 1421–6 for a critical speech by Sir Gilbert Parker MP.

128 For Mozambican labour on the Rand, see Duffy, *A Question of Slavery*, p. 141.

129 Harold Temperley and Lillian Penson (eds.), *Foundations of British Foreign Policy: From Pitt (1792) to Salisbury (1902)* (Cambridge: CUP, 1938), pp.

512–16. Sylvanus Cookey, *Britain and the Congo Question, 1885–1913* (New York: Humanities Press, 1968), pp. 56–131.

130 Richard Langhorne, "Anglo-German negotiations concerning the future of the Portuguese colonies, 1911–1914", *Historical Journal*, vol. 16, 1973, p. 369.

131 For the 1898 Anglo-German Agreement v. ibid., pp. 361–7.

132 FO 367/384, 31120/12, note by Grey for Cabinet, 17 July 1912.

133 FO 367/284, 30828/12, Grey to Earl Granville, 1 Aug. 1912. See also Prince Lichnowsky, *Heading for the Abyss: Reminiscences* (London: Constable, 1928), pp. 270–4.

134 FO 367/342, 7899/13, memo. by Crowe, 12 Feb. 1913. See also Glyn Stone, "The official British attitude to the Anglo-Portuguese alliance, 1910–1945", *Journal of Contemporary History*, vol. 10, 1975, pp. 730–1 and John Vincent-Smith, "The Anglo-German negotiations over the Portuguese colonies in Africa, 1911–1914", *Historical Journal*, Vol. 17, 1974, p. 626.

CHAPTER NINE

The Anti-Slavery Game

Britain and the Suppression of Slavery in Africa and Arabia, 1890–1975

SUZANNE MIERS

SLAVERY IN AFRICA IN THE LATE NINETEENTH CENTURY

Slavery you say is bad. I agree that it is bad, but slave labour is to the interior of Africa what steam-power is to your country. In your great factories where steam is used, is all well with the employees? Is there not much misery and suffering? Well, if the angel of God came and saw the unhappiness of your factories and said: "this must not continue – abolish steam", would you think it a wise decree?

With these words Zubayr Pasha, one of the great slave and ivory traders in Sudan in the nineteenth century,[1] put in a nutshell the problem that faced the British and other colonial rulers, as they conquered large areas of Africa late in the century. Slavery was not only widespread but it was the only means of mobilizing labour and the slave trade kept it mobile.

As each new region was conquered, the officials appointed to administer them faced the temptation to play the anti-slavery game – to make it seem as though action was being taken to eliminate slavery while in fact doing as little as possible. The whole central part of the continent had no roads and no draft animals. Travellers wound their way on foot, walking around obstacles. Communications were limited to drums which passed the news from one area to another. There was no currency. Most exchanges were in kind. Although in some areas cowry shells were used and as the early Europeans conquerors discovered much could be bought for a spoonful of salt. Most Africans were content to provide food for themselves and their families by working their own land. There was almost no wage labour. In this situation slavery was a treasured institution. As an Ethiopian was to lament as late as 1972: "It is only the younger generation of today that has not known the sweetness of slavery . . . a slave is your property, just like money in your pocket . . . you could send him anywhere, sell him at any price, or even give him away . . . this was not a secret business but a sacred one."[2] Moreover, it was to be found in almost all levels of society and took many forms. Slaves might be high officials of state, trusted warriors, valued concubines or lowly agricultural labourers.

To the British public, however, slavery was an anathema. From the day in 1807 when Britain outlawed its own slave trade, it assumed leadership of the international anti-slavery movement. It was not alone in outlawing the traffic, Denmark preceded it and the United States outlawed the American trade from the same year. Britain, however, played the leading role in policing the seas for slavers and waged a long struggle to negotiate a network of treaties with other nations binding them to end the traffic under their flags, in order to prevent this lucrative trade from simply flowing into their hands.[3]

While this naval and diplomatic struggle was in progress, the slave trade and slavery were spreading rapidly in Africa beyond the reach of naval action, stimulated by the growing demand for ivory and other exports. New research shows that by the middle of the nineteenth century slaves and ivory were being exchanged for western arms and ammunition in the great lakes area in the heart of the continent. The impact of the trade was not simply commercial. It transformed social and political relations.[4] People increasingly came to be seen as commodities – human capital – to be bought, sold, and even bred. Slaves were used as agricultural labour, as porters, canoe paddlers and traders. Rulers used them as government officials and soldiers. Women, who formed the bulk of the slaves, were wanted as concubines, wives, farm hands, servants and porters, as well as bearers of children. Chiefs and kings built up their power by using slave soldiers. They cemented the loyalty of their subordinates by giving them slaves, and they augmented the numbers of their subjects by accumulating captives. Women were particularly valuable in matrilineal societies as the children they bore to their owners belonged to their father's lineage and were under his control. Even young children could be used to run errands or serve as currency, becoming more valuable as they grew older.[5]

As slavery spread into new areas it stimulated social and political change. Relations between rulers and ruled, hitherto largely based on mutual respect and reciprocity, were now increasingly based on force as kings and chiefs built up slave armies and used slave labour to augment their wealth. Slaves were exchanged for arms and ammunition. Wars became more devastating. Unknown numbers of men, women and children were sold into the burgeoning slave traffic. This trade and the wars that supplied the captives spread through much of eastern, central, southern, western and northern Africa. Thousands of slaves were exported across the Red sea to Arabia and the Persian gulf. Victims from central Africa were marched across the Sahara to the Mediterranean and sent on to the Ottoman empire. From north-west Africa the trade reached southwards into central Africa, joining the long established traffic from the interior to the west coast, which had supplied the transatlantic trade until it ended with the abolition of slavery in the Americas during the nineteenth century. After the end of this traffic, the trade fed a rising internal market in western Africa, as slaves were increasingly used to produce goods for export and local consumption.

The last decades of the nineteenth century were a period of wars and political turmoil as the slave and arms traffics spread into the heart of the continent. In the ensuing instability, individuals might be enslaved, freed and enslaved again more than once in their life times. The increasing traffic was devastating new areas at the very time in the 1880s that the European colonial powers were signing treaties dividing up the continent. As they started to conquer their new colonies, they faced a dilemma. The European public expected them to suppress the slave trade and ultimately slavery, particularly as a conference held in Brussels, at British instigation, in the winter of 1889–90, had been held to reach agreement on a common policy against the trade.[6] The problem for Britain was to ensure that the other colonial powers also attacked the slave trade. Otherwise the valuable traffic in ivory and other export goods would automatically flow towards the territories of those who tolerated it. Moreover, colonial powers ready to use slave labour would have the advantage over those who sought to replace it with a free wage labour force, which was bound to take time to develop.

As the British established themselves in new regions, they outlawed slave raiding and trading. Small scale kidnapping or buying, mainly of women and children, continued underground throughout colonial rule, but the pathetic caravans of slaves, roped together, weighed down with goods on their heads, the women holding babies and trailed by exhausted children, soon vanished from British Africa.

The problem that remained was what to do about slavery itself. The temptation to ignore it and to use slaves for imperial projects was considerable as officials with scant resources were expected to make their territories produce goods for export and become self-supporting as soon as possible. For the British the problem was particularly important since the public also expected them to lead what was seen as a world-wide "crusade" against slavery and the slave trade – a crusade which Britain had led since 1807. Slave raiding and trading were used to justify wars against Africans who resisted British rule.[7] For the British public the end of slavery was an integral part of a package which included the imposition of peace, the rule of law, the development of a free market economy, and the spread of Christianity. The public expected slavery to end with the establishment of British rule.

Moreover, a small, but very vocal society, known in the late nineteenth century as The British and Foreign Anti-Slavery Society,[8] founded in 1839, and dedicated to ending slavery throughout the world, constantly reminded the government and public of Britain's anti-slavery role. It was a pacifist, largely Quaker, society, which wielded considerable influence through its contacts in Parliament, with government officials at home and in the empire, and with missionary societies. It was quick to report lack of zeal against the slave trade and slavery. Through its members and sympathizers it could raise embarrassing questions in Parliament, and it had a proven ability to mount impressive propaganda campaigns. It was not the only humanitarian organization concerned with ending slavery but it was the most vocal and prominent.

Africa was not the only part of the rapidly growing British empire in which slavery was entrenched at the time of the British conquest. Across the Red sea, it was widely practised in the Aden Protectorate and in the small shaikhdoms along the Persian gulf,[9] whose external affairs Britain controlled. The British established bases in these areas mainly to command the route to India – the largest and most valuable of their territories – the very heart of Britain's empire. It was in India, where slavery was widespread and took different forms, that, earlier in the nineteenth century, the ruling East India Company had hit on a solution, which was to become standard in the empire in all areas which were not designated crown colonies. In the latter slavery became illegal and could not openly be tolerated. But in the vast territories which the British called "protectorates", they simply declared that slavery had no legal standing and that all persons born after a certain date were free. Slavery was not actually outlawed but no claims over slaves could be brought to court, or, in theory, to British officials. Since only existing slaves remained in servitude, it was hoped that the institution would die out slowly without sudden disruption to the economy. In some protectorates, slave owners were even assured that they could keep their slaves.

This posed a dilemma for early British administrators. Many of them, and many of the Christian missionaries, who had preceded them in some areas, believed that Africans would not work unless they were enslaved. Land was plentiful and most Africans preferred to provide for themselves and their dependants by tilling their own soil rather than working for wages. Moreover the British, like the other colonial powers, did not have the resources to risk alienating the slave holding élites, whose cooperation they needed to maintain agricultural production, to serve as rulers or chiefs to keep the peace and man the lower echelons of government.

Hence in many areas slavery was tacitly tolerated for years. This was justified by the claim that African slavery was "benign" – meaning devoid of
the cruelties that had characterized slavery in the Americas. Hence, the
argument ran, slave raids and the slave traffic should be suppressed as soon
as possible in the interests of orderly government, but slavery itself could
be allowed to die out gradually.

However, runaway slaves posed a problem for administrators. Many
slaves took advantage of the disturbances during the wars of conquest to
leave *en masse* as the colonial armies advanced. Colonial officials tried to
halt the exodus and discouraged slaves from leaving their owners, except
in cases of flagrant cruelty. Once their administrations were established,
however, they could refer fugitives to native or Islamic courts, or send
them to Christian missions. In the case of women both the courts and
missionaries tried to find them husbands, who were encouraged to pay
their owners for them in lieu of bridewealth. Child slaves were placed
with "reliable", usually meaning Christian, families, or were sent to
Christian missions. A few homes were also established for freed children.
Male slaves posed a more difficult problem. They were often urged to
ransom themselves and in some cases were given work by the colonial
governments so that they could earn the necessary money. In others officials simply withheld help, hoping that this would force fugitives to
return to their owners.[10] In many cases they actually returned runaways,
risking a prison term for supporting slavery. No official, however, was
ever prosecuted for returning a slave, although in some areas, such as
Northern Nigeria and the Sudan, it was common practice.[11]

Colonial officials were in no hurry to alienate masters or disrupt the
local economy by informing slaves that they were free. In the east African
hinterland, in Northern Nigeria and in parts of Sierra Leone, for instance,
slaves did not know they could leave their owners for many years after
the British conquest. Owners, when they heard they could not legally
stop their slaves from leaving, tried to prevent them from hearing the
news and from reaching the few British officials on the ground to demand
their freedom. Once slaves knew they could not be forced to stay with
their owners, some left. Many others renegotiated their terms of service.
Their actions depended upon the extent of their desire for freedom and
their assessments of their prospects as free persons. These depended on
their age, gender and grievances, on whether they could gain access to
land, tools or livestock to make a living independently, on whether they
could find a chief or colonial official anxious to welcome them into his
territory, or on whether wage labour was available.

In this equation much depended on the local colonial officials. Their
attitude depended partly on their views on slavery. These were personal
and varied greatly. Thus in Muslim Sudan an official complained that

"every inspector has his own ideas and acts in accordance with them alone: one will go to any lengths to recover [runaway slaves], another is rabidly anti-slavery".[12] Even more important than their personal views was their assessment of the danger of disrupting the economy and provoking rebellion if slaves left their owners *en masse*. Colonial officials could help slaves gain their freedom by giving them land or jobs, or they could refuse help and try to get them to return to their owners. In cases of ill-treatment a district officer was expected to protect them, but he might try to keep the matter quiet by helping them slip away undercover of night. He could also avoid responsibility by referring the case to native or Islamic courts. In the case of women the courts would try to find them husbands who would pay their owners to free them. For the bridegroom this had the advantage of allowing him to acquire a wife without paying bridewealth or being answerable to her family for her welfare, and in matrilineal societies their children would be under his exclusive control rather than that of her kinsmen.

BRITISH OFFICIALS AND THE LABOUR QUESTION

To complicate the situation for colonial officials they needed a mobile labour force to attract European businesses and farmers to develop their territories and make them self-supporting as soon as possible. They needed roads, railways, docks and telegraphs, as well as a permanent administration. Since they did not have the resources to pay wages high enough to attract labour, they introduced their own form of compulsory work – forced labour. This was unlike slavery because in theory it applied only to younger men and was for a limited time. It also carried no social stigma. To the conscripts, though forced to leave their own fields, often at crucial times, to work on colonial projects, it often seemed that they had merely exchanged one form of bondage for another. A district officer on tour, for instance, might demand porters from the local chief, or men might be conscripted to work in mines, or forced to build roads or docks from which it might be years before they saw any advantage to themselves. In settler colonies land was taken from Africans, many of whom were forced into reserves, and the best land was given to European farmers. Many Africans became squatters on white estates and had to work, part or full time for the white settlers.

The worst scandals in colonial Africa took place in the areas adminis-tered by other powers[13] but during the First World War, the British conscripted men to serve in the East Africa Carrier Corps and tens of thousands died from disease, overwork, exposure and malnutrition.

SUZANNE MIERS

New Post-War Anti-Slavery Treaties and the Anti-Slavery Society

In the last decade of the nineteenth century and the first decade of the twentieth colonial officials were much concerned with slavery. By the outbreak of war in 1914, however, it was no longer a serious problem. After the war, when the victors met to negotiate the peace treaties, most of them, in common with the general public, believed that the slave trade in Africa, and the export traffic, had been virtually eliminated. They, therefore, abrogated the Brussels act and replaced it with three new treaties signed at St. Germain-en-Laye in 1919. One of these contained a single clause binding signatories to try to "secure the complete suppression of slavery in all its forms" and to end the slave trade; while the covenant of the new League of Nations bound members to "secure and maintain fair and humane conditions of labour" in all their territories. These were weak clauses. They set no time limit for ending slavery and did not define either its forms or "fair and humane conditions of labour".

However, the International Labour Organization (ILO) was founded in 1919 to improve labour standards around the world. Its great weakness, though, was that it could not force governments to sign its conventions or carry out their provisions. If they did sign them they could, and did, delay applying them to their colonial territories claiming that conditions were not yet "suitable". In practice, therefore, these agreements left the colonial powers free to take action against slavery only if they wished to do so.[14]

Foreign Office Policy, the Anti-Slavery Society and Slavery in Ethiopia

No further steps against slavery would probably have been taken had it not been for the Anti-Slavery Society. Its Secretary from 1910 to his death in 1940 was John (later Sir John) Harris.[15] He was particularly adept at gaining public support and pressing reluctant governments to protect labour.

In October 1919 Foreign Office officials were appalled to hear that slave raiding and trading were rife in southwest Ethiopia and were spreading into British East Africa (later Kenya and Uganda), in regions Britain claimed but had not yet occupied.[16] The bearers of this bad news were two British commissioners, Majors Henry Darley and L. F. I. Athill, who had been sent out by the Foreign Office to demarcate the border between Ethiopia and British territory. Foreign Office officials were anxious to defend British interests in Ethiopia against the rival machinations of France and Italy. Hence they were reluctant to take any action which might upset the weak Ethiopian government and enable the Italians and French to gain commercial and other concessions. They tried to ignore the unwelcome news and to throw doubt on the veracity of their own commissioners, who had walked for many days through the British southern Sudan on their way home and had seen the devastation wrought by the raids and even inspected the camp of the raiders, who were at that moment raiding for slaves and cattle in British East Africa.

To the consternation of the Foreign Office, however, articles on slavery in Ethiopia were published by Darley and others with the backing of the Anti-Slavery Society. The foreign secretary, Lord Curzon, was attacked in the House of Lords and showed complete ignorance of the subject. Acutely embarrassed, he demanded that his officials supply him with full information. A reluctant Foreign Office complied and hastily took action to free the slaves owned by employees of the British legation in Addis Ababa.[17] This created a domestic crisis when the wives of some of the employees refused to free their slaves, many of whom they had acquired in childhood. The British consul was appalled when the employees divorced their wives in order to keep their jobs. However, his employees said they would easily find more amenable wives. A consul was also hastily appointed to Maji to watch the frontier and report on slavery. He and his successors soon confirmed that slaving was rife in the whole region.[18]

The main interest, however, of members of the Foreign Office was not to allow the slavery issue to interfere with British relations with the weak Ethiopian government, since this would give France and Italy an advantage in the quest of all three powers for influence and concessions. Moreover, the British were hoping to get permission from Ethiopia to construct a dam on Lake Tana in order to provide power for the development of the Anglo-Egyptian Sudan. This episode is of interest, showing, as it does that under some foreign secretaries, policy was largely determined by officials whose aims were to defend British interests as they saw them. The slave trade would have taken second place to these interests had the Anti-Slavery Society not brought the matter to the attention of Parliament and the public. However, in the long run, all that was achieved was that Ethiopia passed some laws against the traffic and promised action, but little changed until the Italian invasion of 1935. Slavery was only finally outlawed in 1942, after Britain occupied the country during the Second World War.

Consular Manumission in Arabia

Dramatic evidence that there was also a lively export trade in slaves across the Red sea was furnished in June 1922, when the Royal Navy captured a ship carrying thirty Ethiopian slaves, mainly young women and children to Arabia.[19] This trade was reviving,[20] encouraged by the ruler of Hejaz, who was taxing it. As a devout Muslim, he had no intention of suppressing slavery or the slave trade, both of which were legitimate under Islamic law. The country's main source of income was the pilgrimage (*hajj*) to Mecca and the other holy places. This annual "rain of gold" brought thousands of pilgrims to the Hejaz every year. Slaves, regarded as the most profitable investment, were bought and sold openly as part of daily business. Many were destitute pilgrims. Others were children or servants of pilgrims or other travellers. Many were kidnapped. The buyers ranged from poor herders in the desert to rich merchants and officials.

When Arabia was part of the Ottoman empire before the First World War, the British not only patrolled the seas and searched dhows for slaves, but their consul in Jedda claimed the right to harbour and ask the authorities to free any genuine fugitive slaves who reached the consulate. With doubtful legality, the consul continued to exercise this right after the war when Hejaz was independent. This was greatly resented by slave owners and was an embarrassment to the rulers. The consul had to tread carefully, and a routine was established to prevent the arrival of every fugitive from creating a diplomatic crisis. When a male slave arrived at the consulate, often hotly pursued, he was searched to ensure he was not a criminal. He was then carefully interviewed to establish that he was really a fugitive slave. If satisfied that he was, the consul would ask the authorities to free him, and would then try to send him back to his homeland. Many of those captured in childhood, however, did not remember their origins, and the consul had to guess this from their appearance. If they seemed to be from the Sudan or western Africa, he would call on the government of the Anglo-Egyptian Sudan to pay for the repatriation of its own nationals, and to take in the others. He would then send them by boat to the Sudan. If they looked Ethiopian he would either send them to the Italian consul, who rarely cooperated, or try to arrange for their return to Ethiopia. Some were mere children. Women fugitives posed problems as the consul had nowhere to house them while he checked their stories to ensure they were not runaway wives or daughters. He would usually tell them to sneak back home, and come back when a boat was expected on which he could embark them for the Sudan or Eritrea. Generally the matter could be handled with tact and delicacy, but sometimes the authorities refused to free the slave and the consul would have to sneak him or her personally on a boat leaving the Hejaz. He was not given funds to pay the fares and quarantine costs of the fugitives and had to milk the Nigerian Repatriation Fund founded to help destitute pilgrims, unless they were Sudanese in which case the Sudanese authorities paid their expenses.[21]

By August 1925 Hejaz had been invaded by Abdul al Aziz ibn Saud (henceforth Ibn Saud), the ruler of Nejd. In the disorders of the war, twenty fugitives had been repatriated in a month, and furious owners began charging them with theft. The consul feared they might suffer amputation if they were convicted in a Shari'a court. The king of Hejaz, promised to end slavery when the war was over if the British would stop harbouring fugitive slaves. The then foreign secretary, Austen Chamberlain, refused this deal, fearing an outcry in Britain. Thus the consulate remained a haven for fugitives until after Ibn Saud conquered Hejaz and established his rule over much of the Arabian peninsula in what became the kingdom of Saudi Arabia. He imposed peace and protected pilgrims from being kidnapped and sold into slavery. Moreover, demand for slaves was slowly dropping as slave retainers were no longer needed for security and cars were replacing slave camel drivers.

However, consular manumission was only finally given up after long negotiations and a crisis in 1931 when a slave of Ibn Saud appealed for manumission. The king believed that the British had agreed not to try to free his own slaves and asked that the slave be returned. The foreign secretary, Sir John Simon, himself a member of the Anti-Slavery Society, was prepared to risk a diplomatic incident by sending a ship to embark the fugitive by force. In the end the matter was settled by the consul sneaking him onto a British sloop which happened to be in harbour. Consular manumission in Saudi Arabia only ended when new agreements were reached with Ibn Saud in 1936. However British political officers continued to manumit fugitives in the tiny Arabian states of Kuwait, Bahrain, Qatar and the Trucial States, whose foreign policy Britain controlled, and in the Aden Protectorate. It was also exercised by the consuls in Muscat and Oman (now Oman) where slavery was legal until 1970.[22]

An episode of particular interest is the suppression of slavery in Qatar. This was the result of the initiative of the political officer, Michael Benson Jacomb. Before the development of the oil industry, the royal family had been deeply involved in slaving. In 1951, taking advantage of their sudden oil riches, Jacomb reminded owners that the slave trade was illegal and made it clear that slaves could appeal to him for help. The eventual upshot was that the shaykh freed all slaves and paid some compensation money to their owners.[23]

SUZANNE MIERS

THE LEAGUE OF NATIONS, THE FOREIGN AND
COLONIAL OFFICES, AND SLAVERY

In 1924, as the result of hard lobbying in Geneva by Harris, the newly-established League of Nations asked all members to report on slavery in their territories. This was a watershed in the anti-slavery cause. For the first time there was an international body to which the question could be referred. Not all powers were members of the League and not all members replied, and many of those that did were less than truthful. In some cases the reply turned on the definition of slavery. The resident in Aden admitted that slavery existed in the protectorate but claimed that slaves were better off than the free poor and would resent being freed. Since much of the protectorate had never been visited by a British official, this was not even an educated guess.[24]

The League proceeded to appoint a temporary slavery commission to inquire into slavery everywhere. The British foreign secretary hoped this would be a short-lived body appointed by governments, from which they would take instructions.[25] However, the secretary-general of the League, determined not to have a committee packed by the colonial powers, appointed seven "independent members" chosen in consultation with their governments to represent all the African colonial powers, France, Portugal, Italy, Belgium, with the exception of the British member, Sir Frederick (later Lord) Lugard. He was so well known and had promoted himself so vociferously as an expert on slavery, that the British government was not even consulted about his appointment. This was to prove a fateful choice, for Lugard, unlike most of the other members of commission was truly independent of his government. He had had considerable experience of slavery in both east Africa, where he participated in its conquest using slave soldiers, and later as governor of first Northern Nigeria and finally of all Nigeria. In this capacity, he had pacified the country and developed policies which led to what has been called a "slow death" for slavery.[26] However, unlike many of his contemporaries, he believed that Africans would work if they were offered sufficient incentive.[27] Also on the commission was a member of the ILO, and a representative of "the black race" from Haiti, who provided the nearest thing to the "slave voice".

The commission began work in 1924. Its discussions illuminated the difficulty of defining slavery – a term used to cover a multitude of practices restricting personal liberty. Unable to reach a clear definition, the commission simply listed in its report all such practices, including debt-bondage and forced labour. The most fruitful result of its deliberations was its recommendation that the League should negotiate a new treaty to abolish the legal status of slavery, and serfdom, and to declare the maritime trade piracy. None of the colonial powers wanted such a treaty, however, Lugard forced the hand of the Foreign Office by presenting a draft convention to Viscount Cecil, who convened an interdepartmental committee with representatives of the Colonial, Foreign and India Offices, the Board of Trade, the Admiralty and the Ministry of Labour, to ensure it did not infringe any British interests. The first step was to downgrade the proposed treaty to a protocol, which did not have the same force as a convention but would show the world that Britain was still committed to end slavery. They accepted Lugard's proposal that slavers on the high seas should be treated as pirates, but rejected the banning of forced labour, debt-bondage and the forced extension of contracts. They watered down other provisions and weakened the draft still more by allowing signatories to exclude some of their territories from its provisions, or to reject some articles. This was largely to avoid attacking the labour practices in some of the states ruled by Indian princes and other rulers in the British empire. Cecil thought this emasculated draft weak enough to be accepted by the other colonial powers. To ensure that Britain gained credit for proposing it, he presented it to the Sixth Commission of the League Assembly. It then went to a drafting committee, which to his dismay met in private, depriving the British of possible kudos in the press should they be unable to carry stringent measures against the opposition of the other colonial powers. After more redrafting by these powers, the treaty finally emerged as the slavery convention of 1926.[28]

This was a landmark in the anti-slavery battle as it outlawed "slavery in all its forms", thus including a wide range of exploitative practices and opening the way for the attack on those considered "analogous to slavery". It did not name these or establish any means of enforcement, or set a date by which slavery should end. The proposal that slavers on the high seas should be treated as pirates was eliminated. The British were well pleased, however. They hoped their "leading role" in getting the treaty at all "would be appreciated in the world at large" and that other powers would be blamed for the weakness of the convention.[29]

However, revelations of slavery in the British empire, of among others, a traffic in slaves from Ethiopia to the Sudan, of raids into Kenya, and of little Chinese girls being sold into slavery as domestics in Hong Kong and Singapore, kept public interest alive. Harris, who was given to exaggeration, estimating that there were still four to five million slaves in the world,[30] urged the Foreign Office to revive the temporary slavery commission. In November 1931 Sir John Simon was appointed Foreign Secretary. He was a vice-president of the Anti-Slavery Society, and his wife was on its committee. The society now boasted three peers, as vice-presidents, and the archbishops of Canterbury and York and a number of other bishops and reformers among its members. Britain duly called on the League to establish a permanent commission with powers to call witnesses and conduct on the spot investigations. Needless to say, this was opposed by the other powers and the measure nearly foundered on the grounds of its expense. It was saved by Harris who arranged for the Anti-Slavery Society to provide some of the money, together with the Italian *Societa Antischiavista d'Italia*. The same powers were represented on this committee as on the last, except that Spain was added. Portugal sent a woman to placate increasingly vociferous women's groups; the Haitian delegate was not included; and the ILO only sent an observer.

This meeting of the committee of experts on slavery in 1932 was particularly acrimonious owing to friction between the British and French delegates. However, it had an important result. Its information was so manifestly inadequate that it recommended the establishment of a permanent slavery committee. This body, known as the Advisory Committee of Experts on Slavery was established in 1933 – the centenary of the British Emancipation Act which had outlawed slavery in all British colonies, which was being commemorated by a number of events around the country. The committee, funded by the League, was to meet every two years "if necessary". It was purely advisory, its proceedings were to be confidential and it could only receive information transmitted by governments. For the British it was to have totally unexpected results because, to Lugard's dismay they appointed as their representative a retired official from the Malayan civil service, Sir George Maxell – a choice they would soon regret. He had never been to Geneva and knew nothing about League procedure, but he set about his work with a determination to get at the facts and to enhance the value of the committee rather than defend his government like his colleagues.

Maxwell dominated the committee from 1935 to its last session in1938. He engineered extra sessions so that it met annually.[31] He demanded full information on progress towards the elimination of slavery in British territories and he presented his colleagues with as much information as he could whittle out of the Colonial and India Offices about slavery in the empire. He badgered these offices into producing honest reports. By forcing them to inquire into slavery where it still existed in British possessions, he succeeded in getting new policies enforced. In Northern Nigeria, for instance, where slavery was still widely practised he forced the government to declare all slaves free.[32] In practice this did not prevent owners from receiving payments and exacting services from former slaves, but this was now illegal. Maxwell's aim was to concentrate on those persons who had themselves been enslaved and secondly on hereditary slaves. He hoped to pass various questions included in the wide definition of slavery, such as *mui tsai,* the use of little girls as unpaid domestics by the Chinese, to other League bodies such as the Advisory Committee on Social Questions, and debt-bondage, peonage and serfdom to the ILO.

The result of Maxwell's prodigious efforts and the failure of his colleagues to produce much material on slavery in their own territories gave, as the Foreign Office complained, the impression that slavery was a "peculiarly British affair".[33] They were not sorry when the outbreak of war in 1939 put an end to the committee's life.

Britain and the Slavery Question, 1945–1975

By the end of the Second World War much had changed. Harris, who had led the anti-slavery campaign with such vigour in the past, died in 1940. His successor as secretary of the Anti-Slavery Society was Charles Greenidge, a retired colonial official. Less than a year after the end of the war, he began lobbying the United Nations (UN), which had now replaced the League of Nations, for a permanent anti-slavery committee. For the next fifty or so years the struggle for the suppression of slavery *in all its forms* was carried on against the background of the Cold War. The ideological divisions of the ensuing rivalry resulted in deep disagreement between the Eastern and Western blocs as to the meaning of "freedom" and "human rights". To the Soviets they meant primarily freedom from want, from discrimination, as well as equal opportunity, the right to employment and education. To the Western bloc they meant freedom of expression and religion, freedom from arbitrary arrest, rights to political protest and other components of the rule of law. Each side had its vulnerabilities and its strengths. The United States was particularly vulnerable on questions of discrimination. Britain was attacked for colonialism and the Soviet bloc for its lack of political and religious freedom. All discussions took place in an atmosphere of intense rivalry as each side sought to win support among the uncommitted nations, the number of which proliferated as the European empires broke up into independent states.

As in 1919, it was generally believed that slavery barely existed if at all. This was an idea that Greenidge set out to eliminate by lobbying UN delegates, making public speeches, writing pamphlets and generally drumming up support for a permanent advisory committee on slavery.[34] The Foreign Office opposed it on the grounds of expense and the fear that it might lead to demands for other committees. Getting no response from the Foreign Office, Greenidge sent a memorandum claiming there were five million slaves in the world, as well as twenty million Russian slave labourers, and twenty million Amerindians in debt-bondage. Officials did not believe him, but their hands were forced when he persuaded the Belgian delegate to propose the establishment of a UN committee to inquire into slavery in all its forms.[35] The British decided that they would have to support an investigation into slavery but wanted it to include other forms of exploitation such as peonage and forced labour in the communist bloc to divert attention from their satellites in the Persian gulf and from the Aden Protectorate, where classic slavery continued.

Eventually the Ad Hoc Committee on Slavery was established and met in 1950–51. To the dismay of the Colonial Office, Greenidge was a member. In response to pressure from women's groups a half-African, half-French woman was appointed. In line with UN policy to try to get members from the five areas in which the UN divided the world,[36] the other two members were a Chilean and an American. This committee proved a disaster. Its members spoke no common language. Peru, Colombia and Chile, incensed at the inclusion of peonage as slavery, managed to get the second session cancelled. Finally members could not agree on a common report and submitted two reports, one of them by Greenidge.

Greenidge now followed Lugard's example and presented his government with a draft convention, supplementary to that of 1930. As in the past the Colonial Office did not want the convention and feared that a number of its provisions would be objected to by colonial governments, many of whom now had their own legislatures. The problem lay in what were designated practices "analogous to slavery". Many of the provisions of the draft were to protect women and children, including establishing a legal age for marriage. These involved interfering with "native customs" – always a problem for the Colonial Office and it officials.

There followed long and complicated discussions in Britain as comments were received from the ILO, the UN secretariat, the Anti-Slavery Society, women's groups, and government departments. A consensus had to be reached over such questions as the distinctions between forced labour, slavery, serfdom and debt-bondage. Each state was henceforth to police its own ships, ports, airfields and coasts. The outcome of the discussions was the signature of the supplementary convention of 1956 to complement the 1926 convention. In order to get this treaty the British had to give up their long held right to search foreign ships for slaves. In practice this meant little since the Royal Navy had not been patrolling the seas for slavers since 1939. Moreover there were no treaties giving them the right to search ships flying the flags of Saudi Arabia or Iraq, or of the newly independent states such as Pakistan or India.

The result of the 1956 convention was that the definition of slavery now officially included debt-bondage, peonage, forced marriage, and adoption for exploitation. To protect labour further the ILO adopted the Abolition of Forced Labour Convention. The main defect of these treaties was that, as in the past, there were no mechanisms for their enforcement – a fact that drew scathing comments in the press.[37]

For some years after the signing of the 1956 convention, the slavery question was in abeyance. It was revived by an agitation for a UN commission of inquiry by a vocal group of non-governmental organizations (NGOs) including the Anti-slavery Society. This was now led by Thomas Fox-Pitt, who publicized some cases of slavery and then played a trump card by appealing to the British public to write to their members of parliament (MPs) demanding action from a reluctant government. He was incensed that Britain, hitherto, the leader of the anti-slavery cause, was now upstaged by the president of Egypt, Gamal Abdul Nasser. Since in 1962, Saudi Arabia and then Yemen had abolished slavery, the only areas in which it now existed were the British satellite states on the Persian gulf and Britain's ally Oman. The NGOs demanded some mechanism for implementing the slavery conventions. Britain finally agreed to the appointment of a special *rapporteur*, Mohammed Awad. He compiled a questionnaire for governments which was sent out in 1964, asking for information on slavery, debt-bondage, serfdom, forced marriage and the exploitation of children.[38] Only seventy-eight states out of a hundred and seven answered. Most denied there was any slavery in their territories, a claim that was refuted by the NGOs.

Chattel slavery, which had all but ended in most countries, was no longer the main problem. Most forms of servitude now were practices like forced labour, debt-bondage, forced marriage, child marriage and the inheritance of widows. Even the payment of bridewealth was denounced by women's organizations. All were long standing customs in which governments did not wish to interfere. Other problems were the adoption of children in order to exploit them, the use of unpaid child labour in often hazardous employment and forced prostitution. Awad recommended the appointment of a UN committee to examine evidence and suggest action. Britain reluctantly supported this.

However, the proposal was defeated. It was opposed by the Russians and the USA and by Waldo E. Waldron-Ramsay, Tanzania's representative at the UN, who in a clever move persuaded his colleagues to add to the definition of slavery to be referred to the Commission on Human Rights "the slavery-like practices of apartheid and colonialism". This ended British official efforts to lead the anti-slavery movement for the moment, while it increased the interest of the newly independent states. Eventually the UN's Economic and Social Council (ECOSOC) referred the question to the Sub-Commission on the Prevention of Discrimination and the Protection of Minorities and in 1974, with British support, it appointed a Working Group on Contemporary Forms of Slavery drawn from members of the sub-commission. Like its predecessors it had no executive powers, but it heard evidence in public, hence it was valued by NGOs. It sat from 1975 until its dissolution in 2006, by which time it had collected a great deal of material and made many recommendations.

Unlike its predecessors, its members were not experts on slavery as those of the League of Nations had been. Gone were the days of experienced officials, like Lugard, Maxwell and Greenidge, who forced reluctant government departments to produce information and sometimes to take action, and who initiated anti-slavery conventions. Gone too were the many administrators, particularly in Africa, who tackled the difficult task of keeping the peace and at the same time suppressing slavery. Gone were the consuls in Arabia and the executive officers in the Gulf States who dealt with runaway slaves. Their efforts to combat slavery are now a proud memory.

However, the present Foreign and Commonwealth Office and its officials abroad still rescues young girls forced into arranged marriages in Arabia, Pakistan, India and elsewhere.[39] Moreover they combat modern forms of slavery, such as the trafficking of eastern European women and children into forced prostitution in Britain, or the importing of victims of wars in Sudan ostensibly as servants but in reality as virtual slaves.[40] Whereas in the past slavery was to be found first in colonies and then in protectorates, today slavery in various modern forms is to be found in Britain itself and is the concern of a number of government departments.

Notes

1   Quoted in Frederick D. Lugard, *The Dual Mandate in British Tropical Africa,* 5th edition (London: Frank Cass, 1965), p. 365. For his career see *inter alia* Richard Gray, *A History of the Southern Sudan 1839–1889* (Oxford: OUP, 1961).
2   Alessandro Triulzi, *Salt, Gold and Legitimacy: prelude to the history of a no-man's land, Bel Shangul, Wallag , Ethiopia (ca. 1800–1898)* (Naples: Universitario Orientale, 1981), p. 136, quoting the district governor of Asosa, Ethiopia 1972.
3   For a discussion of these treaties see Suzanne Miers, *Britain and the Ending of the Slave Trade* (London: Longman, 1975), pp. 9–117.
4   For a recent study of the impact of the slave and arms traffics on the far interior during the nineteenth century, see Henri Médard and Shane Doyle (eds.), *Slavery in the Great Lakes Region of East Africa* (Oxford: James Currey, 2007).
5   Many references could be cited, but for children see particularly Fred

Morton, "Small Change: Children in the 19th Century East African Slave Trade", *Children in Slavery through the Ages,* vol. i (Athens OH: Ohio UP, forthcoming 2009), eds. Gwyn Campbell, Suzanne Miers and Joseph C. Miller.

6 For a detailed study of this conference and its results see Miers, *Slave Trade,* pp. 229 ff.

7 Médard and Shane, *Slavery*, pp. 231 ff.

8 This society, which still exists, has had several changes of name. Today it is called "Anti-Slavery". Here it will be called the "Anti-Slavery Society". For further discussion of its impact, see Suzanne Miers, *Slavery in the Twentieth Century: The Evolution of a Global Problem* (Walnut Creek, CA: AltaMira Press, 2003), pp. 62–5.

9 These were Kuwait, Bahrain, Quatar, Abu Dhabi, Dubai, Sharjah, Ajman , Umm al-Qaiwain, Ras al-Kaimah, and Fujairah.

10 For examples of the official attitudes and solutions to the problem of fugitive slaves, see Paul Lovejoy and Jan S. Hogendorn, *Slow Death for Slavery: The Course of Abolition in Northern Nigeria, 1897–1936* (Cambridge: CUP, 1993), pp. 31 ff.

11 For examples of the actions of officials, v. ibid.

12 Taj Hargey, "*Festina Lente:* Slavery Policy and Practice in the Anglo-Egyptian Sudan", *Slavery and Abolition*, vol. 19, no. 2 (1998), pp. 250–72.

13 The worst were probably in the rubber producing areas of the Belgian Congo during the reign of King Leopold II, as well as in the French Congo, and in the Portuguese colonies. For a recent discussion of some of these questions with further references, see Kevin Grant, *A Civilized Savagery: Britain and the New Slaveries in Africa 1884–1926* (London: Routledge, 2005).

14 For more detailed discussion of the peace treaties and the ILO and their impact see Suzanne Miers, *Slavery,* pp. 58–62.

15 On Harris, v. ibid., pp. 62–5.

16 Ibid., pp. 66–76.

17 Ibid., pp. 66–72.

18 The National Archives (TNA), FO 371/5501, Hawkins to Lockhart, letter, 20 March 1921.

19 For further information on slavery in Hejaz, see Miers *Slavery,* pp. 87–99.

20 For a brief description of the Red Sea slave trade, v. ibid., pp. 76–8.

21 For consular manumission and further sources, v. ibid, pp. 87–94, 179–183, 254–60.

22 Ibid., pp. 339ff.

23 Ibid., pp. 340–1.

24 For slavery in the Aden Protectorate, see Suzanne Miers, "Slave Rebellion and Resistance in the Aden Protectorate in the Mid-Twentieth Century", *Slavery and Resistance in Africa and Asia* (London: Routledge, 2005), eds. Edward Alpers, Gwyn Campbell and Michael Salman, pp. 99–108.

25 Miers, *Slavery,* p.102.

26 Lovejoy and Hogendorn, *Slow Death.*

27 For Lugard's views on slavery, see Lugard, *Dual Mandate,* pp. 354–425; for

his instructions to administrators see Lugard, *Political Memoranda,* 3rd edition (London: Frank Cass, 1970), pp. 216–48.

28 For a detailed discussion of the negotiations leading to the signature of the convention and the British role in them, see Miers *Slavery*, pp.121–30.

29 Ibid., p. 130.

30 He was guessing.

31 For a more detailed study with archival references, see Miers *Slavery*, pp. 278–94.

32 Lovejoy and Hogendorn, *Slow Death*, pp. 280–3.

33 Miers, *Slavery*, p. 290.

34 Ibid., pp. 317–20.

35 Ibid., p. 320.

36 The Western democracies, Eastern Europe, Latin America, Africa and the Orient.

37 Ibid., pp. 326–31.

38 Ibid., pp. 361–6.

39 See *inter alia* David Barrett, "Girls as young as nine taken from school to marry overseas", *The Sunday Telegraph*, 28 September 2008.

40 For an example, see Miriam Ali-Kamouhi with Jana Wain, *Without Mercy: A Mother's Struggle Against Modern Slavery* (London: Time Warner Books, 1996).

Index

'Abduh, Muhammad, 136–7, 138
Abdul Mejid, Sultan, 103
Abdülhamid II, Sultan, 112
Aberdeen, George Hamilton-Gordon,
    4th earl of
  Anglo–Brazilian disputes, 12, 50, 52,
    54, 70–1
  Anglo–Portuguese disputes, 12
  anti-slave trade diplomacy, 20
  attitude to Portugal, 69
  Bandinel's appointment to commis-
    sion, 25
  Britain's diplomatic relations, 12
  ending of coastal raids, 69
  Luanda offer to Jackson, 64n
  Parnther's allowance, 27
  slave trade in Muslim world, 94
  Texas issue, 88–90
  Turnbull's appointment to Jamaica,
    57
Aborigines' Protection Society
  labour in Portuguese west Africa, 167,
    170, 171, 173, 174
  see also Anti-Slavery and Aborigines'
    Protection Society
Abyssinia, 98, 109
  see also Ethiopia
Aceh, 131
Acland, Francis, 184
Acre siege (1799), 13, 133
Activo (Brazilian brig), 49–51
adat, 127, 132
Addington, Henry Unwin, 21, 22, 28,
    29
Aden Protectorate, 199, 205, 206, 210
Admiralty, 1, 32, 74, 84, 171
Advisory Committee of Experts on
    Slavery, 208
Advisory Committee on Social
    Questions, 209

Africa
  Anglo–German agreement (1886),
    163n
  Anglo–German agreement (1890), 40n
  British dominance of slave trade, 2–3
  British efforts to stem supply, 3, 67–8,
    77
  development of trade, 67–8, 84
  English slave trade (17th century), 2
  historic slave trade routes, 67, 198
  impact of slave trade on society, 2,
    197–8
  labour laws, 147–51, 152, 154–6, 159,
    160
  Portuguese slave trade (15th century),
    1–2
  runaway slaves, 200–1
  slavery as treasured institution, 196–7
  see also east Africa; individual
    colonies/countries; west Africa
African Institution, 82, 83–4, 86
Ahmad Bey, 132
Ahmad of Pahang, Sultan, 126
Aix-la-Chapelle congress (1818), 8, 85
Alexander I, tsar of Russia, 85
Algeria, 132
Algiers, 67
Ali Pasha, 104
Allen, William, 85
Almada, José d', 180, 181
Almeida, José, 177
Alston, Francis, 30, 32
American civil war, 12, 20, 32, 58, 66,
    78, 95
Americas
  European discovery and
    colonization, 2
  labour laws, 143–4
  mixed commission courts, 11
  slavery, 2, 7, 10, 94, 198, 200

215